A Father's Son

A NOVEL

Richard Harris

ISBN: 1484921674
ISBN 13: 9781484921678

Produced with the support of the City of Toronto
through the Toronto Arts Council

To Matt

And in Loving Memory of
Frederick John Harris (1944-99)

"Words such as love, passion, duty, are so continually used they grow to have no meaning—except as coins or weapons. Hard language softens. I never knew what my father felt of these 'things'. My loss was that I never spoke to him as an adult."

—Michael Ondaatje, *Running in the Family*

Autumn

1

Hanging around 53 Division for hours on end sucked, but getting driven to Dad's place in a crappy yellow police car *really* sucked the bag. While at the cop shop, I had to wait around someone's desk the whole time, doing pretty much what Dad calls "the square root of nothing." When Mom had been pulled over and handcuffed outside her Pontiac Grand Am, it felt like a dream. It was only when an officer told me she'd be arraigned in court next week that it began sinking in. Even though I had no idea what "arraigned" meant, I knew it was bad because he asked if I had somewhere to go in the meantime. There was no chance I'd move back with Mom's psycho boyfriend, which meant I'd have to stay with Dad.

The sun was setting when the police car pulled over to the side of the road, across from Dad's building, a concrete eyesore in the centre of Toronto. To the north was the country's richest neighbourhood; the south was a bunch of streets and alleyways full of hookers, drug addicts and bums. Officer Brady opened his door and I took that as my cue to get out. Inside Dad's building, I scanned the black rubber board on the wall. The names, all in white lettering, went from CHERNOVSKY to KAO to RHEE to GONZALEZ. Officer Brady moved a finger down the glass until he found what he was looking for, MALONEY, R, then entered eight-oh-four.

"Yes?"

"Mr. Maloney? Sir, this is Officer Jeff Brady. We spoke earlier on the phone. I'm here with your son Justin. Would you mind letting us in?"

The door buzzed and we rode up to the eighth floor without saying anything, which was fine by me because I wasn't much in the mood to talk. Hands buried deep inside the pockets of my jeans, I noticed a hole at the bottom of my T-shirt as Officer Brady rapped on the door. When Dad opened it a moment later, a sound escaped from the back of my throat. It'd only been four months since we'd last seen each other, but he looked a decade older. His brown hair was shorter than I remembered and most of it had turned grey, the pockmarks on his forehead more visible than ever. He had stubble all over his face, not in the style Crockett or Tubbs wore it on *Miami Vice*, but more like someone who didn't care about shaving. What surprised me most was how skinny he was. He must have lost at least twenty pounds over the summer. His black dress pants were seriously creased and the armpits of his white button-down matched his teeth, the yellow of a cigarette butt that's been smoked down to the filter. Dad looked, I hate to say it, really sad compared to Officer Brady's crisp uniform and clean-shaven, youthful face.

Directing his eyes from Officer Brady to me, Dad locked his fingers behind him. His glasses were halfway down his nose, which meant he'd been reading before we arrived. "So Merlyn has finally been caught with her hand in the financial cookie jar, has she?"

"Well, as I mentioned to you on the phone, sir, your wife—"

"My ex-wife, Officer."

"Sorry, your former wife—"

"The term 'ex-wife' has a much more incontrovertible feel to it, does it not?"

Officer Brady's jaw went rigid. "Your ex-wife," he went on, frustrated, "was arrested and charged with cheque kiting and driving under the influence this afternoon, sir."

The fact that Mom was sitting in a holding cell somewhere in the city and up on some pretty serious charges didn't seem to faze Dad. He stared down at his loafers, nodding to himself: "*Sunt pueri pueri, puerilia tractant.*"

"What was that, sir?"

"Kids will be kids? You reap what you sow? Something along those lines. In any event, my ex-wife always had a penchant for decadence but, sadly, never the means to attain it. Legally, at least."

"Mr. Maloney, have you been drinking tonight?"

"That, sir," Dad said at once, "is none of your business. Now, if that will be all, thank you for bringing my son home."

If he was offended, Officer Brady did a pretty awesome job of hiding it. He looked at me, and for a few seconds I thought he might try and say something uplifting like they do in those made-for-TV movies. But in the end he just turned around. To be fair, there wasn't much he could say. *I'm sorry your mother was arrested, half-wasted no less, and then locked up? I'm truly sorry, but you're going to have to move in to your father's latest shoebox?*

Dad pulled his foot away from the bottom of the door as I walked in. Classical music was playing in the background, one of those depressing pieces he liked listening to in the evenings. The place reeked of smoke, its painting-less walls the colour of egg yolk. A cigarette burned in an ashtray beside Dad's record player. This bachelor apartment was the smallest place he'd lived in since the divorce, and I'd spent time at all of them. It was about five hockey sticks long and a little less than that wide. Aside from a bed, a TV, a desk and a grey sofa, the only other thing in the room was a dresser separating the bed from the couch. Directly across from that was a puny little kitchen. Dark grey curtains were drawn closed against the balcony windows. Something seemed to be missing to this whole scene, though I couldn't put my finger on it.

"It obviously goes without saying that you will take the bed, Justin." Dad extended an arm as a waiter might when taking a person to their seat at a restaurant.

"Where are you going to sleep?" I sat down on the wool blanket covering the bed. Dad walked across the room, picked up his glass and drained it with one bend of the elbow. "The chesterfield will suffice."

I looked over and saw a book on one of the cushions, and that's when it hit me. "Dad, where are your books?"

He refilled his glass. "Extraneous at this point in my life, I'm afraid."

"What does that mean?"

"Extraneous? It comes from the Latin, *extrāneus*, meaning 'external' or 'foreign'. I suppose you could say 'unnecessary' in layman's terms. Anyway, you must be hungry, no?"

"Dad, I'm serious. Where are your books?"

He took a sip of his drink. "I sold them."

"What about your first editions?"

"They're now the property of a literary establishment on Queen West." I could hear the regret in his voice. "In any event, why don't I put something together while you regale me with tales from your Homerian odyssey today?"

Dad would read to me at night when I was a kid, the *Oxford English Dictionary* never far from my side. Anytime I didn't understand something, he made me look it up and highlight both the word and the definition. His feet would be up on the bed as he made me repeat each new word, over and over, until I pronounced it correctly. I'd developed a pretty insane vocabulary by my tenth birthday; not a lot of fifth graders knew the difference between "erudite" and "pedantic." That, of course, was all fine and dandy until kids at school began making fun of me. Things really went south with the teasing in grade six, the same year Dad caught wind of Mom's affair and moved out.

When I changed schools in grade seven, going from a downtown public school to an uptown private school on a hockey bursary, I saw it as a chance to reinvent myself and never use big words again. That was 1986, the same year I switched AAA hockey teams and started playing for the Young Nats. More important, that was also when I got my braces off. It was a pretty wicked feeling to smile again without being called "brace face," "metal mouth" or "tinsel teeth."

"Oh, come now," Dad said, rattling me out of my thoughts. "You're a growing boy. There must be something here you want." Dad seemed bent on feeding me, but I wasn't hungry. Stress turns my stomach into a web of knots. The tremors in my arms and hands come next.

"I mean it. I'm fine."

"Come now, Justin. I have quite a lot to choose from. Let your father provide you some sustenance on this abhorrent day when your mother—"

"I told you already! I'm fine!" The words came out harsher than I'd meant them to, yet Dad didn't seem too bothered. He topped himself up as he studied me. "What!"

He did some stupid thing with his lips he thought made him look all cool. Dad calls it a "stalemate" when two people look at each other and neither one says anything. I call it "being annoying." Our own stalemate ended when the fire alarm went off all through the building. The noise made my head throb and forced me to cover my ears. Dad drained his glass in one fluid motion.

"Should we get out of here?" I yelled.

Dad grinned. "It's a false alarm."

"What?"

"False alarm. Pun intended. Nothing to worry about, kiddo."

Uh-oh.

Dad only called me "kiddo" when he'd really had one too many.

A few seconds later, the stupid thing stopped ringing. I lowered my hands, scared it would go off again and make me jump out of my skin.

"See? Momentarily obstreperous, that's all."

"You mind if I watch TV?"

"I'll turn off the music for you."

I wanted to say thanks, but I was pissed off at my mother for abandoning me today and at my father for living in a place built for the Smurfs. I hit ON, wondering if he had cable or not. When I flipped through the channels, ABC, CBS, and NBC were all there.

Nice!

Dad removed the record with both hands and slipped it into a case. As he crouched down, sounds popped out of his joints, like tree branches snapping. He returned the album to its home, a red milk crate he kept under the desk. On TV, Ron MacLean and Don Cherry were talking about tonight's preseason battle between the Leafs and Oilers, Edmonton's first game since trading Gretzky last summer to the Kings. Dad grabbed his desk chair and dragged it towards the TV. I put my back up against the wall and let my feet hang over the bed as Toronto skated to a four-two victory over the defending Stanley Cup champions.

2

We drove over to Tony's place to pick up my stuff the next day. The trip there was uneventful, the conversation between Dad and me as short as it usually was when we weren't talking hockey.

"Burger or fried chicken for lunch?" he asked.

"Burger, I guess."

"Harvey's or McDonald's?"

"Harvey's."

Dad nodded. "Want to grab something now or later?"

"Can we get my things first?"

"Indeed."

When we arrived at Tony's bungalow, Dad couldn't resist taking a potshot at Mom. "*This* is what she moved on to?"

Tony's house was in Little Italy. On a street with pretty nice houses, Tony's crapbox bungalow was rotting from inside-out. As we pulled up and Dad turned the car off, I noticed the eavestrough had come loose at one end of the roof. Dandelions dotted the small front lawn, each one a landmine warning.

"Want me to come in and help you pack your stuff?"

"No. I'm good."

"You sure?"

"Yeah."

If there is truly a God, please have Tony out of the house right now.

Not only was Tony home, but he knew nothing about what had happened over the last 24 hours.

"Where the hell'a you and your mother been, huh?" he said from his chair in front of the television, where he was watching a WWF match between "Macho Man" Randy Savage and some skinny pecs nobody. "Ya think you two can come and go here like this is a god-damn hotel? This is *my* home and that means *my* rules, ya little shit." Tony flew out of his seat, beer bottle in hand. "I swear to God, if that slut has hooked up with someone else..." Tony raised a finger and pointed it at me. "I'm gonna give ya five seconds to fess up to what you and your sidekick have done behind my back or so help me God I'm gonna slap ya into next week."

Tremors.

Tears formed in my eyes. I rubbed them away with a shaky hand as I tried to tell the biggest loser on Earth what had happened: "She was arrested"; "I'm moving to my Dad's"; "I need to grab my clothes." This only made Tony angrier. He looked around and zeroed in on the bookcase, which, instead of books, had a bunch of things Mom had collected over the years, including a small glass horse, a handmade doll, and something called an "amphora" that she'd bought in Greece with Dad on their honeymoon. Tony grabbed the fancy vase, smashed it against the floor, then paced back and forth. "Well? What are ya waitin' for? Go grab your shit." Frozen in place and shaking, I didn't move until Tony yelled, "Now!"

My blood, or at least my skin, felt like it'd turned to ice. Tony had a habit of taking out his problems with Mom on me. The more she screwed up, the worse he got with me. I fetched two big bags from my closet, stuffing one of them with clothes and loading the other one up with school books, my Walkman, a bunch of cassettes, and some stuff I wanted to save, like an autographed picture of Mario Lemieux and a puck Dad had caught at a Leaf game. Down in the basement, I zipped up my hockey bag and raced back upstairs. Tony was watching TV again, the curtains drawn closed. He didn't turn around and offer to open the front door as I struggled to get all three bags out at the same time.

As soon as he saw me, Dad got out of the car and helped put everything in the trunk. I'm not sure if he could sense how upset I was or see that my eyes were puffy and wet, but I was inside again before he could ask. Leaving behind my posters and trophies didn't bother me that much; the aquarium was different. These fish were my first pets, and as someone who'd never had a dog or a cat, the angelfish and guppies meant a lot to me.

Keep your head down and don't look anywhere near him.

The weight of the six-sided aquarium when it was full of water blew me away. It was basically impossible to move faster than an injured turtle without spilling a drop. On the edge of freedom, I tried getting my hand around the doorknob while balancing the aquarium on one wrist. This was costing me precious seconds, a ticking time bomb waiting to go off behind me. No matter how hard I tried, I couldn't find the strength to turn the old brass knob. I looked outside the grimy panes of glass on the upper part of the door and saw Dad sitting behind the steering wheel, taking pulls from his flask. I put the aquarium down, propped the door open, and hoped Tony didn't lose his mind because of how long it was taking me to get out of his stupid house. Without meaning to, I groaned when lifting the aquarium. I knew the second I did, Tony had the excuse he needed to go seriously bonkers.

Swallowing hard, he chugged his beer and leapt out of his chair. "Hey!" he yelled as I let the door close behind me.

Get to the car. Get to the car. Get to the car.

"Hey!" Tony was racing my way. "I'm talking to you. What am I supposed to do with your mom's shit, huh?"

Careful now. You're almost there...

Tony cut me off from the side and snagged the aquarium from me easily, twisting his body and throwing it high in the air like a discus.

One Mississippi, two Mississippi…BOOM!

Glass shattered when it hit the ground, water and fish sent rushing down the street. Dad came flying out of the car. He lowered his head and charged Tony, bowling him over with a football tackle. The Italian Stallion went down hard, shouting, *"Vaffanculo!"* Locked together on the grass, they pulled and punched and kicked and spat. Elbows, knees, fingernails, hands and feet were all in play. I looked at the fish now dying on the pavement, their bodies flipping from side to side.

When Dad and Tony eventually fell off each other, they lay on their backs, huffing and puffing. Tony had more blood on him, most of it coming from his damaged nose, but Dad had a shiner and a whole bunch of cuts and scrapes all over his face.

Tony was the first to get up from the grass. He marched into his home and slammed the front door. I helped Dad to his feet and got him in the car. Before starting the ignition, he looked over at me and said, "I don't think he would have made a very suitable step-father."

The blue Plymouth Volare limped over a speed bump and into the arena's parking lot. The car was a hand-me-down from Grandpa Robert, Dad's dad. Although he was the source of my middle name, I knew pretty much nothing about him except what Mom had told me over the years; Dad never, ever, ever talked about him. When Grandpa had a stroke and couldn't really take care of himself anymore, he moved in with us, as Grandma Ellie had already passed. The strongest memory I have of that time was near the end of grade four. Mom was in the kitchen and Dad was at work, which meant I had to keep an eye on Grandpa. We were in the living room. He was sitting in Dad's reading chair, staring off into space, and I was on the sofa reading a Hardy Boys story. Suddenly he waved me over with a limp hand. I flipped *The Crimson Flame* over to mark my spot (Dad says dog-earing a book is sacrilegious) and shuffled over to Grandpa. He motioned for me to come closer, as if he wanted to whisper a secret into my ear, but instead he just slapped me across the cheek. It wasn't a hard slap, more like a gust of wind hitting you in the dead of winter. I backed away, more confused than I was hurt.

Now, as Dad turned the steering wheel and looked for somewhere to park, a cigarette dangling from his mouth, I lifted an elbow up onto the padding and rested my chin on the palm of my hand.

"What are you thinking about there, Rodin?" I ignored his question. "Believe that game Koharski called last night?" This was typical Dad, switching gears and bringing it back to hockey whenever I kept quiet. "Bloody miracle the Maple Laughs won with that yahoo at the wheel."

"Yeah."

Dad found a parking space and slid the car into PARK. (I wasn't sure whether he hadn't noticed or simply didn't care, but he'd parked in a spot reserved for handicapped people.) He pushed the car lighter in and tried to get it to stick. Even though it was dark out, I could tell the bruising around his eye had swelled up in the hours since the WrestleMania extravaganza at Tony's place. Looking at his battle scars now, I felt the tiniest sense of pride. It wasn't as if he'd saved the day, but Dad had, in a way, come to the rescue. He stubbed out his cigarette and then, just as quickly, lit another one. We both sat there, lost in our thoughts.

"You should get going. Less than half an hour until you're on the ice."

"Yeah."

"Meet you in the lobby afterwards?"

"Sure."

There are two types of rinks you walk into as a hockey player. One is where the entrance and the lobby are sealed off from the actual ice skating surface. Take North Toronto, our home arena. You're more likely to smell cigarette smoke or perfume in the lobby than anything connected to hockey.

Then there are places like Forest Hill, where the pungent, unforgettable, gorgeous smell of hockey gloves, wood bench stands, Zamboni exhaust, rubber pucks and the sweat guys have worked up over a game or practice smack you in the face like an uppercut the moment you pass through those doors. At Forest Hill, the lobby's at the opposite end of the entrance, over by the dressing rooms, so in the time it takes you to reach the door that separates the warm snack bar from the cold arena, your head is already in the game.

That night, we were at Forest Hill: crappy ice surface, *awesome* smells.

In practice, the coaches worked us hard. Our first game was a week away and some of the guys were still hurting from the long summer off. Dad was the only person in the stands. He sat on the home side. Now and then he drank from his flask, which he kept tucked inside his suit jacket. I'd hoped his being so many rows up would hide his injuries, but everyone was on me after practice.

"Hey, J.R. Did you beat the tar out of the Rickster or what?" Keith said. This drew a few laughs from the room as guys got undressed, wiped down skate blades, and changed into fresh shirts. I might have been captain of the team, but that didn't mean I was safe from being the butt of a joke now and again.

"What happened, Baloney? Did the Rickster get in a bar brawl? He should get an eye patch for that shiner. They're totally coming back into fashion, you know." Ryan laughed a little too hard at his own joke as he looked around to see if anyone found him as funny as he did.

"Yeah, you could use a little help in the fashion department yourself, fagnuts," Dean said.

"You got a problem with the way I dress, Burks?"

"No. Chicks dig skin-tight acid-washed jeans, Delacrotch."

"Look who's talking, shit-for-brains. Just last week I was spanking my frank while thinking about your mother, 'cause I saw her at the Scarborough Town Centre wearing her leopard-skin mini-skirt and trying to bag all the locals." Our team's very own Cam Neely, Ryan Delacroix had two unique talents off the ice: making terrible jokes and keeping things light in the dressing room.

Dean wiped a tear from his eye. "I'm just sayin', is all."

"Hey, Delacock," Michael Bolton chimed in, "I heard your mother—"

"No, *your* mother!"

"—entered an ugly contest and got turned down 'cause they weren't accepting professionals."

You could tell Ryan wanted to top that one, but an explosion of laughter drowned him out. Realizing his moment had passed, Ryan knew he was screwed and so looked to get out of the team's crosshairs. "Yeah, well, anyway, maybe Baloney won't play like such a Euro any-more now that he's got his first KO under his belt, eh?"

On our way to the apartment, Dad played coach and talked about what "needed to be improved upon," saying, "Someone's got to talk to Atkinson's kid about how often he goes down on shots." Dad almost never called anyone on my team by their first name. A player was always so-and-so's "kid" or so-and-so's "brat," depending on how rich his parents were. "He's got a five-hole wider than a prostitute's—"

"Dad!"

"I'm being serious. You could drive a Zamboni through the gap in his pads. You scored on him 23 times tonight." Dad's ability with numbers was frightening, as was his ability to remember them faster than he could drain a glass of whiskey. "And what's going on with your third line? They can't even break out properly."

"It's still early in the season."

"Well, this is the year you've got to start thinking more long term, as in you need to be playing on a winning team so the scouts notice you."

"I *am* playing on a winning team."

"Right. And I have a bridge in Brooklyn for sale."

"What does that even mean? You've been using that dumb line since I was born and I still have no idea what you're actually saying. You know what? Forget I asked. Great. You've got a bridge in, whatever, New York City for sale. Wonderful. Can we drop this now?"

"I told you already. You should have tried out for the—"

"Stop it, would you? I'm sticking with the Nats."

We pulled over to the side of the road, across from what Dad calls "Hooker Harvey's," and he asked me to run in and grab us dinner. After today's fiasco, we'd skipped lunch and gone straight home. Dad poured himself a massive glass of liquid courage and I made myself a slice-of-cheese-and-mayonnaise sandwich.

"Fine."

"I'll take a cheeseburger with ketchup and relish and some onion rings." He pulled out his wallet, which was in worse shape than any of my ratty T-shirts, and handed me a five-dollar bill.

"Dad, what do you expect me to get with five bucks?"

Reluctantly, he pulled out two loonies from his pants. "Better?"

"No comment."

We ate in opposite corners of the apartment. I devoured my two burgers while watching a lame movie, one of those feel-good stories about a high school girl overcoming the trauma of not being named homecoming queen and then snagging the cool guy with the cool car at the end. With their sparkling white teeth, her supportive parents offered up the right advice at the right time and with just the right amount of tenderness —and all nicely wrapped with a pink bow on top.

Afterwards, I hopped in the shower and let the hot water soothe my aching muscles. Dad didn't have any of those fancy shower gels that made Mom's bathroom smell as nice as a summer garden. All he had was a bar of soap, which didn't lather very much or feel particularly smooth against my skin.

"Fall asleep in the shower there, Mr. van Winkle?" Dad asked when I got out, steam following me from the washroom.

"Huh?" I searched through one of my bags for a T-shirt and a pair of track pants.

"You were in there for the better part of a revolutionary war."

"I didn't know I had a time limit."

"Hydro is not included in the rent at this abode, young man. And the longer you're in there depleting the Great Lakes of their greatness, the higher our bill at the end of the month."

"Sorry." I had no desire to go down this path. According to Mom, Dad had been a tightwad since they'd met and didn't ever want to spend a dime on anything, except when it was on booze and smokes. He liked to constantly remind me how money didn't grow on trees and that I couldn't come to him for handouts like I was a union member or civil servant.

There was a chill to the air (Dad didn't use the radiator unless it was deathly cold outside), so I threw on a Patagonia fleece. As I breathed in the heavy smell of fabric softener, I thought of Mom. Whenever she did the wash, she put three sheets of Bounce in the dryer and my clothes came out smelling all fresh and brand-new. Thinking about the arrest now, and the look of terror in her eyes when the cops hauled her off, I couldn't decide whether I felt sorry for her or angry that she let this happen. I was see-sawing between these two emotions and flipping through my school notebook when my heart sank. "Oh, man…"

Dad looked my way from the sofa. "Problem?"

"You could say that, yeah."

"Of a personal or academic nature?"

17

"I forgot I had an essay due in history tomorrow. Crap, crap, crap!"

"And what, may I ask, is it on?" Dad put his book down while I skimmed through *Canada: 120 Years in the Making* and counted the number of pages I was supposed to read.

"Something about the Battle of Abraham Plains."

"The Battle of the *Plains of Abraham*," Dad corrected me. "Yes, indeed, that defining moment in French history when the *merde* really hit the fan and Louis XV, *le Bien-Aimé*, lost his North American *bijoux*," he said in his crappy French accent.

I wasn't interested in listening to him ramble, but I was in a bind because I didn't have the time or energy to read through the material and then write a half-decent essay. "All right. I could use your help."

He grinned. "What, precisely, is the subject of the essay?"

"We have to write five hundred words on how the battle played an important role in defining early Canadian history." I put a finger into my mouth. "*Barf.*"

"Yes, well, we're going to look at this essay of yours as an example of…historical irony." Dad scratched his temple and nodded. "And how French incompetence cost them Lower Canada."

It was past one a.m. by the time I got to the last sentence. My brain was a messy blackboard of thoughts by then. I took out the four pieces of paper from my binder, paper-clipped them together, and lay down. Too tired to brush my teeth, I just crawled underneath the covers.

"Sweet dreams, Herodotus," Dad said, liquid hitting glass the last sound I heard before falling asleep.

3

As usual, Dad was up early. I made myself a slice-of-cheese-and-mayonnaise sandwich for breakfast and added mustard to it for no other reason than I thought it might give me more energy. Dad was reading the paper when I asked him for some money.

"I thought lunch was covered by your tuition," he said, taking a sip of his Bloody Caesar, which had a stalk of wilting celery in it.

"It is, but I can't exactly walk to school from here. Can I have something for the subway?" I said, flipping the hair out of my eyes.

He handed me a twenty-dollar bill. "I trust this will get you to and fro all month. By the way, make sure you're home in time for dinner. Your father will be playing the role of *chef de cuisine* tonight." I waited for him to go on, certain he'd just told me that summer followed autumn. "What? You don't think your father can prepare a meal that is both delicious and of high nutritional value?"

The trip to school took a lot longer than it did from jerkface Tony's. I was yawning throughout the day, counting down the minutes until 3:10 hit. After our last class, Keith and I went to his place. Not only was he my best friend and the left winger on the first line with me, but he was also the only guy on the team who went to my school. Within minutes of getting in the door, his mom had turkey sandwiches made up for us with more vegetables than I'd seen in a week. Lorraine Fraser was a second mother to me and had been since Keith and I became friends in grade one. Even though she wore sweats around the house most of the time, she was pretty hot for someone her age and was the subject of many a yummy mummy joke in the dressing room during the season. Unlike Mom, who refused to spend more than a few minutes in the kitchen every day, worried she'd burn the place down or slice off a finger, Lorraine took real pleasure in putting on her KISS THE COOK apron and making all of her meals from scratch; ready-made pot pies and frozen dinners were not allowed in her home.

"There's more where that came from if you're still hungry later, boys."

We went to the basement to play video games, each of us with a sandwich and a glass of milk.

"What do you want to listen to?" Keith asked as I plopped down on the couch and began inhaling my food. Hercules, or Herc, the Frasers' yellow Lab, trotted into the room, tongue out and demanding some attention. Keith was standing in front of his awesome stereo, which had two tape decks and a CD player built into the same unit.

"Whatever."

"Then Halen it is." The title track to *1984* came on as he passed me a controller and jammed *Space Harrier* into the Sega Genesis game console. At the far end of the basement was a two-in-one pool/Ping-Pong table, making Keith's house the coolest place to hang out. The Frasers weren't exactly rolling in it like the parents of a lot of guys at our school (Mr. Fraser worked at a bank and Lorraine worked a couple of days a week as an instructor for deaf children), but when it came to their own kids, they were pretty awesome and wouldn't chintz on birthday and Christmas presents.

"Shit!" Keith said as he died his first death in the game.

"Language!" Lorraine yelled from upstairs.

Now it was my turn.

"So, ah…" I said, staring at the TV and lowering my voice, "I've moved in with my dad again."

"Oh, yeah?"

"Yeah." I maneuvered my space harrier guy around some fireballs. "On Saturday."

"What gives?"

This is where it got tricky. I'd been stressing out about how to tell Keith the news without coming across as a dork or a wuss. It's not like I wanted to fib (*fib* sounds way better than *lie*), but that's the thing I'd been realizing today: sometimes you needed to stretch the truth a little here and there about stuff like your parents. Otherwise, people think you're totally uncool. "My mom moved out of Tony's place." I was at the end of level one and battling some futuristic beast.

"So why didn't you go with your mom?"

Opening up about Mom's arrest and what that loser Tony had done wasn't an option. "I thought it'd be better to be with my dad for the hockey season. He drives me to all the games and stuff." A massive insect tore through me and it was Keith's turn again.

"Things been okay with the Rickster so far?"

"Yeah. You know. Same as usual."

Keith cleared level one. "So what really happened with his black eye?"

Fib/lie—truth/fib—lie/truth…No whammies, no whammies, no whammies…Stop!

"He got in a fight."

"Like, at a bar?"

"Yeah."

The next song was "Jump" and I sang along in my head while watching Keith continue his journey through the game's Fantasy Zone.

21

I get up, and nothin' gets me down
You got it tough, I've seen the toughest around
And I know, baby, just how you feel
You got to roll with the punches and get to what's real

"Dickpill!" Keith had just lost his second life and it was my turn again. "We should play something else."

"Hold your harrier, dude. I've still got two more lives." My guy began flying where he'd left off.

"That really sucks you had to move again. That's, like, what? The 10th time since the divorce?"

"Something like that."

Level two was clear.

"I want to play, too," Victoria said. Keith's ten-year-old sister was standing at the bottom of the stairs, as if waiting for permission to enter.

"Beat it, Vic."

"I'll tell Mom."

"Scram!"

"Mommy!" Victoria yelled as she rushed up the stairs, Herc right on her heels.

Keith and I went through another round of *Space Harrier* and then played our latest addiction, *Ice Hockey*, on his Nintendo. We'd won a game each when I said I had to leave.

"J.R.! It's a best-of-three series. You're breaking my balls here!"

"Language!" came a warning from upstairs.

"Seriously, man. Just one more game."

"Sorry, I've got to split."

Upstairs, as I put my shoes on, Lorraine asked if I wanted to stay for dinner.

"I've actually moved back with my dad and he's cooking us a big meal tonight," I told her.

"Well, always know that we love having you over to eat with us, Justin."

"Long day at the office?" Dad said from the kitchen when I walked in.

"Yeah. I was at Keith's." I put my knapsack down. The air smelled of stuff that didn't register with me. "What are you making?"

"It's a surprise. I need fifteen more minutes, though. Can you hold off for that long or are you starving?" Dad walked out of the kitchen, a cigarette between his fingers and a white poufy thing on his head. I laughed. "Your father is determined to be equal measure educator and equal measure provider. Tell you what, kiddo," he said, pouring himself a drink. "Clear off the desk and pull it out into the middle of the room, will you?"

Besides the desk chair, the only thing to sit on was one of those white foldable pieces of crap that made me feel like a kid it was so low to the floor.

"So what is this?" I asked when Dad put the plates down on the desk a while later, the dumb hat still on his head.

"Breaded veal cutlet with artichokes and scallops."

"Which ones are the artichokes?" Dad took a seat, lifted his fork and pointed to the cactus thing. "And, ah, how are you supposed to eat it?" For me, vegetables were something you put on sandwiches and this thing had definitely not been on any sandwiches or subs of mine.

"Like this." He peeled off a slimy, mushy leaf and licked it. "Artichokes are high in fibre, potassium, calcium, iron and phosphorus. I've also prepared lemon wedges for your veal, or you can try your father's homemade aioli."

Ai-what-ee?

I started with the veal cutlet, which cracked under my knife like glass. The lemon didn't make it any better. I put a little of Dad's white sauce on it, but that only made me drink half my water to kill the taste of garlic in my mouth.

"Go ahead and try the scallops. They're a wonderful source of omega-3 fatty acids and vitamin B12. And they're excellent for your cardiovascular system."

I had another sip of water and then tried the scallops.

Gross.

Then I had one of the alien arms from my artichokes.

Shoot me now.

Lowering my cutlery onto the plate, I drank some more water and kept my eyes angled towards the floor.

"Justin," Dad said, taking off his ridiculous hat. "I know it's not cooked perfectly, but these things really are excellent for you. And while they may not delight your palate, I implore you to finish your meal."

"I can't."

"You *can't* or you *won't?*"

I flipped my hair to the side. "I'm sorry." I was in what Dad calls a "Catch-22." "It's not your cooking. I've had an upset stomach since the mystery meat they served us at lunch. Plus, Lorraine gave us a snack earlier and I'm not eating a lot these days anyway so…" Each word that tumbled out of my rotten mouth had me digging a deeper and deeper hole, which apparently I'd be sleeping in when the evening was over.

"Do you know why there is no such thing as a list of reasons, Justin?"

Oh, boy. Here comes the lesson.

"Because in life you either have one adequate reason or a list of excuses."

After he was done eating, Dad dumped all the leftovers into the garbage, then sat on the sofa and read a paperback as thick as a Bible while I scoured the frying pan with a plastic spatula. The veal actually burned so badly it had formed a new layer of crud on the stupid thing.

When the dishes were clean and put away, I went over to the TV and watched *The Wonder Years*, a new show I'd seen a couple of times. Fred Savage was pretty funny, but Olivia d'Abo was the real reason I watched it.

"I heard from the police yesterday," Dad said out of the blue. I lowered the volume. "Your mother, the Right Honourable Merlyn Abbott, was arraigned in court today." My heart started racing. I hated the way he was talking so casually, like Mom had been pulled over for speeding or forgot to pick up something at the market. "It would seem she has been granted a reprieve from the real world and will get to spend sixty decadent days living on the taxpayers' dollar."

"What do you mean?" Tremors ran up and down my arms.

"I'm sure your mother's adamantine tragedy will lead her to pursue a more virtuous life in the future. Tragedy, after all, is the invisible hand that spawns reflection, and reflection bears its fruit in the deepening of one's character." He took a haul off his cigarette. "In short, she will be a guest at a women's detention centre for the next two months. Don't worry, though. She'll be out before you know it and running amok, as, of course, she's prone to do."

"Where exactly is she? I mean, which...which *detention centre* is she in?"

"I can't recall the name. I didn't write it down."

"What do you mean you didn't write it down?" I said, furious.

"Justin, I beseech you to remember that I'm still your father."

"And she's my mother, Dad. You don't think I have a right to know where she's been...locked up?"

His hand steady, Dad emptied his glass with a flick of the wrist. "I don't know."

"You don't know? You don't *know*? She's my mother and you—"

"Stop it!" he said, a hint of anger to his voice. "Get a hold of yourself, Justin."

Dad's tone surprised me, even scared me a little. "I'm going out for a bit," I said, jumping to my feet.

"As you wish."

Out in the hallway, I was waiting for an elevator when a Chinese girl around Victoria's age passed by and said they were both out of order. She was walking the length of the scuzzy yellow and brown carpet as if on a tightrope, each foot placed carefully in front of the other as she stared at the floor.

"How do you know that?"

"They break down all the time. See?" she pointed. "The buttons have no light on."

"A perfect end to a perfect day," I muttered. On my way to the closest staircase, the girl told me I should take the stairs at the other end.

"Why?"

"Those ones smell like cat pee." She raised her hand to point in my direction but still wouldn't lift her pigtailed head.

"Thanks," I said, going past her.

"You're welcome."

I walked around the neighbourhood for almost an hour, one minute wishing Dad a slow and miserable death, the next wondering how crappy Mom must be feeling right now. My knowledge about detention centres or jails or prisons—whatever they're called—came from nothing but TV and movies, and that scared me.

Turning the corner onto Dad's street, a thought occurred to me: he'd gone and played the role of chef with all the fancy food tonight because he'd wanted to show he cared about my health.

Feeling like a turdball, I rushed back to the apartment, bent on apologizing, but when I got there the place was empty. Dad's book was on the couch, smoke from a recently stubbed-out cigarette hanging in the air like a dark cloud. When he hadn't returned by eleven, I brushed my teeth and went to bed.

The next morning, Dad was asleep when I got up. My alarm going off didn't wake him and neither did me scurrying around the apartment. After showering and putting on my stupid uniform—a green jacket, grey dress pants and green tie—I hovered near the entrance and debated whether I should wake him up. In the end, I convinced myself I could say sorry later and that he probably needed the extra zzz's.

I wasn't really paying attention in any of my classes, partly because they were boring, but mostly because I was trying to figure out how to track down Mom. Not really sure it would solve anything, I headed to 53 Division after school. An older guy with a grey 'stache asked if he could help.

"I'm wondering if Jeff…if Officer Jeff Brady is here."

"I can certainly check for you, son."

"Thank you."

"May I ask your name?"

"Justin Maloney."

He got on the phone. A moment later I heard him say "Uh-huh" a couple of times. "I see," he concluded, then hung up. Looking at me again, he explained that Officer Brady was out on patrol.

"Do you have any idea when he'll be back?" My hands were fiddling with the bottom of my tie.

"I'm not sure when his shift will be ending, son, but I can give him a message if you want."

"Ahh…" I didn't want to leave my phone number because there was no way I'd let Dad handle another call from the cops. "No, that's okay. I'll come back some other time."

4

When I got home on Saturday, after a couple of hours spent playing video games down by the Eaton Centre, I had hoped to have the place to myself and do some homework. Instead, I unlocked the front door and found Dad and my cousin Dale huddled over the desk, which had been pulled close to the sofa. This could only mean one thing: *Third Reich*.

"Justin!" Dale said. "*Hisashiburi!*" He got up from his chair and hugged me. Though he had a little less of his dirty blonde hair than last time, he looked pretty good otherwise. What stood out to me more, however, was how much I'd grown since last Christmas. He'd always been taller than me, but now we were eye to eye; I might've even had an inch or two on him.

"How are you?" he asked, hands on my shoulders.

"Ah, you know."

"*Aikawarazu da ne.*"

I laughed weakly and looked down, secretly in awe that he could speak a language as cool as Japanese, even if I had no idea what he'd said.

Dale was ten years older than me. He was Uncle Adam's oldest child of three (he had one sister and a half-sister). Like a big brother, he'd shown me how to do cool things as a kid like make homemade Roman candles and, most recently, he'd taught me how to drive his *stick shift* Datsun 280ZX. Four years ago, he moved to Japan after graduating from university, and was now teaching English in Tokyo through something called the JET program. One of the first things he did when he got there was send me a copy of *Shogun*. Ever since then, I pictured Dale as a modern-day John Blackthorne, slaying babes in their kimonos when not teaching.

"Come on," Dale continued, "join Uncle Rick and me for some World War II banter. Your father is rewriting history at the Battle of the Bulge this very minute. Apparently his strategy is one that Hitler should have paid heed to. He's decimating my armies and turning Europe into a brave new Germanic world as he implements *die Neuordnung Europas*."

Some of my earliest memories are of watching what Mom called "a colossal waste of time" and what Dad called "the only reason I stay sane." As a teenager, Dale would come over a lot on weekends. He and Dad would then spend Saturdays and Sundays moving little square pieces around a board. This game was also the background for a huge fight between Mom and Dad. I think Dale was sixteen and Dad had just poured him his first drink. "Better to enjoy Mr. Walker in the company of responsible adults than to be doing so on one's own," Dad said.

"He's a minor, Rick! Sweet, gentle Jesus in the garden. What do you think you're doing? Do you have any idea what Adam would say if he saw you pouring booze down his son's throat?"

Dale didn't say a word, didn't touch his glass. I watched from the living room, not really understanding what all the fuss was about because it was just a *drink* after all.

"Merlyn, dear, this matter does not concern you. Dale and I are having our first adult moment and it would be much appreciated if you'd leave us in peace to carve up Europe."

Mom put her hands up to her temples and tapped the toe of a high heel. "Then carve up Europe without polluting your nephew, won't you?"

Dale pushed his seat back, as if to say he'd be happy to leave the room and let my parents have this conversation in private. "Dale, stay right where you are. My wife is being a zealot and will not take away from our time together."

"A what?" Mom blasted.

"A zealot, dearest. You've reached a critical boiling point in that lovely head of yours and I fear that if you don't relax with a cold glass of white wine, you might melt down as spectacularly as Chernobyl."

Whatever Chernobyl was, it really set Mom off.

"Rick Maloney, get off your ass and into the kitchen this very second."

Dad hunched himself closer to the board and moved some pieces. Dale's eyes were moving back and forth between Mom and Dad.

"Rick?"

A couple of seconds passed, then Dad clapped his hands together and said, "Aha! France is now mine, just as it was the **Führer's**!" He raised his glass. "Dale, to history not being revisionist in any way, shape or form."

Mom put both hands over her face, as if praying, breathed in deeply, and then flipped the board over and sent tiles flying onto the floor, scaring the crap out of me.

"Now, Merlyn, is that behaviour that becomes the mother of a child? I hate to point out the obvious, but that is precisely what little children do when they don't get their way."

"You son of a bitch! How dare you!" Then, with a Jekyll and Hyde switch in personality, Mom leaned over and put a hand on Dale's shoulder. "Would you mind giving me and your uncle Rick a sec?"

"Dale will do no such thing," Dad said as he began picking up the cardboard pieces off the floor. "We will simply pretend this transgression never took place."

"How would you like a glass of Suntory, Justin?" Dale said, rattling me from my thoughts as he reached for a bottle on the floor.

"I'm, ah…I'm okay. Thanks."

"You sure? This is the very best Nihon has to offer."

Dale held the bottle in one hand like a trophy and flashed me a smile worthy of Chuck Woolery on *Love Connection*.

"Nah. I'm good."

He cracked the plastic wrapping off the top and poured two glasses.

"So, how long have you been in town for?" I asked Dale as he and Dad studied a board that was as complicated to me as integers and fractions.

"A week. Quick trip this time. In and out," he answered, his attention focused on the armies below him.

"How's Japan? Still awesome?"

"Still awesome."

"When are you leaving?"

"Huh? Oh, tomorrow afternoon. I'm taking a JAL flight to Tokyo."

"A what flight?"

Dale didn't answer me right away. He moved some pieces around and then said triumphantly, "If Churchill were alive today, he'd be grateful for erasing that stain called Gallipoli from his record and stopping your Panzers in their tracks, Uncle Rick." He clapped his hands and looked up at me, dazed. "Oh, Japan Airlines. I'm flying out of Pearson at 3 p.m."

"Damn it!" Dad said, opening his pack of Rothmans Blues. "I'm out of cigs. I'll be right back."

When Dad was gone a minute later, Dale removed an envelope from his jacket. "This is for you, Justin." I knew exactly what was inside. Since moving to Japan, he mostly gave me cash for birthdays and

Christmases, or sometimes just as random gifts on visits to Toronto. In the beginning, I'd get fifty dollars each time, but lately it'd become a hundred bucks. Sure enough, when I opened the envelope and peeked inside, I saw what Dad called a "Robert Borden." I didn't take it out because Mom taught me that handling money in front of others was rude.

"Thanks," I said, flipping the hair out of my eyes.

"My pleasure. Now, tell me how school is." He took a small sip from his glass, which, unlike Dad's, had ice in it.

"You know, fine."

"Keeping up with your grades?"

I laughed. "It's the start of the year, Dale."

"True enough."

"And hockey? Your father tells me you're captain again this year."

"Yeah."

"Impressive." Dale studied me the way adults did when they were about to get all personal. "He told me about your mother as well." My cheeks, I'm sure, were burning red. "I'm sorry," he said. I scratched my head and flicked the bangs out of my eyes. "But can I tell you something? This is going to make you stronger. I know it sounds clichéd, but this is going to make you a better person. You've got a bright future ahead of you. You're the best hockey player I've ever seen and it's going to take you somewhere spectacular."

"What, like Japan?" I joked.

Dale didn't laugh. "You've got a shot at the pros. You're *that* good. You have a gift. What you do on the ice," he said, looking out the window at the cement balcony, "is something most kids dream of and never come close to."

We were both quiet. In record speed, Dad was through the door, a cigarette already lit and between his lips. "Now that the Desert Fox has returned, I can resume my destruction of the Allies in North Africa."

"I'm afraid Field Marshall Montgomery will have something to say about that, Uncle Rick."

Third Reich was one of those games that took days to finish, and just before we sat down to watch the 100m final, live from the Seoul Olympics, at a little past midnight, Dad and Dale were in another deadlock.

"Come on, you guys! The runners are at the starting line."

I wasn't that into the Olympics, but this was a special night. Ben Johnson was racing against Carl Lewis, the gold medallist four years ago in Los Angeles. Dad and Dale took their sweet time stumbling over to the TV.

"Seriously! It's about to begin."

The runners were doing that horse thing where they kick their legs as they bend down, their weight supported on the ends of their fingers. I was on the edge of the bed, bouncing up and down. The guy with the gun raised his arm as Dad and Dale finally took a seat beside me. Exactly 9.79 seconds later, Ben Johnson crossed the finish line first. Noise erupted in the apartments around us. The three of us were jumping around like a bunch of kooks when the announcer said a new Olympic and world record had been set. Ben Johnson ran around the stadium with a Canadian flag in his hand as we high-fived each other.

"Now *that* was something!" Dad said. "Dale, I propose we celebrate this proud national moment with a nightcap."

"Finer words'er ne'er spoken," Dale said as he gave me a hug, his arms draped around me all sloppy like an octopus. "I'm gonna call ya from Tokyo more regular, see. I've been a bad cousin. Bad, bad cousin." He belched. "But things are gonna change. Uncle Rick?" he said, looking at Dad, who was putting on a cardigan older than me. "Are we ready to rape and pillage?"

"Judging by your performance in *Third Reich* today, I believe that is all you are good for."

Dale laughed as he looked at me again. "Now, 'member to geep yer stick on the ice. Shoo' fer de net and don' le'anyone gi'ya shi'n de corners."

"I won't," I said, grinning.

"An''member t'always geep yer stick on de ice!" Dale added, looking over his shoulder and walking out the door.

5

"Good morning, Justin," Lorraine said, smiling at me through the rearview mirror as I got in the back seat of her car. When she found out from Keith that I'd moved in with Dad, she'd offered to drive me to school every day.

"Morning."

"Dude, did you hear the news?" Keith twisted around to look at me.

"No. What?"

"They raped Ben Johnson of his gold medal for—"

"*Stripped*, Keith," his mother said. "He was *stripped* of his gold medal."

"Anyway, they flushed his medal down the toilet when he got busted for 'roids."

"Holy moly. So who gets the gold now?"

"Carl friggin' Lewis," Keith said as he slumped down in his seat.

In first period, Mr. Nash gave us back our history essays. I got a B-. "Do I detect a hint of prejudice against the French, Justin?" I looked at him, not understanding what he was getting at. "Your theory on how the French stabbed themselves in the back linguistically was weak. More to the point, it was irrelevant to the scope of the assignment. The reason you didn't get a lower mark is that you infused your argument with enough historical facts to warrant a decent grade."

"What do you got against the Frenchies?" Keith said from behind me.

"And you, Mr. Fraser, have the distinction of receiving a lower grade than your classmate here." Mr. Nash slipped the essay not into Keith's hands but onto his desk, which shut him up pretty quickly.

On our way out of class, I overheard Mitchell Bachman, the smartest kid at school, say to someone else that I probably plagiarized my essay. Keith also heard the comment and decided to fight this battle for me.

"Screw you, *Botch*man. What's your problem anyway?"

"It's a sham the school lets you get away with what you do."

"And what's the sham, numbnuts?" Keith had turned around and was glaring down at Mitchell from many inches above.

"Relax, guys," I said. Keith tended to let his anger – and his ego – get the better of him when riled up. By that point, a bunch of other guys were huddling around us in the hallway.

"No, you ask dipstick here what he meant."

Keith pulled his fist back and Mitchell flinched, raising his forearm up in defence. "Psych!"

Lowering his arm, a look of hurt and anger on his face, Mitchell said, "It's sad, really. You jocks on your hockey bursaries get a free ride here."

Keith's chest expanded. "Us jocks?"

I knew Mitchell was pushing his luck with Keith. "Mitchell, take a pill, okay? Keith? Keith, damn it! He's just…"

"What?" Mitchell said. "A nerd? A loser?"

"That's not what I was going to say."

"Then what, Justin?"

Keith couldn't control himself any longer. He rammed Mitchell into the lockers, making him drop a binder and some pens. Keith's finger was aimed at the middle of Mitchell's chest. "Watch it, *Botch*man."

"Keith, quit it." I tried to squeeze myself between the two. My best friend had a temper and was way too big and strong for his own good, but I knew he would never hurt me.

"You're both goons," Mitchell hissed, picking up his binder and pens, and scurrying down the hallway.

That night was our first game of the season, an away one. While we got dressed, AC/DC's *Back in Black* played on Ryan's ghetto blaster. No one was saying much. I think everyone just had pre-game jitters. "You Shook Me All Night Long" was playing when Mr. Wainwright asked Ryan to turn down the volume.

"Gentlemen, we are the favourites to win the division this season. How do I know this, you ask?" He scanned the faces of the guys opposite me. "Because I decided we're the favourites, that's why."

Everyone laughed.

"The onus is now on you, and you alone, to prove the naysayers wrong." He paused and started counting on his fingers: "We have the skill, we have the drive, and we have the heart to go to the provincial championships this year. And, gentlemen, I believe in you all. You are the nineteen most talented hockey players in your age group. Go out there tonight and show everyone why you are the team to beat this season." Another chorus of yells rang out. Everybody was fired up. "Tim?" Mr. Wainwright said to our starting goalie. "Lead us out, will you?"

Guys slapped each other all over the place, on shoulder pads, girdles, helmets and face masks. I stood by the door and hit everyone's shin pads with my stick as they made their way out. The last player to leave the dressing room, I launched myself onto the ice, just like Mark Messier or Wendel Clark would, with one single goal in mind: to win.

The stands were packed. With so much adrenaline rushing through us, we started off a little shaky and took two dumb penalties. We killed off one of them, but got burned on the other.

One-nothing for the bad guys.

For those first fifteen minutes, I was having a brutal time concentrating. I made dumb passes and missed the net when I had all the time in the world to shoot. I tried to focus, but my mind was either picturing Mom sitting all alone in a cell or thinking of my crappy living situation. But when Dad really started giving it to the refs from the stands, I lost it. Him yelling at one of my games was nothing new, but he was really bad tonight, maybe because he was super-loaded or maybe because I was playing like a piece of pooh. I kept thinking, This is unfair. *Yeah, well life isn't fair, kiddo,* Dad's voice said inside my head. Then I thought of something Mom told me when I was a kid: *Why does the only luck that comes my way have to be bad luck?*

…then I gave the puck away in the neutral zone, completely out of it and forgetting there was a game going on. The other team went in on a two-on-one and, thank God, didn't score. Dean played it perfectly, cutting off the pass between the two attackers like it was no big deal.

Mr. Wainwright benched our line for the next shift and that just made me angrier. This was my favourite sport, the one time I got to leave behind my problems from school and life and family and new zits popping up on my forehead every day, and all I could do was think about the stuff that happened over the last week.

Unfair, unfair, unfair. It's not FAIR!

"You okay, J.R.?" Keith panted.

"Fine."

"Then let's get out there and kick some ass, all right? Put a puck around that skidstain of a freaking goalie."

"Sure."

There was a little under a minute left in the period when Mr. Wainwright sent us out for our next shift. The face-off was in their end. I lost it and raced to the corner to steal the puck from their defenceman, but the stupid thing got caught up in our skates. Then Keith came in and tried to chip away at it with his stick. No dice. Their defenceman was playing it smart, trying to run out the clock. That's when one of their players demolished me against the boards, the Plexiglas shaking as my helmet crashed into it. I crumbled to the ice.

The buzzer went, signalling the end of the first, but I was too mad to be done yet. I got up and shoved the player who'd hit me. He pushed me right back, in the unprotected gut area, which kind of winded me. I was about to launch myself at him when Keith buried the jerk. A wicked player, Keith was more than our enforcer: he was my personal bodyguard on the ice. With one solid push against the guy's facemask, the loser flew into the boards and onto his ass.

We got an earful from Mr. Wainwright during the intermission, and Keith and I started the second period in the penalty box. I got two minutes for roughing, as did the wanker from the other team, but Keith got a double minor. Yet again we'd be shorthanded. There was an upside to this, though. When Keith got out of the box, our line was fired up. I could tell Mr. Wainwright was pissed at me, but by the middle of the period, our line had found our stride and evened things up—I took an amazing pass from Luc Garnault, and drilled it over the goalie's right shoulder. Damn, did that feel good.

Going into the third period, the score was tied three-three. The other team took a tripping penalty five minutes in, but we couldn't take advantage of the power play. With a couple of minutes left on the clock, I deflected a zinger from Dean that found the back of the net. Final score: four-three for the good guys.

Afterwards, Mr. Wainwright was anything but satisfied with our win. "Can someone tell me where our D was tonight? Joel, Randy, Dave," he said, spinning in their direction. "Congratulations. You three are officially on my shit list." The three defencemen stared at the floor as they got chewed out. They knew they'd stunk the joint out and, more than anything, they'd let Timmy Atkinson down, giving up three breakaways. "I mean, honestly. Three goals on eleven shots? If we spring that many leaks against any other team we're gonna go down faster than the bloody *Titanic*."

When Mr. Wainwright and the two assistant coaches left, the room was pretty quiet. You could see the disappointment on everyone's face. Ryan Delacroix broke the silence: "We need to stay positive, boys." It was a harmless comment, but then he finished by saying, "Maybe a little Lorraine burger could help us feel better."

I understood what Ryan was doing, we all did, but it was the wrong time to bring up the yummy mommy jokes.

"Up yours, assface," Keith fired back. "You want to think about something, Delajockstrap, think about this: score much?"

"Yeah? Here's one for you: suck dicks much?"

Keith stood up. "Bring it on—"

Ryan stood up. "You're not gonna—"

"Guys!" I shouted. "We won, all right? We got a W and that's what matters. Let's build on that. Our first home game is coming up." Nobody said a thing as I stood up and chucked a shin pad into my bag. "Let's bring it to the arena on Friday night and pound those...those... *fuckers* into the ground."

There was a stunned silence. Dean looked to his left, then his right. "Ahh...am I crazy or did Baloney just *swear*?"

Ryan sat down and Keith did the same a second later. Laughter started to break out, slowly at first, like the first popcorn kernels snapping in a microwave, but soon the whole dressing room was a wave of smiles and wisecracks.

"Jesus," Timmy piped up. "If Baloney can swear, then anything really is possible!"

It was true. I'd never said the F word out loud before.

Keith grinned at me. "Well, I'll be a mother freakin' horse's ass. It really is a miracle."

"That you're a horse's ass or that Baloney swore?" Ryan said.

"Listen, you wanker, if I'm a horse's ass then you're—"

"—a sweat-stained jockstrap served up in a dirty ashtray?" Michael Bolton yelled from the corner.

Ryan whipped an elbow pad at M.B., who returned the gesture at once. Then the rest of the guys got into it and equipment flew every which way. I ducked down, smiling as I calmly unlaced my skates, not a tremor running through my arms.

On the way home, Dad pointed out the obvious, but I didn't have the energy to argue. I just stared out the window, my chin propped up on my hand, while he ranted. "You guys aren't back-checking hard enough. You've got a bunch of pylons out there on defence and Atkinson's kid isn't helping matters. You've got to play two-way hockey, kiddo. All of those Al Iafrates out there on D aren't going to win you the Provincials this year playing like that." I blinked so slowly it felt like time stood still. When I didn't say anything, Dad pressed on. "You've got to be more like Pat LaFontaine out there, you know, two ways, end-to-end hockey."

Before turning off my light and going to sleep, I reached for my Oxford English Dictionary and flipped to the word that had been gnawing away at me since the game.

un·fair

adjective

1. characterized by inequality or injustice
2. dishonest or unethical

Definition one fit my situation with Dad to a T, while definition two was pretty much what I thought of Mom. Fuming, I put a pillow up against the bookshelf and leaned back, closing my eyes and just trying to breathe normally.

How had everything unravelled so quickly?

I wasn't blind (I think) or completely ignorant (I hope), and so I looked up one more word.

un·grate·ful

adjective

1. unappreciative; not displaying gratitude; not giving due return or recompense
for benefits conferred

I looked over at Dad on the couch and felt kind of bad. He hadn't asked for this situation to be sprung on him, and Mom probably had no idea she was heading to the slammer. Reading the definition again, I wondered if I was the ungrateful one. Years ago, whenever Mom complained about something and she and Dad had a fight about it, he'd say, "Shit happens, dear. Then you pour yourself a drink and get on with it." Mom had her own version, which she'd say when I couldn't understand why something bad was happening, like when she lost her job at the clinic (budget cuts, she said) and gave me a sad smile, explaining, "It is what it is, baby."

Now, as I looked at Dad in his happy place—drink on a coaster, a cigarette in one hand and a book in the other—I finally understood what they were getting at and realized something else. Ever since

Mom's arrest, it had dawned on me how much I hated my new reality and the *unfairness* of it all. My parents would a never say it in a million, billion, trillion years, but I knew that the word I'd just looked up described me perfectly.

The same Chinese girl was tightrope walking down the hallway when I got back to the apartment from school the next day.

"I hear you're this, like, famous hockey player," she said as I put my key in the door.

I looked over my shoulder and waited for her to continue. When she didn't, I asked, "Who'd you hear that from?"

"Your dad. He talks about you with everyone in the building."

"Hey."

"What?"

"Come here." She tightrope walked over. "When?" I asked. Her hands were crossed over one another as she stared down at the carpet.

"When what?"

"When did my dad tell you that?"

"I don't know." She started twirling her pigtails. "Maybe a day or two ago."

"Well, I'm not." I don't know what irritated me more, that Dad was talking about me to strangers in the building or that this girl thought I was a famous hockey player.

"That's not what your dad says." She kicked at the floor with the heel of her shoe.

"What's your name?"

"Kim Jung-ho."

"Well, Kim—"

"No. Kim is my family name. You can call me Jung-ho."

"Right. Well, my name—"

"—is Justin. Justin Maloney. Your dad named you after a Roman emperor." She still wouldn't look at me.

"How old are you?"

"Ten."

I nodded. "Right. Well, it's been nice meeting you. I'm going inside my apartment now, okay?"

I pushed down on the door handle.

"Do you know how to swim?"

I kept the door open with a hand raised above my head. "What?"

"Could you teach me to swim?" Her heel was still kicking at the pukey carpet.

"Why? Do you have a pool in your apartment or something?" I asked through a laugh.

"We could use the one upstairs." That's when Jung-ho finally looked at me.

"What are you talking about?" There was no way this crapstain building had anything as fancy as a swimming pool.

"On the top floor. There's a *biiiiiig*, wide pool," Jung-ho said, spreading her arms far apart.

"Is it clean enough to swim in?"

"Why not?" Her almond-shaped eyes had this look to them that said, *Are you crazy?* "It smells like chlorine. That's good, right?"

"It smells like chlorine," I repeated slowly. "Right. Listen, I'd *love* to help you out and all, but I'm kind of busy these days."

"Please, Justin. I don't know anyone else who can swim and I really, really, really want to learn." She stopped herself and then added, "Your father says you're very kind. He used a big word like ben-*something*-lent when he talked about you."

Even when he wasn't around, Dad made me want to tear my hair out. "Benevolent?"

"Yes! That's it! How do you pronounce it?" You'd think I'd doubled her allowance, she looked so happy.

I said the word again and she repeated it. "What does it mean?"

"It means someone who's very…someone who helps others."

"I see."

I breathed in deeply through my nose. "Okay. Tell you what. Let me check the pool later on. If it's clean enough to swim in, then, yes, fine, I'll teach you. Drop by around four p.m. tomorrow, okay?"

"You promise?"

Holy smokes. There's no end to this kid.

"Yes. I promise."

We shook on it and then she slid her palm across mine. "What's that for?"

"It's a photocopy of our promise."

Unbelievable.

That night I asked Dad about the pool upstairs, having checked it out for myself earlier. As Jung-ho had said, it was a big, wide pool that reeked of chlorine. "How come you didn't tell me we have a swimming pool in the building?" We were both eating Kraft Dinner, Dad's drenched in salt, mine floating in pepper.

"You never asked."

"How was I supposed to ask about something I knew nothing about?"

"Socrates would disagree with you." I exhaled loud enough to snuff out a candle. "He believed the sum knowledge of the universe is contained within our souls and that the only way to access it is through a specific line of questioning."

"You know, if I wanted some…*nebulous* answer I wouldn't have asked you in the first place."

The corners of Dad's lips turned up. "Nebulous?"

"Yes, as in your vague, unclear answer is not appreciated."

"I haven't heard you use a sixty-four-thousand-dollar word in quite some time."

"Would you get over it?"

"I'm very impressed."

"Whatever. Is there anything else I should know about this building?"

"It has four fire exits."

"That can help me!"

"That's very helpful."

"You're infuriating."

Dad grinned. "I've always loved that word. It does a much better job of conveying one's vexation than 'annoying' or 'bothersome'."

Jung-ho held me to my "photocopy." After making myself a ham sandwich on Wonder Bread, there was a knock at the door. A four-foot-something girl in a fuchsia one-piece bathing suit and yellow thongs stood in the hallway. In one hand she had a brown towel; in the other, she had nose plugs, earplugs, a pair of blue goggles, and two of those inflatable arm thingies.

"Let me get my trunks and a towel. Do you want to come in?"

"I'm not supposed to enter strangers' apartments."

"But I'm not a stranger."

This made her think. "No. I can wait out here."

Upstairs, we had the pool all to ourselves. As sunlight streamed into the room through the windows, I dove into the water and made my way to the shallow end. When I tried to get her to jump in, Jung-ho wouldn't budge. Yesterday she was begging me to teach her how to swim, and now she wouldn't even get in the water.

"It's okay," I said, keeping my frustration in check. "Jump in. I'll catch you. There's nothing to be worried about."

"I'm scared."

I climbed out of the pool, took a seat at the edge and let my legs dangle in the water. "Tell you what. We don't have to actually go in the water today. Why don't we just look at it from here?"

She nodded half-heartedly. I extended a hand towards her, keeping it there until she grabbed it and sat down beside me. I could tell her heart was racing like a racy race car, but I had no idea how to make a frightened ten-year-old girl settle down. "So," I said. "What do you feel like talking about?"

Jung-ho dipped a finger into the water, as if testing whether it was real or not, and asked me if I liked her name. I was going to make a joke about George Bell and how out of left field her question was, but I could tell she was serious.

"Yeah, but…I don't really know a lot of Chinese names."

Jung-ho looked at me with that same *Are you crazy?* look she'd given me yesterday. "But I'm not Chinese."

"Oh. Right. What are you, then?"

Jung-ho didn't miss a beat. "Canadian."

"Okay. What I meant was…" I didn't really know how to finish my question because she clearly looked Asian. "Umm…where are your parents from?"

"Korea."

"Hey, they're hosting the Olympics right now!" I said, proud of knowing a single thing about the country.

"Everybody knows that."

Not exactly the response I'd expected. "Right. Anyway, why did you ask me if I like your name?"

"Because I hate it."

Jung-ho explained how her father had given her a boy's name before she was even born. "It's supposed to bring some kind of good luck, I guess. I wasn't good luck."

"Why?"

"Because I'm a girl!"

"Oh."

"It's not so bad at school because no one in my class is Korean. But when we go to church, everyone laughs at me. Sunday school is the worst. That's where all the mean kids are."

I didn't say much as we kicked our feet around in the water. I'd ask her a question now and again, though she seemed happy to tell me about herself. Jung-ho, her parents and her older brother were from Seoul and moved to Toronto in 1982. Koreans almost never have a chance to swim, she explained, and now that she lived in Canada, she wanted to learn how. "Don't girls your age want to play hockey or soccer or, I don't know, hopscotch?" I asked.

"But Canada is *fillllled* with water," she said, her arms open wide. *She did have a point.*

After our "lesson," we rode the elevator down. When we got off, Jung-ho reached for my hand and we walked the length of the corridor together. Jung-ho knocked on 802, two doors down from Dad's place, and lit up when she saw her father.

"Daddy!"

Mr. Kim looked sternly at me and then at his daughter. "*Awdee kassawtnee?*" he asked in a rough voice.

"I went swimming," she replied proudly.

"*Maw?*" her father scowled. "*Suyung haraw kasawtdago?*"

"Yes." Jung-ho slowly lowered her head and looked wounded, her lips turned downward. I had no idea what Mr. Kim was saying, but it was obviously not very good. "Justin was teaching me to..." Jung-ho started, then trailed off.

"You not leave apartment without Daddy's permission," he said in a thick accent. I guess that last part was for my benefit because he then switched to Korean again. *Teukhee natsun waegook sarameerang. Aratjee?*"

"*Nae,*" she said in a nasal voice.

Her father grabbed his daughter's hand from mine, and as the door closed Jung-ho craned her head towards me, fear and sadness in her eyes.

Well, I guess the swimming lessons were officially over. I hoped Jung-ho wasn't in too much trouble, or that at least her dad wasn't going to make a big deal out of it.

Sometime after dinner, there was a knock at the door. "It's not going to answer itself," Dad said from the desk, where he was busy fiddling with his record player. I got off the bed and opened the door.

Jung-ho's father was standing in the hallway, a box of apples in his hands. "I am Mr. Kim. I am Jung-ho's daddy. Excuse me, but Jung-ho tell me about your swimming course at pool. I make mistake when you come to my door. Please, you receive apples." He handed me the wooden crate full of Granny Smiths. "Jung-ho so proud of you, like elder brother. I am sorry." Before I could respond, he walked away.

"Dad?"

He looked over at me as the door squeaked closed.

"I have some good news. We finally have some fruit in the apartment."

6

At our home opener, we were a quieter bunch in the dressing room than last game. Still, everyone was pretty intense as they got ready. Even Ryan wasn't cracking jokes as we listened to *Appetite for Destruction*. Mr. Wainwright gave a short pre-game speech, telling us we had no one to impress tonight, no one to make proud, other than ourselves. He went over a couple of power play and penalty killing options, and then left with the assistant coaches. Nobody said much at first. We were all lost in our own thoughts. "Five goals, boys," I found myself saying. "Five goals."

Most of the guys were looking down at the floor. Their heads snapped up a moment later when Keith echoed, "Five goals! You heard Baloney. We get five goals tonight."

"No," I said with sudden confidence. "We *win* by five goals. We bury them and the season *officially* starts tonight."

In warm-up, I skated around our end nice and casual. No rush. Some of the other guys were blowing by me. Dean was lined up at the hash marks with a whack of pucks. As the player with the hardest and arguably most accurate shot on the team, he often drilled a bunch of rubber at Timmy while the rest of us stretched hamstrings, twisted our torsos, and lifted sticks high above our heads. Then the whole team joined in and helped get Timmy ready in net, firing pucks at him from all different angles. I'd vowed to myself before the game that I was going to leave Mom and Dad in the dressing room, so to speak, and that the next forty-five minutes belonged completely to my team. It wasn't about life being unfair or me being ungrateful for thinking the things I did. It was about scoring goals and helping us win.

At the end of the first period, it was four-nothing for us. We were off to an epic start. Dad was screaming his face off, a little louder than usual. If given the chance, I'm sure the ref would've given Dad a five-minute major for being a loudmouth and a game misconduct for staying on his case every play. Fortunately, fans can't get penalties or else our team would've been camped out in the box every game.

Frustration started coming through on my end in the second period when we couldn't get the puck out of our end and some guy on the other team slashed me across my forearms. I looked at the ref and was thinking, *How could you not call a slashing penalty? That's so unfair.*

The whistle blew when Timmy smothered the puck under his glove. I skated to the bench and started muttering to myself. Keith and Luc probably thought I was demented or something, but all I was trying to do was tell myself to stop using that word *unfair*: not on the ice, not at school, not at home.

The face-off was in our end, on Timmy's left side. Mr. Wainwright left our line on to take the draw. I looked at Dean as I glided to the face-off circle and gave him a little cue, signalling a set play we'd worked out. It was subtle, but Dean was a heads-up defenceman. Lowering my back to ninety degrees, I waited for the linesman to drop the puck.

The rubber never actually hit the ice.

I knocked it cleanly to Dean from out of mid-air and made a beeline towards centre ice, trying to split the other team's defence. By the time both their D started turning on a dime, I'd already blown past them. Dean made a tape-to-tape pass and before I'd even crossed centre ice I was on a breakaway. Some guys get all nervous when they're in all alone. Not me. I can read a goalie pretty well from as far away as the blue line and this time was no different. He was buried in his net and not bothering to challenge me. His pads were locked together, so the five-hole was out of the question. But when you stay stuck on your own goal line, you're inviting a sniper to come in and fill any part of the net he wants.

As I came up on the hash marks I said to hell with it. This one's for Mom and Dad and life being unfair and it is what it is and shit happens and you pour yourself a drink and get on with it. I wound up and fired the hardest slapshot I could muster. For a second, it was quiet throughout the arena because the goalie hadn't moved. Nobody knew where the puck was until the ref caught up to us and pointed to the back of the net, blowing his whistle and indicating a goal.

The parents in the stands went wild. Our team went crazy. The goalie had no idea what had happened and was still standing stock-still in his net. Apparently the puck had flown over his right shoulder at Mach speed and he never saw the piece of rubber zing by him.

Mr. Wainwright wasn't one of those coaches who slapped players on the shoulder pads or gave them taps on the helmet during the game. He was always really focused, thinking of line combinations and who to put out next and how best to adjust to the other team's strategy. But when I swung my legs over the bench and took a seat on our team's lumber, panting like I'd just run the hundred-yard dash, Mr. Wainwright bent down and whispered in my ear, "Gutsiest breakaway I've ever seen, Justin."

When the final buzzer sounded at the end of the third period, the scoreboard read:

HOME: 9 VISITORS: 0

Nine different players found twine. Timmy Atkinson got his first shutout and when Ryan said it was "a coach's wet dream of a game" afterwards, the dressing room went bonkers. I just kind of kept to myself, proud that we'd shown we could annihilate another team on the ice this early in the season, and that my lame pre-game talk might have had something to do with that.

Mr. Wainwright, who announced his shit list empty of any names, managed to crack a smile as well, which was no small feat on his part. Most of the guys were roaring as they tried to outdo each other with yummy mummy jokes, a Metallica song playing in the background as we got undressed. I knew everyone was in physical pain, this being only our second game, and the room probably smelled worse than a months-old dirty sock found at the back of a closet, but we'd won the game. Except for Michael Bolton, who'd attacked the other team's blue line in the third period like a human shield and taken a slapshot off his skate (and who would now be out at least one game with a bruised ankle), the rest of us would just go home and smear RUB A535 all over our aching muscles.

For me, the only crappy part about playing hockey was the end of the game, when I took off my helmet and knew the sweat and grease and oil from my hair was only making the zits on my forehead worse. That night was no different. I'd wash my face at the arena and then go home and scrub my forehead hard with soap and still nothing would change. That Clearasil Acne Treatment Cream crap was only for girls, and I didn't know any other way of making a mountain range more like flatlands once again. People always told me it was nothing more than puberty, but then I looked at Dad's forehead and the bumps which had never gone away, if for different reasons (he had shingles when I was a kid). That would be me, I thought, removing my jockstrap and zipping up my bag: I'd be forty-five years old and still too self-conscious to lift the hair off my stupid forehead.

In the lobby, I asked Dad for a dollar. He hummed and hawed, a cigarette hanging from the corner of his mouth as he frisked himself in search of a loonie. Keith and I walked to the other end of the arena to get our well-deserved reward. When we got there, we breathed in the smell of hot dogs and popcorn, the staple food of every hockey arena snack bar. Behind the counter was a hot blonde our age with light green eyes and a tall dude with bad acne scars all over his face. The babe ended up serving us. "Hiya. What can I get you?"

"I'll take a large strawberry Slushie," Keith said, leaning on the counter with both elbows and grinning.

"And what can I get you?" she asked me. A smile cropped up on her face as a pair of dimples appeared at the same time. Momentarily arrested by those dimples, I forgot what I'd wanted to order. "Hello? McFly? Anyone home?"

I brushed the bangs out of my eyes and said I'd have a small raspberry Slushie. When she went to get us our drinks, Keith gave me a kick from behind and hit my knees, almost making me buckle.

"Ow! What was that for?"

Keith had a goofy grin and refused to take his eyes off Snack Bar Girl.

"For the record, these two flavours are *waaay* inferior to orange Slushies," she said, giving us our drinks. "Now, is that together or separate?"

"Sep—"

"Together." Keith handed over a twenty-dollar bill.

As we made our way to the lobby, Keith and I debated how hot Snack Bar Girl was and averaged out our two answers, coming up with a nine-point-one. Keith said her one fault was that she was too skinny. "You need your head examined," I told him. "If she's too skinny, what the heck is Cindy Crawford or Paulina what's-her-face?"

"Not even in the same league, J.R."

"But they're both thin as rakes."

"And they both have ICBMs for tits, something Snack Bar Girl is definitely lacking."

Lorraine congratulated us on our win when we came through the doors of the meeting area, where Dad and a bunch of other parents hung around waiting for their kids, half of them smoking up a storm. "Excellent game out there, Justin. Best player of the night if you ask me."

"What am I, chopped liver?" Keith asked.

"No, my darling. You also had a fantastic game." She screwed up Keith's hair before turning towards Dad and saying, "Rick, a pleasure as always."

"Lorraine, you will continue to be the most civilized aspect of my hockey-going experience."

Lorraine laughed as she and Keith followed us out of the arena and towards the parking lot, my best friend and I both carrying our bags with one strap, which was the cool thing to do.

"Hell of a game out there tonight," Dad said as he turned the ignition and the engine groaned to life.

"Thanks."

"Five points is nothing to be shy about."

I ignored Dad's comment.

"Your power play was tremendous. I don't know if I'd have Garnault's brat out there for it, though. Perhaps replacing him with Fernesky's kid could benefit both you and your line as a whole." Dad was the only person who called Mike Fernesky by his real name. Everyone, including the coaches, called him Michael Bolton because of his super-stylish mullet.

"Dad, we won nine-nothing and scored on three of four power plays. I think that pretty much confirms everything was working perfectly tonight."

"I'm just saying that there is always room for improvement. For example, did you realize that you won but fifty percent of your face-offs tonight?"

I looked over at Dad. "Can't we focus on the good stuff? Please?"

"You had a fantastic game, Justin, but even the great ones can be improved upon."

"Fine. Great. Whatever."

"Very well, then. We'll brush tonight's mistakes under the proverbial doormat and wallow in our victory."

"Thank you."

"You're welcome."

On our way to the apartment, we stopped at Kentucky Fried Chicken. Dad said we were celebrating tonight's victory with extra coleslaw and fries. We ate in our separate corners of the apartment, Dad reading a hardcover book with an angry-looking guy on the front while I watched *Some Girls* on TV. Towards the end of the movie, Dad threw his book to the floor. Startled, I looked his way as he pulled on a cigarette so hard I thought he'd inhale the stupid thing. Tremors ran up and down my arms like aftershocks.

"There is nothing more aggravating than revisionist historians who try and skew the past with their far-flung theories and hyperbole." He drained his glass. "I'm going to The Last Resort for a nightcap. There, I will attempt to rid my memory of the drivel I have just been subjected to. Remember one thing in the future, Justin: Ivory Towers are for the mentally weak and infirm. Good night."

I'd forgotten how upset Dad could get about things like questionable calls in a game or authors he didn't agree with. His outburst also reminded me how quickly my body could turn seismic. I'd first noticed my tremors in grade six, the year Mom and Dad split. They mostly started in my arms, running from my shoulders to my fingertips. Sometimes they even affected my chest and legs. When it got really bad, I could hardly talk because my throat would be vibrating like a plucked guitar string.

Mom took me to see our family doctor, who in turn sent me to a neurologist called Dr. Marcenkowski. She diagnosed me with essential tremor, explaining how a benign tumour on my brain was most likely the cause of my shaking at times of severe anxiety. She said it wouldn't stop me from living a normal life, though. As Dr. Marcenkowski was writing out the prescription for propranolol, a beta blocker that would slow down my heart rate and hopefully quell the tremors when they were at their worst, she asked if there was anything happening at school that could be leading to higher-than-usual stress levels. I was too embarrassed to tell her how kids were making fun of me because of the big words I used in class. Then she turned to Mom, who was sitting beside me, and asked if there were any problems at home.

"As in, am I allowing my son to be harmed in any way?" You could tell Mom was steamed about that question.

"Not exactly, no. I meant, is there anything going on at home that might lead to Justin becoming more anxious?"

Mom straightened her back and folded her arms. She had a look of mistrust on her face that I'd seen before, sometimes with my teachers and other times with people like dentists and doctors. "Well," she began, looking down and picking at a nail, "me and Justin's father recently separated." She raised her head, annoyed, and added, "but I can't imagine how that would affect Justin with respect to his condition."

in·fat·u·ate
verb (used with object)
1. to inspire or possess with a foolish or unreasoning passion, as of love.

I'd been doing a science assignment when I dropped everything and needed to know exactly what the word meant, as I was having a brutal time getting Snack Bar Girl's dimples out of my thoughts.

Maybe more pathetic was that I'd been consumed with "foolish *and unreasoning passion*" all weekend about someone whose name I didn't even know.

I daydreamed about how all sorts of things would happen when *she* worked up the courage to introduce herself to *me*. She'd play with a strand of her hair, too nervous to look at me, while I confidently threw my head back and gave a deep, hearty laugh. She'd be tongue-tied, my tremors nowhere in sight. I'd ask if she wanted to see a movie and her surprise would only be surpassed by her joy. She'd ask if I were free this weekend, and as I gazed at my perfectly filed fingernails, I'd respond with, "Yah. Why not? Can't hurt, right?" In one version of this altered state of reality, she'd swoon; in another, she'd lean towards me, real slow, and we'd kiss like Molly Ringwald and Michael Schoeffling do at the end of *Sixteen Candles*. I'd feel every groove of her lips when they met mine. They'd be soft and warm, the taste of her lip balm lingering in my mouth for hours. It would taste as sweet as honey. No, oranges. She'd said she loved the taste of orange…

"What are you thinking about there, Romeo?" Dad asked me. He was reading a newspaper on the couch. I must have spaced out and become a zombie while going through my demented fantasy.

"Nothing." I cleared my throat.

"I saw your friend today by the way. She says she'd love to see you again."

Gulp.

"You actually saw her?" I said, my heart beating at a Formula 1 pace. "What did she say? Did she, like, ask about me?"

Please say she wanted my phone number. Please, please, please… Wait, how on Earth could Dad know about Snack Bar Girl?

"She says she'd love another swimming lesson. And I must say, I find it quite admirable that you've decided to become a mentor. It can have a life-altering effect, you know. She told me she'd make herself available at your earliest convenience."

Meteors came crashing down to Earth.
"Thanks. I'll keep that in mind."

Mom had been locked away for twelve nights the next time I headed over to 53 Division to see if I could get some answers about her detention centre. So far she'd popped up in my thoughts mostly at random times, like when I was smelling the fabric softener in my clothes or skating down the length of the ice or flipping through a dictionary. To be honest, I wasn't even sure why I felt this need to go and see her when I knew it would be embarrassing as all heck for the both of us. And really, what was there to talk about? Knowing her, she'd make sure to keep the entire conversation focused on me, but if movies were anything to go by, the last thing I wanted to do was look at Mom through some hockey arena Plexiglas thing and talk to her on a stupid phone, almost as if we were on opposite sides of the planet.

I don't know. Maybe it was the only child syndrome thing kicking in. Like me, Mom didn't have any brothers or sisters, and as with a lot of my buddies' parents who were the same age, she didn't exactly have a ton of friends. That made me sad. Actually, it made me feel sorry for her—and that feeling sucked the big one. While I hated it when anyone felt sorry for me, I had a soft spot for people that I cared about who were in a tough position. There was probably a super-smart person in the past like Freud or Socrates or Florence-freaking-Nightingale that had a name for this "condition," but when you grow up without any siblings, you become more independent from a younger age (I remember cooking my first meal, a grilled cheese and tomato soup, in grade three). At the same time, you learn the power of support and helping others in a different way, especially when your parents get divorced and neither one has the time to devote all their attention to you because they're working every day.

The same older guy with the cheesy 'stache was there at the front desk when I got to the police station, and yet again Officer Brady wasn't around. Before I had time to turn around, he asked, "You're Justin Maloney, right?"

"Yes," I said hesitantly.

"I've got a message for you." He handed over a piece of paper that was folded in half. "This is for you, son."

Only when I was outside, sure no one was looking over my shoulder, did I open the letter and read it.

Dear Justin,

I hope your father relayed the details of my phone call, but Sergeant Ross told me you dropped by last Monday. I'm not sure if you want to talk, but I'm always around if you do. I'll include my home phone number below.

By the way, I called the detention centre (address below) and they informed me they have visiting hours every Saturday and Sunday from 2–3 p.m.

Please let me know if I can be of any other help.

Sincerely,
Jeff Brady

Breathe.

According to the address he'd given, the detention centre was in Brampton. I didn't know exactly where that was, though I knew it was far enough away from downtown Toronto to make getting there pretty much impossible. There was no way I'd ask Dad to drive, as he'd be happier to go a day without drinking than take me out to visit Mom.

On the subway, I thought about those times in grade seven and eight when I'd lived with Dad. Every time Mom would phone to see how I was doing, she'd be happy listening to my boring stories about hockey and school. I kept things short, partly because it was weird talking about stuff like that over the phone with Mom and partly because I was pissed at her for sending me to live with Dad. The only way to show her my disappointment, I thought, was to stop telling her about my life.

When the elevator doors opened on the eighth floor, Jung-ho was tightrope walking her way down the corridor. "You're late," she said matter-of-factly.

"I had to take care of something."

"Something important?"

"Yeah."

She went quiet as I fished out my keys from the bottom of a pocket. "Can you teach me how to swim today?"

The keys rattled in my hands as our eyes met. Frustration over Mom's effed-up situation and how I'd ever figure out a way to visit her in *there* were eating away at me. I was about to tell Jung-ho I needed to chill out for a bit and sort through some crap; we'd go swimming another day. Now that I had Officer Brady's phone number I wanted to call him at once and solve this whole detention centre problem. Then again, Sergeant Ross had said he was out on duty. I looked at Jung-ho's almost expressionless face and guilt got the better of me.

"All right. Go and get your things." Jung-ho lit up and clapped her hands.

Minutes later, Jung-ho was waiting for me in the hallway. She had on the same bright-pink swimsuit as last time, and was holding her nose plugs, earplugs and arm thingies. We went up to the pool and as I'd guessed, we didn't end up swimming. We sat at the edge of the pool and made mini-whirlpools with our feet. We talked about safety rules, about not running anywhere around a swimming pool, making sure she was always with someone who could swim really well and, ideally, that a lifeguard was present. Then we practiced how to use our arms and legs to keep from going under. This made Jung-ho giggle.

"You look like a funny monster when you do that."

I grinned. "Maybe I am a funny monster," I said in a Dracula-like voice, waving my arms all around her.

Jung-ho shrieked in delight and began kicking water on me. I lowered myself into the shallow end and started splashing her with water, my arms going all over the place in the air as I let loose a gruesome *ha ha ha* that made Jung-ho howl louder each time I did it.

"I am the boogeyman," I said in my fake scary voice. This set Jung-ho off even more.

"Eek!!!"

Her legs were thrashing around the water awkwardly. At first, all she wanted to do was soak my face. (She did a pretty good job of blinding me with all the chlorine getting in my eyes.) But her kicking motion soon became more controlled, almost as if she were treading water.

Before getting out of the pool, I rubbed my eyes to lessen the sting and slicked my hair back, blinking several times and grateful that this ten-year-old girl had been able to take my mind of Officer Brady, Mom, the detention centre and everything else stressing me out. I lifted myself out of the pool and sat down beside Jung-ho again, feeling lighter than I had in a while. "You just had your first swimming lesson," I told her with not a little bit of pride.

"What do you mean?" Jung-ho was taking off her floatation thingies from her arms and not paying much attention to me.

"That kicking motion you were just doing, when you were splashing me with water, that's half the battle. You'll need to learn how to use your arms in the water, but you now know how to kick under water pretty good."

Pretty "well," Justin! I could hear Dad saying. I made that mistake a lot and he always burned me on it.

"Really?"

"Truly and for true." Jung-ho was ecstatic. "You'll be doing that on your own in the pool in no time. Believe me."

We dried ourselves off and while waiting for the elevator, Jung-ho took my hand in hers. For a second I worried her father would freak out again, then remembered the box of apples.

Dad wasn't in the apartment when I got back. Not knowing how long I'd have the place to myself, I took out Officer Brady's letter from my blazer and read it over again. I picked up the phone and my arms were surprisingly steady as I dialed the number. A woman answered.

"Hi is Mr.…is Officer Brady home."

"May I ask who's calling?"

"It's Justin. Justin Maloney."

"Hold on one second, Justin," she said. "I'll go and get him for you."

"Thank you."

A few seconds passed and then a man's voice said, "Hi, Justin."

"Hi."

"Sergeant Ross told me you got my letter today."

"Yeah." I was twisting the phone cord in my hand, wrapping it around my wrist as tight as possible. "Thanks."

"Don't mention it. How've you been these last couple of weeks?"

While I got what Officer Brady was trying to do, I didn't feel like getting all personal with him.

"Ah, you know, fine. Listen, I was wondering. How far is Brampton from Toronto?"

"From where you live?"

"Yeah. Yes, I mean."

"Jeez," he said, exhaling loudly. "In good traffic it might be half an hour, forty minutes out. If you try during rush hour, though, you could be looking at closer to an hour and a half."

"And the TTC doesn't go out there, right?"

"No, I'm afraid it doesn't. There might be a GO train or Greyhound bus that goes out there, but it would probably be a pain in the butt and cost more than the subway."

"Yeah," I replied, feeling defeated.

There was a long pause. "I could give you a lift out there if you want." I spun my hand the other way and the cord started to come undone from my wrist, the blood returning to my fingers. "Umm, yeah. That would be…it's just, you know, I don't know how else to get out there."

"I tell you what, Justin. I'm off this Sunday. How about if we drive there in the afternoon? I could pick you up around one-fifteen."

"Yeah, sure. That would be great." For some reason, I struggled to get the next part out. "Thanks a lot."

"Don't mention it, Justin."

As I was saying goodbye, I heard the sound of a key going into the doorknob, so I quickly hung up.

"Were you on the phone?" Dad asked, crouching down to pick up a massive plant in a white pot.

"Yeah. Just got off with Keith."

"Come help your father, will you?" He walked in with part of the Amazon rainforest in his hands, while I grabbed the three bags he'd left in the hallway. "And how is your *socius criminis*?" Dad asked, adjusting the plant (or whatever you called something that big) on top of the dresser.

"What? He's fine. I don't know. Same as always."

He turned and grinned, showing off the plant like one of those babes on *The Price Is Right* does when there's a great new dishwasher or a set of golf clubs to bid on. The plant was so big it kind of split the room into two parts.

"Now we have our own separate quarters," Dad said.

In the kitchen, I left the groceries on the counter and asked what the special occasion was.

"What makes you say that?" Dad asked while pouring himself a drink.

"I haven't seen you buy this many groceries since, I don't know, forever."

"Nor have you seen me buy these in an eon." Dad pulled out two packages from a plastic bag.

"Steak?"

"Filet mignon, no less. And I'll be serving them with mashed potatoes and green beans."

Our favourite meal. Well, it was for Dad and me when I was growing up. Mom really liked some fish called tilapia but would only make it on nights when Dad worked late because he loved fish as much as he did biased hockey refs and Harold Ballard. I unpacked the rest of the groceries, putting the jar of Cheez Whiz and pack of cheese slices in the fridge; the Campbell's soup cans, Kraft Dinner boxes, and Chef Boyardee tins went into the cupboard above the sink.

Looking over towards the desk, I saw that Officer Brady's letter was just lying there. I managed to scoop it up before Dad saw it, though he did ask me in a casual tone of voice what I had in my hands as he refilled his glass in the miniscule kitchen.

"It's a school assignment. That's what me and Keith were talking about."

"What Keith and *I* were talking about."

"Right. Keith and *I*."

Dad took the steaks out and showered them with Worcestershire sauce. I couldn't help but notice that he only washed up *after* rubbing the filet mignons with his hands. "By the way, your father landed his first major corporate client as a freelance accountant today."

"Congratulations."

When I was younger, I had a pretty good idea what my parents did for a living: Dad worked at an accounting firm and Mom was a homemaker. When they split in '86, it got a little more complicated. Mom got a job at a clinic doing clerical work and Dad, having been canned by the firm a year earlier, began freelancing as an accountant. I had no clue what "clerical work" really meant and thought "freelance" might be something like volunteering.

"I'm going to let those fine specimens marinate for an hour. Can you hold off that long?"

"Huh? Sure," I said without really thinking as I stuffed Officer Brady's letter into the middle of a notebook.

Dad moved over to the sofa with a paper in his hands and sat down. "Excellent. In the meantime, I shall entertain myself with news of the ongoing circus south of the border. By the by, are you talking about the U.S. election in school these days?" Dad asked, unfolding a copy of the *Globe and Mail*.

"No."

"Messrs Bush and Quayle are putting on quite the show. Dukakis and Bentsen might be lulling the American people to sleep with their Nytol-worthy rhetoric, but I must say, Mr. Quayle provides several nuggets of sage wisdom every time he opens his mouth and does something other than masticate."

I tuned Dad out while sitting on my bed. With the small jungle now growing on top of the chest of drawers, he couldn't see if I was paying attention or not. Busy replaying the conversation with Officer Brady in my mind, I felt good about what I'd done. Sunday would be hard and it would be embarrassing (at least for Mom and me), but it was almost certain I'd be the only person who'd visit her while she was in the detention centre, and I figured that'd make her happy.

"Did you hear me?" Dad said, a ridiculous snicker to his voice.

"What? No. Sorry."

"Mr. Quayle has outdone himself yet again. He was quoted as saying, 'The future will be better tomorrow'. Ha!" Dad folded the paper and clapped his hands. "I love it!"

7

"Hiya," she said, chewing on some gum. She put her elbows on the counter and leaned forward. "Wait! Let me guess." She closed an eye and pointed to Keith, her hands locked together like a gun. "Large strawberry Slushie." The gun moved my way. "And a small raspberry Slushie."

"Nice!" Keith exclaimed.

"No!" I said, throwing them both off.

"What the France?" Keith knew I always got the same flavour.

"I thought I did really good," she said, looking crushed.

"No, you did. I mean, you're right. I usually get raspberry—and I did last time—but, well…I thought I'd mix it up tonight."

"But you don't know how to mix it up." Keith had a deadpan look on his face.

"What can I get you, then?" she asked.

"I don't know. I thought I'd try, you know, an orange Slush Puppy."
Dimples.

"One large strawberry Slushie and one small orange Slushie coming right up."

Keith kicked me in the back of the knees.

"Ow! What's your deal?"

"Me? I've got no deal. You, however, seem to have a raging case of—"

"Hey," I said as quietly as possible through clenched teeth. "Keep your friggin' trap closed, would you?"

Like last time, Snack Bar Girl was busy serving someone else moments after giving us our drinks and that fantasy I'd had about how we'd properly meet and exchange names went down the drain again.

Lorraine wasn't around when Keith and I returned to the lobby. When I asked where she was, Dad said she had to leave early. "Your sister," he explained, looking at Keith, "has been sick the last couple of days, I'm told."

"Yeah, but I didn't think it was that serious."

"You know lionesses: overprotective of their cubs at the best of times. I'm sure everything's fine. Nonetheless, she has asked that I shuttle you home."

During the ride, Dad and Keith yapped away about the Leafs and the Gretzky trade and who they thought were strong Cup contenders this year. I sat quietly in my seat, amazed at how excited Dad could get when talking to someone my age.

"Thanks for the ride, Mr. Maloney," Keith shouted from behind the car after hoisting his bag out of the trunk when we got to his place.

"My pleasure."

Keith walked up my side of the car and tapped on the window. I rolled it down as he said, "Say, J.R., you want to swing by tomorrow afternoon and play some vids?"

"Yeah. Cool."

"Give me a call before you drop by."

"Will do."

"I must say," Dad said as we pulled out of Keith's driveway. "I find him the most engaging of your friends."

"You like him because he's as nuts about hockey as you are."

"No, it's more than that. He's a well-grounded young man with a solid *thymos*."

I shook my head. "I'm not talking to you anymore."

"Justin, that's not very polite."

"Yeah, well, speak English, then. By the way, I need a new stick." In the second period, I was hit from behind in the corner while digging for the puck, the butt end of my lumber snapping as it rammed hard into my stomach. Dad lost his marbles when the guy only got two minutes for boarding. There were lots of boos coming from our side of the stands, but Dad was the only one telling the ref where he could put his whistle. I knew our team couldn't be penalized for Dad's outburst, but I'd seen a parent from another team led out by police a few years earlier when the father wouldn't stop abusing the referee, not just with a slew of swear words either. He was actually throwing crap onto the ice surface, which is when someone called the cops and the guy was kicked out of the arena. I never did learn if he was arrested or simply told not to go inside again, but I prayed the police would never have to escort Dad out of an arena.

"Those things aren't cheap, you know."

"What do you want me to do? He hit me from behind!"

"I'm not saying it was your fault. Just be more vigilant with your sticks in the future. Ensure you get the maximum use out of them while we bankroll the Canadian timber industry which, I might point out, is just one big Crown corporation."

"Yeah. Sure. I'll be more vigilant in the future when I get decked from behind."

"Don't be insolent, young man."

On Saturday, Dad and I went to Wendy's for lunch and then drove to Canadian Tire. I tried to convince him to get me more than one stick so we wouldn't have to keep coming back every time I broke one, but all he said was that the more a person had, the more they wanted.

"Dad, I'm not trying to be greedy. I want to save us more trips in the future." I put myself in his shoes before going on. "Every time we come here, the more you have to spend on gas. Plus, it takes you away from your work, which is also losing you money in a way, isn't it?"

"Justin, all you're doing here is trying to sell wool to a shepherd. Now pick out a stick and let's vamoose."

Argh.

Keith and I ended up having the ultimate games day. He had a basketball net in his driveway and we played one-on-one until we were both drenched in sweat, Keith having won all three games. We moved inside to play best-of-three rounds in Ping-Pong and then eight-ball. Keith took the pool games two-one but I smoked him two-nothing in Ping-Pong. By the time we moved to the TV room, Mr. Fraser was outside on the deck barbecuing hamburgers.

"Okay, boys. Come on up. Dinner's ready," Lorraine shouted from the kitchen. We'd just started a game of *Super Mario Bros.* and had to pause it right away or else get an earful from Lorraine, who was pretty serious when it came to mealtime. Everyone was expected to drop whatever they were doing, even Mr. Fraser, wash up and report to the dining room table.

After eating so many lunches and dinners eating alone in front of the TV over the last month, this felt pretty awesome. Keith and I were on one side of the dining table, and Victoria, who still wasn't feeling all that well, sat across from us.

"Sweetie," Lorraine said to Mr. Fraser, "will you pass the salad when you're done?" Holy crapola, I thought. Salad? Leafy greens with cucumbers, tomatoes, onions and avocado? I couldn't remember the last time I'd seen so many vegetables in one bowl.

"So, Justin," Mr. Fraser said, "Keith tells me you've started the season flying out of the gates."

As much as I appreciated that the Frasers tried to make me feel like a part of their family, it made me uncomfortable when they singled me out like this. I never liked being the centre of attention, especially in someone else's home.

"Yeah, we've done pretty well so far."

"I'd say undefeated is more than 'pretty well'," Lorraine said, smiling.

"Well, me and Keith—sorry—Keith and *I* have been connecting on the power play."

"Rippin' it up is more like it, J.R. We've been blowing pucks past goalies."

"Why do we *always* have to talk about hockey when Justin is over?" Victoria grumbled. Although prone to getting pouty when she was sick, this kind of reaction was exactly the reason I hated talking about myself at their house.

"Love, we don't solely talk about hockey when Justin is over," Lorraine explained in a soft, gentle voice.

Victoria crossed her arms. "*Hmph.*"

"How's your mother doing by the way, Justin?" Lorraine asked, lifting her fork to eat some salad and looking my way.

"Great. Good. Thank you."

Don't freak out. She doesn't know. Keith doesn't know. Mr. Fraser doesn't know. Victoria doesn't know. Everything's okay.

"Have you been able to drop in and see her recently?"

"Huh? What, sorry?" Okay, now I was panicking. Victoria was stabbing her plate with a fork and trying to get some attention, which Keith's parents were having none of.

"Your mom. Have you seen her since you moved back in with your father?"

"Oh. Right. No. Not yet. She's, ah…she's been super busy, you know."

Victoria dropped her cutlery and a clanging sound rang out. Instinctively, we all looked at her.

"Sorry. I didn't mean to—"

"Why are you such a retard, Vic?" Keith said, cutting off his sister, who looked hurt by the comment. "Can't you even hold a stupid fork and knife?"

"Keith," his mom said, an edge to her voice. "Don't insult your sister."

"But Vic's a special needs retard."

Tears began welling up in Victoria's eyes.

"Keith, so help me, if you want to eat the rest of dinner by yourself upstairs in your room, keep it up. Otherwise, I don't want to hear another word from you unless you have something nice to say," Lorraine said, the warning not an idle threat.

Scared the Frasers would keep asking about Mom, I tried to change the subject, telling Keith's dad he'd done a wicked job with the burgers. "These are your best yet," I said. "Really, really fantastic."

"You know what the secret to a great hamburger is, Justin?" Mr. Fraser asked, dabbing at the corners of his mouth with a napkin.

"Let me guess, Dad. Your magical hands?"

"I'm not going to deny I have magical hands." Mr. Fraser grinned at his wife. "But it's more than my gifted hands that sculpted the burgers you're enjoying, Keith. The key is to never slap your meat around before it gets on the grill."

Keith burst out laughing. "Dad, who wouldn't want to slap their meat around before making dinner?"

"Language!" his mother said at once. "I don't want to hear that kind of thing at my dinner table, Keith Lloyd Gordon Fraser. Am I clear?"

"Sorry."

"Anyway," Mr. Fraser went on, "don't *throw* the meat around. Get the freshest ground beef you can and then make small indents in the middle of your patties, about half an inch deep. That way you get an evenly cooked burger, like the one you have tonight. See, ordinarily it's the middle of the burger that's the least cooked because the outside cooks faster than the middle, but when you make these small indents it reduces the surface area of the hardest part to cook. And voilà!"

"Dad, you are, without a doubt, the biggest geek when it comes to cooking." Keith glanced over at me. "Everything's a freaking scientific measurement or amount or…or…Bunsen burner with him."

Keith didn't always make sense when he got riled up.

Two burgers, a supreme helping of potato salad, one corn on the cob and a full plate of salad later, I tapped out. "Thanks so much for the great meal. It was amazing," I said to Lorraine.

"Don't be such a kiss-ass, J.R. My mom's already got the adoption papers written up."

"Hey! What did I warn you about with the language thing?"

"You said not at the dinner table, and I'm now standing in the kitchen." Keith grabbed a box of Oreos and had them taken away just as quickly.

"And you will also watch your language in my kitchen. No cookies for you tonight."

"Oh, man. Mom, seriously, this is not cool."

Lorraine handed us each a bowl of fruit.

"*Your* dining table, *your* kitchen…what part of this freaking house is mine?" Keith moaned.

"None," Lorraine said and winked at me.

Keith and I played Nintendo and Sega games for a while and then watched two movies from his massive library of videotapes. We started with *The Shining* and ended the night with *The Princess Bride*. I have no idea what time I got home, but I know it was late because, for the first time since I'd moved in, Dad was asleep before me.

"Late night, Señor Quixote?" Dad was standing beside my bed, a drink in one hand and a cigarette in the other. The sand in both eyes made it hard to open them and focus clearly as I lay on my side, the blanket pulled up all the way to my chin. Dad was wearing a cardigan, his usual white dress shirt underneath, and a pair of khaki pants I hadn't seen on him in years.

"Huh?" I muttered, though the word—or the sound of something *similar* to a word—barely made it out of my mouth, the phlegm in my throat making it hard to swallow.

"You're lucky your father is not as strict as some of the Floor Fellows who kept watch over me in university." Dad returned to the kitchen, where, from the smell of it, he was making bacon and eggs. The one good thing to come out of Mom and Dad's divorce was a curfew my friends were super-jealous of. While most guys my age had to be home on weekends by eleven or twelve at the latest, Mom and Dad had become pretty lax with that. I think it was their way of trying to score points with me and make up for their split. "I trust you were not roaming the malignant downtown core of our troubled city," Dad said a minute later.

"No. Keith and I had a video game Olympics and then watched a couple of flicks." I swung my legs over the side of the bed and sighed heavily. My watch said it was half past eleven, but it felt like I hadn't been asleep for more than a few minutes.

"You know, those things aren't good for your eyes."

It was too early to argue. "Do you have any plans today?" I asked, hoping I could slip out unnoticed to see Mom. Truth is, I didn't really want to have to lie to Dad about where I was going.

"As a matter of fact, I do, thank you for asking."

"And?"

"And what?"

He was unbelievable. "And what are your plans?"

"Well, you and *I* are going to the Toronto Marlies game this afternoon. They're playing the London Knights at one-thirty and your father," he said, making his way to my bed with his wallet and pulling out two tickets, "secured two seats in the—drum roll, please—gold section. I was going to keep it a surprise until we actually arrived at Maple Leaf Gardens, but I thought I'd start your day off on the right foot. Now, how would you like your eggs?"

My hunger vanished, as did my desire to get out of bed. "Umm... however you're having them."

"Good man." Dad was in the kitchen again, smoking a cigarette with one hand and turning the bacon over with tongs in the other. "Sunny side up, it is, then. And do you want your bacon crispy or tender?"

Each time he opened his mouth I died a little more. "Whatever's easiest."

"Ha!"

"And one or two pieces of toast."

Shoot me now.

"One. Thanks."

Lying to Dad for the sake of seeing Mom was possible. But this changed everything. I couldn't very well tell him I was going to a friend's or had to do homework when he'd gone and bought these hockey tickets. I groaned and rolled over. A second later, Dad was hovering over the bed with his Caesar and a cigarette, asking if I was okay.

My mother, the wannabe caregiver, now in a detention centre; my father, the absent parent, now doting on me like a concerned nurse.

"I'm fine. It's fine. Everything's fine," I said, facing the wall and refusing to turn over.

Dad pulled out the desk, removed all his papers and the record player, and set it with paper napkins and cutlery. He was pretty talkative this whole time, a regular "Chatty Cathy," as he liked to say. He seemed happy just to flap his old gums as he went on and on about the starting lineup for the Marlies. Halfway through the meal he looked up and asked if I was feeling all right. I had my fork on the tip of a yolk, toying with it. I'd eaten a slice of bacon and then lost my appetite.

"Something on your mind, kiddo?" The yolk popped and oozed all over my plate, like watching the sea come rushing into shore. Dad put down his knife and fork. "Where were you last night, Justin?"

"What?"

"What did you *really* do last night?"

"What are you talking about?"

"You're clearly at war within yourself and, what with your late return and teenagers being prone to—"

"Dad," I said calmly, "I was at Keith's all day and all night. I swear."

"Is it drugs? Have you been cavorting with some of those wealthy classmates of yours?"

"Whoa! Dad, slow down. You're way off base here. I promise." He didn't look convinced. "I promise. On my life. Phone Lorraine if you want to." I fiddled with my cutlery and then added, "I, ah—"

"Justin?"

"Dad, hold on. It's not what you think. It's just…I don't know. I mean—"

"It's just what?" Dad was about to put some of the eggs and toast in his mouth when he lowered his fork and instead reached for his Caesar. Then he lit a cigarette.

"I'm supposed to…go and see Mom today…at the, you know…"

There was no point in finishing my sentence. The bomb had already gone off, the damage done.

Dad tapped the end of his smoke against the rim of the ashtray. "How long have you been orchestrating this scheme?"

"Dad…"

"How long?" he said again, this time more strenuously.

I waited a few seconds and then explained how I'd been planning to visit her since last week.

"And you didn't think it relevant to tell your father the moment you hatched this plan?"

"It's not that, Dad." I expected him to be defensive, but all he did was lean back in his chair and wait for me to go on. "I didn't want to hurt you or…disappoint you." I braced myself for the speech I thought was coming, about *the impertinence of such an ungrateful son* and all. *How could I let him down and support a criminal when he'd done so much to make today special for me?* and so on and so forth.

"Very well, then. I'll vacate the premises so you can get ready. I'll see you here for dinner, I trust." He rose from his chair and stubbed out his cigarette without as much as a look in my direction.

"Dad, I never meant to screw up your plans."

"Justin," he said, putting his smokes into his shirt pocket and opening the door, "as you will come to see, everything in life comes at a price. Nothing is free, not a single thing, tangible or intangible. There is an equilibrium at play all the time. For every gain, there is a loss of equal value. For every heart that is broken, one is sutured. It's called balance, and it's the only reason the universe doesn't collapse onto itself at any given moment."

I wasn't sure what you were supposed to wear to a detention centre. Something smart was probably the right call, so I put on a button-down and a pair of khaki pants. I made my way downstairs a little before one-fifteen, assuming I'd have to wait, but Officer Brady was already there behind the wheel of his car.

"Hi there," he said when I got into his Honda.

"Hey."

We headed east on Bloor as I played with one of the buttons on my shirt and tried to work up the courage to thank Jeff. It may have been one measly word, but something about saying it out loud in this kind of situation was totally uncool and embarrassing.

"Thanks," I finally found it in me to say. "For this, I mean…Officer Brady."

"Justin, you can call me Jeff. Just Jeff. Is that cool?"

While something about hearing him say "Is that cool?" sounded, I don't know, forced or fake, it did make talking to him a heck of a lot easier. "Sure."

"Great."

On the way out to Brampton, Jeff didn't pepper me with questions or smother me in adult wisdom. He just let me be and played the radio on low. As I wondered what it would be like seeing Mom again, and whether she'd be disappointed in me for not having phoned or visited yet, I thought back to the day she was arrested.

We had the place to ourselves. After one of their usual weekend blowouts, Tony stormed out of the house, probably off to the sports bar he managed to put back a few. Mom was watching TV with the sound so low it was basically on MUTE when I lugged my hockey bag up to the living room to try on some of my equipment from last season. She was sitting in Tony's piece-of-crap armchair, a cigarette in her left hand and a glass of wine in the right. Mom kept looking between me, checking to see whether my stuff from last season still fit, and the game show she was watching. It was almost as if something colossal might happen on *Press Your Luck* in that fraction of a second she wasn't paying attention to what Dad used to call the "boob tube."

The room was so dark I could hardly see a thing. The lamp in the far corner was on, but barely any light escaped from its shade. Mom was like a vampire when I opened the curtains, raising a hand to cover her face. One of those stupid Whammies with a red cape was dancing across the TV screen. A minute later, when her eyes had finally adjusted to the sun, she asked me what I was doing in a tone of voice all sweet and tender.

"Just seeing if my skates are still big enough for me." Mom blew a tornado of smoke my way. I coughed.

"And?"

"I don't know. I guess I could use a new pair."

Mom gave me a sad smile, stubbed out her cigarette and placed the wine glass on a coaster beside the chair. As she went to get up, she had to catch herself from falling. She recovered quickly and angled her arms in the shape of an L, one hand supporting an elbow and the other covering her mouth. "How about we drop by P.J.'s Sports World and get some new skates, then, hun?"

"Are you sure?" I asked, knowing Mom wasn't exactly rolling in it, especially since her hours at the clinic had been cut.

"Of course, I'm sure. What, you think your old mom can't take care of her baby's needs?"

On the way over to P.J.'s, I started fidgeting with my T-shirt. Obviously, getting new skates was gnarly, but these days Mom was doing something she didn't use to when we bought something. Instead of paying in cash or pulling out a credit card (her AmEx and Visa had been cancelled, though she didn't know I knew because it was Tony who'd spilled the beans one time while ranting and raving about Mom's spending habits), now she was more likely to write a cheque, even if the store said they didn't accept personal cheques.

"What are you thinking about, hun?" Mom asked as we drove down Yonge Street in pretty light traffic.

"Nothing."

"You sure?"

"Yeah," I lied. "Just thinking about the upcoming season and all."

Mom tapped away on the steering wheel to a song on the radio, her multiple rings and bracelets rattling as I wondered what kind of skates to get. A pair of CCMs would be cheaper, but they were totally inferior to Bauers. Wearing my crappy girdle and dinky pair of shoulder pads with stupid saucer thingies on them would be manageable for one more season; buying wanker skates was out of the question.

When Mom dropped me off outside the store, she said she needed to find somewhere to park and that she'd be back in a jiffy. An older guy greeted me as I walked in the door at P.J.'s and asked what I was looking for. By the time the Bauer Supreme 100s were laced up and snug on my feet, I was taking baby steps around the small area of the floor that had rubber padding on it in the rear part of the store. Mom's perfume soon found its way into the room before she did.

"How do they feel?" the sales guy asked, hands on his hips.

"Pretty good."

"They've got a great advanced level of performance. I bet they feel pretty light on your feet as well, eh?"

I nodded. There was no doubt I could break my scoring record from last season with these puppies on my feet.

"Well?" Mom asked, biting a nail. "What do you think? Should we get them?"

"They're kind of expensive."

Mom looked at the sales guy and made this face as if I'd said the silliest thing in the world.

"I meant, would you *like* to get them, hun?"

"Yeah, I guess that'd be pretty cool."

Mom looked at the sales guy's name tag. "Stanley, we're going to take them."

Stan the Man looked stoked, though I think that had more to do with how Mom was dressed. She had on a jean mini-skirt and a white sleeveless top which clung to her chest tighter than Superman's unitard. Her dyed blonde hair was all big and poofy, like Farrah Fawcett used to wear it on *Charlie's Angels*, her blue high heels making her many inches taller than her five feet three inches. Stan took an extra second to watch Mom pass by, his eyes going from top to bottom as he bared his teeth, a set of fangs coloured cigarette-filter yellow.

I unlaced my new skates all nice and slow because I heard Mom asking if she could write them a cheque. This was the worst part of any purchase, especially lately, because she'd do whatever she could not to pay in cash. Lucky for her, Mom had Stan eating out of her hand. She was bent over the counter where the cash register had a sign attached to it that read NO PERSONAL CHEQUES ACCEPTED. Seeing Mom flirt with any guy was gross. With Stan, who was an older version of Ed Asner from his *Mary Tyler Moore Show* days, it kind of made me want to puke.

"I know it's asking a lot," Mom said, "but I left all my cash and credit cards at home. In my wallet, I should say. I rushed out of the house so quickly…well, I only had time to grab my purse and chequebook."

Stan put his hands up and with a jolly old I-don't-make-the-rules-around-here laugh and said there was nothing he could do. I made my way to the stick section of the store so I could try out all the new Titans, Sherwoods, Kohos and Eastons. As I leaned down on each one to test its flexibility, Mom was amping up her routine.

"My darling son had me in such a frenzy—and I'm so forgetful by nature anyway—that I didn't have a chance to look inside my purse. I'm so sorry. Really. I am. I know this goes against store policy, but do you think there's any way this one time, just this one time, you could find it in your heart to make an exception, Stanley?" Mom reached for one of her golden locks and twirled it with a finger. Stan had his mouth open and was going to say something when Mom went in for the kill. "I know, I know, I know. I really don't want to put you in a bind here, Stanley. I used to work in retail so I know this isn't easy. I do. I really do. And if you want me to leave my son here, I can drive home and grab my wallet and be back in a flash. Well, not exactly a flash, see, on account of the fact we don't live that close by. But it's fine. Tell you what," she said, defeated and lowering her voice as she returned the chequebook to her bag slowly. "I'll just go and…scoot home and…"

Stan picked at some food lodged between his teeth using a fingernail, then closed his mouth and gave himself what Mom calls a "mouth wash" with his tongue. If I didn't know any better, Stan was, at that very moment, thinking, *Merlyn Abbott, you have snafued this whole thing and put me in a real pickle full of pickled pickle juice.*

"It's okay," he finally said. "I think we can make an exception this one time. And please," he added, "call me Stan."

Mom looked up and reached for one of Stan's hands, which she clasped between both of hers. "Thank you, Stan. I mean it. I really do."

"Don't mention it, Mrs.…"

"*Ms.* Abbott. Merlyn Abbott. But, please, call me Merlyn."

"Don't mention it, Merlyn. Now, as for the cheque, I *will* need to see one piece of picture ID."

"Then let me find the piece of ID with my most flattering picture." Mom laughed as she rifled through her huge purse. "By the way, Stan, do you have a pen I could borrow? I can't seem to find mine."

Stan handed a pen to Mom, which she managed to drop behind the counter. When he bent down to get it, Mom fished out her license from her wallet. By the time Stan stood up again, Mom had her chequebook and driver's license out. Stan flipped open the two pieces of folded plastic and studied her picture carefully. "I think there's a problem with this piece of identification, Merlyn." Now *this* was something I hadn't heard before. "It says here you were born in 1945. Huh…" Stan scratched the top of his head. "Clearly not the case. Guess someone made a mistake when typing in 1955, eh?" As he grinned, crow's feet cropped up all over Stan's heinous old skin.

On the way back to the car, Mom said all kinds of ridiculous things about my new Bauers—"I'm positive these skates will do wonders for your game" and "You'll skate faster than the Roadrunner out there"—the sort of stuff, basically, no hockey player would actually say. When she was about to unlock the doors of the car, I looked over top of the roof and thanked Mom for the skates. She went all quiet as she tilted her head to one side, her eyes glassy.

"Mom! The doors!"

"Right! Sorry, hun."

Inching the car into traffic, Mom poked her head over the steering wheel as she pulled an illegal left when a gap opened up in traffic.

"Are you hungry?"

"Nah. Not so much."

"Can I make you something when we get home? Maybe a grilled cheese and tomato soup?"

"I'm fine."

She took a hand off the steering wheel and messed with my hair.

"Mom!"

I hated people touching my hair because it was always carefully protecting my forehead, which had broken out into a mountain range of zits last summer. When the bangs didn't sweep across it in just the right way, it was worse than being naked.

Just then, sirens began blaring from a cop car behind us. Mom didn't pull over. Instead, she veered into the left lane, turned and parked behind a pickup truck. She talked to herself nonstop until the officer came up to our car. As she rolled down her window, she muttered, "Sacred heart of Jesus it's hot in here."

"License and registration, please."

Mom's hands were shaking when she gave the cop her license, but then she couldn't find the registration. The officer seemed to understand what was happening and said it was probably in the glove compartment.

"I'm such an idiot." Mom leaned across me with her seatbelt still on. In the two weeks she'd been driving this rental car—ever since her Jeep Cherokee had been repoed—she'd already managed to fill up the glove compartment with Kleenexes, takeout menus, and all sorts of other useless stuff. "Apparently it's me who needs adult supervision." The cop didn't laugh as Mom went through the documents like a deck of cards.

"Ma'am, were you aware that one of your brake lights isn't working?"

"No. I, ah, no…" Mom said, trailing off as she handed the copper her insurance.

"I'll be right back," he added and then disappeared.

Mom jabbered away when we were alone again, rolling up her window and blasting the A/C. She'd be going on about the Indian summer we were in the middle of, then talk about my upcoming hockey season, and then ask about friends I hadn't seen in years. It wasn't as if she needed any answers either; Mom hated silence as much as the dark used to scare the bejesus out of me.

This time both officers came up to the car, one on either side. Mom kept changing her focus from the rearview mirror to her side mirror as she touched her cheeks with both hands. "God, I'm as cold as blue blazes."

"I'm going to have to ask you step out of the vehicle and put your hands on the roof of the car, ma'am," the officer said when the window was down again. I reached for Mom's arm, which was so thin my hand wrapped itself around bone.

"What's going on?" I asked.

"Ma'am? Please step out of the vehicle and place your hands on top of the vehicle."

"Mom!" I screeched, trying to latch onto her, any part of her.

Before she got out of the car, she looked at me and said, "It's okay, baby. I promise. Everything's going to be just fine."

We pulled up to the detention centre around two o'clock. The building was your typical government piece of crap: brown, ugly and completely unmemorable. Even after Jeff found a parking spot, I still had a couple of minutes to burn before I could go inside. He turned off the ignition but left the radio on. Some annoying song from Belinda Carlisle was playing.

"Do you want me to come in with you?" he asked.

"Thanks, umm, I appreciate the offer, but I'd rather go in alone." I looked at my watch, the big hand creeping up on two o'clock.

"All right. I'll stay here, then."

"Right. Well, guess I'll go in now."

There was a lineup inside the facility. Everyone else was a grown man around Dad's age. Most of them wore denim shirts and jeans. Some had baseball hats on. There was a screening process we went through where visitors were frisked and asked who they were visiting. When my turn came, I could see the look on the woman's face change. She had short curly hair and a gut that hung over her belt. "This here your first visit?" she asked in a weird accent.

"Yes."

"Well, it's pretty straightforward, see. There'll be a phone on your side of the glass and one on your mom's side. Pick it up and start talking through it. Easy, peasy, Japanesey. Wash your bum in lemon Squeezy."

I was through security.

While adjusting the seat at my "booth," I wondered what I'd say to Mom. Would I make small talk and pretend like nothing had happened? Should we talk about what would happen when she got out? Neither one seemed any good and left me second-guessing my decision to come out here today.

People began talking into the phones. All the ones like Mom (saying "inmates" wasn't going to happen) wore the same blue uniforms and looked excited to be speaking with the man who'd come to visit them (the only women I saw there were either locked up or doing the locking up). I could make out some of the one-way conversations and there were a lot of emotional things being said. Minutes later, the same woman who'd said things would be easy, peasy, *yada yada yada* came over to see me.

"It's Justin, right?"

"Yes."

"Listen, I, ah, I've got some bad news for you. Your mom, see, she ain't coming out to see you today."

"I don't understand."

"Your mom, ah, she couldn't come out today."

"Wait, as in she's not allowed?"

The guard was finding this hard to explain, but I was finding it harder to believe that they would let me into this joint and then not let Mom and me talk. "See, inmates don't *have to* see their visitors. It's their choice. And sometimes they choose to stay in their cell, for whatever reason. Now, with you, I'm sure there's a good reason. I didn't talk to her directly. She might be sick or unable to get up, but…"

And that was that. The whole day hung on a "but."

"Right."

"I'm real sorry."

"It's fine. I'll just…go home. No big deal."

"Are you sure? Do you want some water or something?"

I knew she was trying to be nice, but I was done here. My day had started out as a disaster and would end as a ten-car pile-up.

"No, thank you. I'll leave now if that's all right."

When I got back to the Honda, Jeff had his seat reclined all the way and was napping. The door was locked so I had to knock on the window. He popped up and looked both ways so fast I thought he might pull a gun on me. When he recognized who it was, he pressed the automatic unlock button and I got in the car.

"That was fast."

I stared out the windshield. "Yeah."

"Did you get to have a good talk with your Mom?"

"Yeah. It's all good. Can we just, you know, go?"

"You've got it."

He started the ignition and pulled out of the parking lot. I put my arm on the edge of the window, my head at the base of my hand, and watched the scenery as it sped by us. When we pulled up outside Dad's apartment and I was undoing my seatbelt, Jeff said that if I needed anything else in the future he'd be around.

I couldn't take it any longer and kind of snapped, like The Champ does most mornings on Q107 (*We have to make some cuts at the factory, Champ, and I don't know whether to lay you or Jack off!*) "Why are you being so nice to me?" I said a little too aggressively. "What did I ever do to make you want to be there for me like some kind of big brother?"

He turned down the radio and put his hands on the steering wheel. "I'm new to the Force, Justin. They teach you in Police Academy not to get attached to your…not to get attached to people. But…see, my mom raised me and my two brothers on her own because my dad got locked up when I was a kid." He stole a glance my way. "I know what you're going through right now and I guess I wanted to help out any way I could."

I waited a second before telling Jeff in a flat tone of voice that Mom wouldn't see me. "It's fine, though. I'll be fine."

"Tell you what. You've got my number. You call if you want to. If you don't need to call, no sweat off my back, no sweat off yours."

"Sure."

"Justin?"

"Yeah?"

He placed a hand on my arm. "Call if you need to. Jasmine, she's my wife, and, well, we're around night and day, okay, big guy?"

Being called "big guy" by Jeff was annoying, but I got that he wanted to help.

"Sure. Thanks for the lift by the way."

"Don't mention it."

Dad wasn't in the apartment when I got upstairs. Even though I had a mountain of homework to get through, I didn't want to deal with any of it, so I sat down on the floor, against the side of the bed, and turned on the TV. I must have been watching one completely forgettable show after another when Dad stumbled in. It was dark out by then and I was eating a bowl of SpaghettiOs.

"Hey," I said as he tried to work the keys out of the door.

"How was your afternoon with Ms. Abbott?" Dad asked, slurring his words.

"Nothing special."

"Is that so?" Dad tripped, almost fell, but grabbed hold of the dresser drawer just in time. When he tried to steady himself, he knocked the Amazonian plant onto the floor. The pot cracked and spilled dirt all over the place. "Well, I'm glad things went so swimmingly." I wanted to ask if he'd ended up going to the Marlies game, but was scared that would upset him. "I'll put myself to sleep with a bed now…on the sofa and find the sleep…that I need to get done."

Sometime in the middle of the night, Dad hurried past my bed and unleashed a waterfall of puke in the bathroom, reminding me of when he'd been fired from his job at the accounting firm. Ever since I can remember, Dad drank. The day he got "let go of," as he put it, however, was the first time I'd seen him so loaded that he threw up. Mom made him sleep on the couch and I'll never forget seeing him lie there, his blanket full of little orange chunks, as I made my way to the kitchen the next morning. Aside from the smell hovering all around the living room, which was rank, I felt bad for Dad and told Mom so over breakfast. "He looks really sick," I said.

"He *is* sick," she replied, scooping out a piece of grapefruit onto a plate.

"Does he have the flu or something?"

"No. He has demons."

8

"Third time's a charm," Dad says. On her third swimming lesson, Jung-ho finally got in the water.

Earlier that day, in history, we were given a thousand-word essay on people and events I'd never even heard of. Two periods later, I was given back a math test I'd failed. Integers were my new sworn enemy. Mr. Ingersoll finished off the class by cracking one of his favourite one-liners: "What do you get when you take the circumference of your jack-o-lantern and divide it by its diameter?" No one put up their hand. I fought hard to keep my eyes open. "Pumpkin Pi!"

Groan.

In the last class of the day, French, Mlle Rochette made me read a passage out loud as guys laughed their heads off. Clearly I'd inherited Dad's knack for foreign languages. To be fair, Mlle Rochette, one of two female teachers at our school, was smoking hot and helped make an otherwise boring class something to look forward to. A twenty-something woman from Quebec, she dressed that class, and each one, wearing a skirt hiked many centimetres above her knees and with heels so high her calves practically exploded out of her pantyhose. She was the source both of urban legends (about who she'd done it with because she'd *obviously* done it with at least one student) and locker room talk before and after phys. ed. class (guys would argue about her bra cup size, the shape of her nipples, how she moaned in bed, etc.)

"Wanna come to my place and play a little *Ice Hockey*?" Keith asked me as we zipped up our knapsacks on our way out of the classroom.

"I think I'll pass this time. I need to, you know, practice my French."

"J.R.! Take a chill pill! You know Mlle Rochette loves breaking your balls because deep down she has this…" Here, he swiveled his hips and put his fingers up to his mouth in the shape of a V. "Deep… down…love…of Justin Maloney's baloney."

"You need help."

"And *you* need to get laid."

In grade eight, no one talked about sex except when gossiping about whose brother had done it. Now that we were in high school, it seemed a favourite comeback for guys when they couldn't think of anything else to say.

"Would you get a life?" I said, marching out into the hall as Keith trailed me.

"Let me guess. You've got a hot date with SBG?"

"Seriously. Give it a rest."

"*Seriously. Give it a rest*," Keith mocked me in a girly voice.

"What's your deal?" I said, spinning around.

"Whoa! J.R., relax. It's a joke."

"Yeah, well, it's not cool." That seemed to shut him up because, as we were leaving school, he said he needed to stay behind and take care of a few things, choosing not to ride the bus with me to the subway station.

The day flashed through my mind as Jung-ho took her first steps into the water from the stairs in the shallow end. I was sitting at the edge of the pool, my feet in the water, when Jung-ho had told me she wanted to go in the water. Surprised, I said we'd go slow and that I'd be there beside her the whole way. "If you get scared, we'll come right out of the pool."

She dipped her toes into the water as I stood in the metre-deep shallow end, looking over at me before taking each step forward. When she got to the bottom of the stairs, her hand still on the chrome railing, she let herself go. I'd seen Herc swim in Keith's pool and Jung-ho didn't look so different at first. Her legs and arms swung madly, thrashing about in the water. Without those little plastic things on her arms, she wouldn't have been able to stay afloat. That didn't take away from her excitement, though.

"Justin! Justin! Look! I'm swimming! I'm swimming!"

While she wasn't technically *swimming*, I didn't want to burst her bubble and so told Jung-ho that she was bound for the Olympics. She was bobbing around like a buoy caught in a storm, so I moved over and placed a hand under her mid-section, bringing her horizontal with the water. "Let's putter around the shallow end, okay?"

When we got out of the pool half an hour later, Jung-ho was heaving and panting and looked like she might fall over from exhaustion. "Are you all right?" I asked, slightly concerned.

"That was fun!"

The end of phys. ed. turned out to be a mess the following day. After class we headed to the change room where we'd left our school uniforms. Ken Chang was the first one to say anything. "Shit! My wallet's gone!" From there, a string of guys echoed the same thing, including me. In all, twenty-four of us had our wallets stolen. Aside from losing the last fifty bucks I had left from Dale's gift, what angered me most was that whoever had pilfered my wallet had also taken my frigging keys.

I stood outside Dad's apartment after school, *knock, knock, knocking* away until I realized where he could be. I headed over to The Last Resort, where (sure enough) Dad was sitting alone at the far end of the bar. We still hadn't talked since yesterday morning when he took off midway through breakfast, so I wasn't sure how this was going to play out. "Ah!" he said as I walked up to him. "Alicia, may I introduce you to Justin, the fruit of my loins."

Holy mackerel. Was he already half in the bag?

The bartender, a tall black woman with killer curves, a raspy voice, and a chest spilling out of her top, shook hands with me, revealing a huge gap between her front teeth. "Darlin', it's a pleasure to meet you. Your dad here's told me so much about you I could write a book." She let out a soulful laugh while saying this. "Can I get you anythin' to drink, good lookin'?" I took a seat beside Dad on a stool.

"Alicia, dear, light of my life," Dad said. "My son will have a ginger ale. And I will have another of the house special, otherwise known as the sweet spirit of cats a-fighting."

Alicia didn't pay attention to Dad's bizarre comment, which made me like her more. "Comin' right up."

"To what do I owe the honour of your presence here today, Justin?" Dad took out a cigarette and lit it. I told him my wallet and key had been stolen at school earlier.

"I thought I told you to be vigilant with this kind of thing."

"Only when getting hit from behind and having a stick jammed into my stomach."

Dad drained his glass. "Well, you can take mine for the time being. Just be careful not to lose this one, or else we'll both be up a creek without a paddle."

Before leaving, I asked Dad if he was still going to be able to drive me to my game tonight.

"Is the Pope Catholic?"

"Right. See you at home."

We won our fifth game in a row, taking sole possession of first place in our division. Although I had a pair of goals and three assists, I wasn't that happy with how I'd played; Mom's no-show at the detention centre was still pissing me off and making it hard to concentrate on anything. It just made no sense why she wouldn't come out and talk with me.

On the way back to the apartment, I answered Dad's questions with mostly one-word answers. He talked about how I had to improve on my face-offs and how Mr. Wainwright wasn't mixing and matching the lines properly. I was staring out the side window, not meaning to ignore Dad, but lost in a maze of thoughts that had no start or end point.

"What's weighing you down, Atlas?"

"Nothing."

"And nothing will come of nothing."

"I'm just tired."

"So it would appear."

I looked into my lap and noticed a new hole in my T-shirt. Mom gets all flustered when she sees me walking around in "ratty clothing," but I don't know how they even get there. I'll wear a shirt for a while, have it washed, and the next thing I know there's a piece of fabric that's come undone, the tiniest piece of skin underneath it visible. That's when it hit me how distant Dad had become in the last couple of days.

"I'm going to pop into The Last Resort for a nightcap," he said as we rolled into the underground parking lot. His voice was lifeless. "I'll see you at home later."

"Dad?"

"Yes, Justin?"

"I'm sorry." We were still in our seats, the engine turned off.

Dad reached into his jacket, took out his flask and drank a good, long swig. "You have nothing to be sorry about, Justin."

"I mean for Sunday. I didn't mean to—"

"There's no need for this."

"No. There is. I just want you to know I'm sorry."

"Very well." Dad took another swig.

"Dad?"

Silence.

I didn't know what to say next. I wanted to say something to mend this hole, something smart and brilliant, something Dad would say in Latin. Instead, a whole bunch of words jumbled themselves together in my mind like puzzle pieces being dumped onto a table.

"Well, then," he said, pulling the lever to pop the trunk as he opened his door. "Until I see you at home later this evening." Dad put my hockey bag on the ground, closed the trunk and walked away.

9

Shock waves rippled through school when our homeroom teacher, Mr. Jenkins, told us Ron Cuthbert's parents had found our wallets in their son's bedroom. Ron had been suspended indefinitely while the headmaster reviewed the incident. When Mr. Jenkins left, everyone started buzzing. In no time the rumour mill was in full swing: *You think it was for drugs?; maybe he's a kleptomaniac; he's definitely got a gambling problem; I always knew he was a cheat and a liar.*

"*Bonjour, mes petits anges,*" Mlle Rochette said, making a dramatic entrance into the classroom with her silky legs. Ron Cuthbert himself could've walked in right now and everybody would've asked who the new kid in class was. For me, I was stuck on one question, not why he did it, but why he'd be stupid enough to leave the evidence lying around his room.

After a five-two victory over the second place team in the division, I looked around the arena for Dad. He'd dropped me off earlier, saying he needed to pop over to Uncle Adam's place and would be back

A Father's Son

before the drop of the puck. I didn't think anything of it until the next game had begun and Dad wasn't in the lobby. I found a payphone and called to see if he was at home. There was no answer. I would've called Uncle Adam's house, but I couldn't remember his number. Ever since Dale had left for Japan a couple of years ago, I never had any reason to phone over there.

Outside, I threw my gear on the ground and then took a seat on the pavement, using the bag as a backrest. The weather was warm for mid-October and smelled of burning wood. The wind helped dry my hair, which still felt greasy. If Dad was in the arena and I hadn't seen him, or if he was on his way right now, this was the safest place to wait. Most of the guys had already left, but Timmy Atkinson and Jamie Longfellow, in typical goalie fashion, were the last ones out.

"You need a lift, man?" Timmy asked.

"No, I'm good, thanks. My dad's on his way."

"Are you sure?" his father said. "It's really no inconvenience at all. You live on Glenrose, right?"

He still thought I lived with Mom at our old place.

"No, really. It's fine. He's probably caught up in traffic or something. He'll be here any minute, I'm sure."

For the next half hour I played out a bunch of different possibilities: Dad was working late; he was drunk at The Last Resort; he'd been in a car accident; he was teaching Jung-ho how to swim. I knew the next game was over when both teams' players began filing out of the arena. Stealing a quick look at my watch, I gave Dad ten more minutes. Unsure whether I had enough money to get on the subway, I leapt to my feet, reached inside my pocket and breathed a huge sigh of relief after pulling out a ten-dollar bill.

"You didn't come around for a Slushie earlier" came a girl's voice from behind me.

"Huh?" I said, turning around.

Dimples.

The door closed behind her as she lifted a shoulder up so the straps of her bag wouldn't fall off. "Your friend Keith swung by for his ridiculously massive strawberry Slush Puppy and I thought you'd be with him."

She was so close to me I could almost taste her scent. "Oh, ah, I took my sweet time getting undressed and then, umm, had to take care of something."

That makes no sense, meathead.

"Are you waiting for someone?" She folded her arms across an oversized sweater, which made her (already thin) calves and thighs seem even skinnier in a pair of black leggings.

"Me? Yeah. My dad's on his way here right now."

"But your game ended over an hour ago, didn't it?"

"Yeah. He's late sometimes. No big deal."

Dimples nodded, unsure. "Okay, then."

"Right."

She turned around and started walking the other way. Pissed off at myself for sounding so idiotic, I punched my palm with a closed fist.

"Say, I'm sure your dad'll be here any minute, but…" She'd spun around and was facing me again. "Do you want some company while you wait?" I went to say something but nothing would come out. "You should close your mouth. You're catching flies." Coming my way again, I nervously did as I was told and ended up biting down on my tongue.

"Ow!" I said, cradling my face with a hand.

"What?"

"I bit down on my…forget it. I should be locked up."

"Tell you what. If we're going to wait, do you mind if we sit on a bench?" She craned her neck in the direction behind me, her arms still hugging her chest tightly. There was a park surrounding the arena, and at the foot of the parking lot was a bench.

"Yeah. Sure." We sat down under a tree, squirrels darting all around us as they stocked up for the winter, one acorn at a time. A full moon was out overhead. The only other light came from the orange lamp-post beside one of the baseball dugouts in the distance. I was trying to think of something to break the ice and when nothing came to mind, I reached into my K-Way pocket and pulled out a bag of chips. "Want one?" I asked, as I opened them up.

"What flavour are they?"

"Salt and vinegar."

"Only the most delicious flavour!"

"Yeah, but ketchup is a close second."

"Whatever," she scoffed. "Ketchup chips are clearly inferior to sour cream and onion."

I made a mental note, adding salt and vinegar and sour cream and onion chips to a list that now included orange Slush Puppies.

"They say you're on track to break the single season point record for the MTHL," she said as she crunched down on a chip.

Say what?

"How do you—"

"Are you kidding? You're all people talk about at the arena. Justin Maloney this, Justin Maloney that. You look as if no one's ever told you this before."

She knew who I was and I didn't even know her name?

"Hey, McFly, your mouth."

I grinned and the pain from biting my tongue returned. But then she smiled and those dimples of hers made me forget about the tiny river of blood flowing in my mouth. "What?" she repeated. When I still didn't answer, she punched my arm. "What!"

"I guess I thought, you know, that nobody really talked about our team."

"They don't talk about your *team*. They talk about *you*. And when you're this, like, super rich and famous player in the NHL one day, I can tell all my friends that I served you raspberry Slush Puppies for an entire season!"

My legs were shaking mildly, tremors going up and down each arm. My mind was like a TV channel in the early morning hours when the shows end and it goes to static. "So you like hockey?" I asked.

"I don't *dis*like it, but I'm more of a summer sports girl: swimming, canoeing, hiking. You know, that kind of thing."

"But you work in a hockey arena snack bar."

You're a douche bag, Justin.

"Sorry, that came out wrong. I meant, you don't work at a swimming pool...or...I'll shut up now." Dad had spent years cramming a dictionary full of words into my head and now I couldn't even string together two sentences without coming across like a donkey's backside.

Dimples on full display, she said, "There aren't exactly a lot of canoeing and hiking clubs to work at."

"Right."

We stayed quiet for a bit. I looked out at the park, the sky, the tree leaves above us. I was desperate to know her name; to say something memorable; to have her see me as cool. We'd demolished the bag of chips when Ali said, "Can I ask you something?"

"Sure."

"Your dad's not coming, is he? Your game ended at, what, eight-thirty? And it's almost ten now. He's probably working late or something, I bet. My dad does that all the time. Tells my mom he'll be home by six and then he'll walk in from the hospital at nine o'clock. Worse still, my mom says she'll be home for dinner and then stroll in the front door as I'm getting ready for bed. Never trust a workaholic to be on time, I say."

"Yeah. You're probably right."

"How are you going to get home, then? Do you live close by?"

"Not exactly."

"Where's your place?"

"You know where Branksome is?"

"It's in Rosedale, isn't it?"

"Yeah."

"Wow, your dad must *really* be doing well if you live down there."

"Right."

"So I guess you'll have to take the subway home."

I nodded.

"I could walk to the subway station with you. If you want, I mean." Suddenly, she looked nervous. "These streets are just so dangerous at night," she added with a tiny grin.

"Yeah. That'd be cool."

There were no awkward silences on our way to Eglinton Station. She told me how she was in her first year of high school at North Toronto and working part-time on weekends at the arena to earn some extra spending money. "I have a healthy disrespect for money," she explained, "but I stopped taking an allowance from my parents because they started putting the most ridiculous conditions on it. They actually wanted receipts— *receipts*!—from where I'd spent my money. Can you believe that?"

"That's crazy."

"There's no reasoning with them, though. They're bonkers about money. But you must have something similar with your dad, right?"

I'd stopped listening and was actually grateful Dad hadn't shown up. He would've gotten out and introduced himself, all hammered and sloppy. Then Ali would've had to watch me climb into the Volare and…

"…Hello? Earth to Justin? Do you agree?"

I tried to remember the last thing she'd said and drew a blank. "Yeah. Totally."

"Well, this is where I get off."

We were at the entrance to the subway. I wanted to rewind the tape and play this whole scene over again. I'd extend a hand and, in a confident tone of voice, say my name and she'd say hers.

"So, I guess I'll see you around, Charlie Brown." She pulled her arms inside her sweater and crossed them over her chest, the weather a lot colder than it had been an hour ago.

"Yeah."

When she didn't move, I said bye with a dumb wave and made my way down the stairs. "Hey," she said as I hit the first step. I turned around. "Your third goal was the best one tonight. The first two were okay, but that last one on the breakaway was pretty special." I didn't have to ask the question. The look on my face said it all. "You think we have anything to do when you're playing? No one moves from their seats. They should put a camera up there in the stands and broadcast it on CBC. People would watch."

Dimples.

"By the way, talk to your friend Keith. He's got something for you."

10

Parents ask me what it's like growing up as an only child. No matter what I say, inevitably the next question is, *Weren't you lonely when you were little?* I'll say it was great, best thing that could've happened to me, and still that lonely question comes up. I didn't have an older brother to fight my battles or a younger sister to pick on when I was in a bad mood. I had myself, which is a pretty good way to get creative when there's nothing else to do. It's also a surefire way to depend a hell of a lot more on your friends. When I was little, mothers and fathers would look at me with this I-feel-sorry-for-you look on their faces, saying how brave and strong I must be to grow up alone. Although I never said it out loud, what I always wanted to tell them was, *Alone? You think I'm growing up alone? I've got 18 brothers on a hockey team who I'd go to the wall for and a best friend who's closer to me than any "real" brothers I know.*

I guess that's why it was sometimes hard for me to figure out Dad and Uncle Adam. If parents assumed it was better growing up with a sibling, then their relationship made no sense because they were always at each other's throat about something, and that something was usually money. On Saturday morning, Dad avoided any mention of not picking me up from the game and instead went off about Uncle Adam as I ate a bowl of cereal. Mom says Dad and Adam have never been close. Things only got "stickier," as she put it, when Grandpa Robert moved in with us for those few months before he passed away. Adam was nine years older than Dad and a businessman that had been rich for as long as I'd known him, but who made a crapload of dinero on the stock market after something called Black Monday a year ago ("more than what all the Reichmanns are worth put together," as Dad put it). Adam and his second wife had a massive house with more bathrooms than we had bedrooms. And although they also lived in Toronto, taking care of Grandpa somehow fell on Dad, which is to say it somehow fell on Mom. That's when Dad and Adam started fighting about money, or at least when they started fighting about money in front of us kids. Sometimes it would be over the phone, Dad calmly telling his brother he was an "ungracious bastard" and informing him where he could stick his worthless money. When it happened in person, Dad wasn't quite as put together. Typically towards the end of a visit, there would be harsh words on both sides. Even Mom would jump into the fray, asking how on God's green Earth we were supposed to pay for Grandpa's care when we were barely making ends meet as it was. Adam would say something along the lines of, I fulfilled my financial responsibility to Dad when I bailed out his insolvent business venture and made sure our mother could put three square meals on the table every day.

By the afternoon, Dad's rant had become real stale, so I walked over to Keith's place to watch Game 1 of the World Series. Lorraine let me in and said Keith was in the basement. I got to Keith's house before Dean, who'd also been invited over, and headed down to the basement, where Keith was already playing *The Legend of Zelda*. Herc was sleeping on the couch so I sat down in an armchair, kicked back and put my legs on a footrest. Keith paused the game and then flicked a piece of folded-over paper at me.

"What's this?"

"I don't know. Okay, fine. I kind of looked at it for, like, a few seconds." I unfolded the message. At the top of the page was a caption that read *I wonder how many wishes a star can give.* Underneath that was the name Ali, written all in cursive, a heart sitting above the letter *i*, and a phone number. At the bottom of the page was a yellow bear with a red top, his arms wrapped snugly around a blue "hunny" jar.

I looked over at Keith in disbelief and asked if this was Snack Bar Girl.

"No, it's not Snack Bar Girl. It's her evil twin." I'm pretty sure I had GULLIBLE GUPPY written across my forehead. "Hello? HELLO! Of course it's Snack Bar Girl, dickweed. And she better have drop-dead friends, pal. Hot like Christie Brinkley and as flexible as that figure skater, Katarina Tit."

I looked down at the note again and analyzed every stroke of the letters, the little heart drawn with care, the stationery she'd used to write this on. Keith threw a controller my way and then unpaused the game. We'd only killed a handful of those annoying Octorok monsters when Dean arrived. I didn't know Dean that well outside of hockey, but the few times we'd hung out he seemed cool. He was a big guy from Windsor whose family had moved to Toronto when his dad got laid off at the Ford plant there. This was Dean's first year with us, and while changing teams is no easier than changing schools when it comes to making friends and being accepted, Dean had done all right. Our coach, Mr. Wainwright, could see the positive energy he brought to the dressing room and to the blue line, naming him one of two assistant captains this season. It sounds kind of dumb, but the first thing that made me like Dean was his Dad's car. At a tryout earlier in the year, Dean climbed out of a white Continental way uglier and clunkier than the Volare. After the tryout, we were taking off our equipment when I mentioned his dad's wheels. This made him smirk. "My dad calls it the General Sherman."

"I don't get it."

"As in the Sherman tank."

We laughed. "Yeah, well, wait till you get a load of my Dad's hunk of junk. It would give a Pinto or a Yugo a run for its money."

With Dean there now, Keith said we should take turns playing *Mike Tyson's Punch-Out!!*

"Nah. I'm over that game. Let's play something else."

"How can you be sick of *Mike Tyson*?" Keith asked.

"It's boring. Besides, we've already finished it. Let's just play *Super Mario Bros.*"

Keith didn't make a big deal of it and the three of us took turns playing a few rounds with Mario and Luigi before Lorraine called us upstairs. She'd made an amazing chicken dish, with peas, carrots, baked potatoes—and homemade fudge brownies! Even Mr. Fraser looked surprised that we were having chocolate for dessert.

"Well, dear," Lorraine said as Keith, Dean and I helped her clear the dishes when we were done, "I have three growing boys at the table and a daughter who's been at me for weeks to have something besides fruit after dinner. I had to cave in one day or another. Now, boys," Lorraine went on as we headed downstairs, "I'll have some popcorn for you shortly, but I'm warning you now: no butter!"

"Mom!"

"*Uh uh uh.* House rules, my dear."

For eight innings, the baseball game was b-e-y-o-n-d *boooooooring*. I probably would've fallen asleep if we hadn't been shooting the commercial breaks away playing *Duck Hunt*. By the bottom of the ninth inning, I was yawning and hoping for a quick end. The score was 4-3 for the Oakland A's and Tony La Russa had brought out his closer, Dennis Eckersley. Keith was at the base of the couch, his eyes glued to the screen. Dean and I sat in separate armchairs, far away from the TV and talking about hockey.

"Damn!" Keith said. "Scioscia popped up. One out." A minute later he moaned that there were two outs. When the next batter walked, I got up. The popcorn had made my mouth dry and I needed some water. Keith grabbed my wrist at the foot of the den. "You're not going anywhere, pal."

"What the…"

Keith pushed the volume up on the remote control. Dodger Stadium was going mental. They were giving the pinch hitter, Kirk Gibson, a standing ovation. The announcers were saying how Gibson had been a scratch for the World Series because of a bad left hamstring and a bum right knee. He limped to the plate and as he took a practice swing, Lorraine casually walked in, arms folded. "I'm not sure if you're trying to go deaf, Keith, but if you don't turn down the TV this instant, you won't be watching it again until you're in university."

Keith lowered the volume.

"Satisfied?" Gibson had just gone down oh and two.

"Keith Lloyd Gordon Fraser, I do *not* like that tone in your voice."

"Okay, okay. I'm sorry." When Lorraine finally made her way back up the stairs, I slid behind Keith on the sofa and watched a slumped-over Kirk Gibson get set for the three-and-two pitch. When he connected, Keith and I jumped to our feet.

"High fly ball into right field," the announcer said. "She is…… gone!" Gibson trotted to first, his fist high in the air. Then he hobbled around the rest of the bases, pumping his arm. Keith and I bounced around the room as the guy on TV, stunned, added, "In a year that has been so improbable, the impossible has happened."

Talk about the understatement of the decade. With a pulled hamstring, a bum knee and an ankle throbbing in pain, a guy Sparky Anderson once called "the next Mickey Mantle" had limped out of the silver screen as Roy Hobbs from *The Natural* and done something inconceivable. Kirk Gibson hadn't just beaten the odds when he blasted his pinch-hit homerun out of Dodger Stadium. He'd rewritten history and showed everyone that the word "impossible" now had two letters that were, as Dad would have said, "extraneous at this point."

Ali, Ali, Ali.
A-L-I.
Ali.

I'd never phoned a girl (like, a *girl* girl) and had no idea what we'd talk about. Dad read on the couch most of the day, ignoring me and taking frequent sips of his drink. When he went out later, I tried working up the nerve to call Ali. That was easier said than done.

Over at Dad's desk, I stared at the phone, now a source of fear. My heart was pumping madly up around my throat. I went over the dialogue in my head so many times I could've written a script. In my version, everything went smoothly. We talked, we laughed. Ali was impressed with my sense of humour and my far-reaching knowledge of everyone and everything. We'd hang up and I'd casually stroll to the bed and pick up from where I left off with my homework. Mom would be released from the detention centre early on good behaviour, Dad would return home and tell me how he'd just won the lottery, and Ali would finish off the night by coming over and giving me a peek at her boobs.

I picked up the phone and put it down just as fast. Reaching for it again, I got it up to my ear, then hyperventilated as I replaced it on the cradle. Tremors started rippling through my arms, so I took 20 mg of propranolol. Then, against doctor's orders, I popped one more pill.

She's going to see through me. She'll see me as weak and poor and stupid and incompetent. She'll ask that I never phone her again and I'll be the source of jokes around the arena for the rest of the season.

That's when a random thought came to me. I remembered Jung-ho taking her first steps into the pool the other day and yelling at me, "Justin! Justin! Look! I'm swimming! I'm swimming!" Breathing a little bit like an asthmatic, I hit the numbers on the phone.

One ring…two rings…three rings…

"Hello?"

"Hi, is Ali there, please?" I'd practiced the line so many times it came out as fake.

"May I ask who's calling?"

"It's Jistin—Justin," I corrected myself, closing my eyes.

"Hold on one moment."

I lifted the white cord to my mouth and bit down on it.

"Hello?" Ali said on a different phone as her mom, I assumed, hung up.

"Hi, Ali?"

"Yeah."

"It's Justin." I swear my voice cracked.

"Hiya!"

"Hey." *Stick to the script.* "I got your note from Keith last night."

"Cool."

"Yeah."

Our first pause was murder.

"I guess you got home safe on Friday night," she said, keeping the ball rolling.

"Yeah. The subway was no big deal, you know." I could actually smell the sweat running down from my armpits. "How was your weekend?"

"Fine. I went out with some friends last night and tried to do a little shopping earlier today. I *totally* need a new jacket for winter, but I couldn't find a thing. It was so annoying."

"I bet."

"How about you?"

I laughed.

That wasn't a joke, moron.

"Last night, I went over to a buddy's house, Keith, you know, the guy you gave the note to, and watched the World Series."

"Ugh. I hate baseball. Was it a good game?" she asked, sounding bored.

"It was okay. The Dodgers won. Well, they won game one, but it was a pretty incredible ending."

"Oh, yeah?" I could tell she wasn't really interested, but what else could we talk about?

"It was kind of epic. Kirk Gibson—he plays for the Dodgers—and he hit a homerun in the bottom of the ninth."

"Cool."

"Yeah." *Pitter-patter, pitter-patter, pitter-patter.* "So what are you up to now?"

"Me? Not much. Just lounging around my room and watching some TV."

"Cool. What're you watching?"

"MuchMusic."

"Oh, yeah? What's on right now?"

"Let's see…Looks like U2."

"Which song?"

"'Bad'."

"Oh, my God!"

"Do you know it?"

"I love it!"

"*Really?*"

And that was the break we needed. Girls my age, I thought, talked about fashion and makeup and Hollywood heartthrobs; guys talked sports and video games. The connecting factor, I'd just discovered, was music. Ali said she listened to everything, from the Cowboy Junkies and the Clash to Enya and the Eurythmics. When she put the question back to me, I had to think for a minute. "You know, Dire Straits, Genesis…*obviously* U2." This last one was the spark I'd been dying for.

"What's your favourite album by U2?" she asked.

I said "Bad" was my favourite song, but *The Joshua Tree* was my favourite album.

"That's so not true!" *The Unforgettable Fire* was totally their best album. Although, I must say, 'With or Without You' is pretty awesome."

"Oh, come on. 'Where the Streets Have No Name' is *waaay* better than 'With or Without You'."

"Not a chance!"

Before getting off the phone, I told Ali my phone number. She said she'd call me next week (Did that mean tomorrow? Wednesday afternoon? Friday night?) and then we hung up, both of us pretty giddy. I knew I was still in another world when Dad got home around dinner and asked, "Why the bravado, Casanova?"

"Huh?"

"You look elated and full of a certain *joie de vivre*."

"You know, I finished all my homework in record time."

"No last-minute history questions for your father?"

"Nope."

"In that case, I shall repose on the sofa and discover how Nicholas II managed to have his family killed in such spectacular fashion by the Bolsheviks."

11

The difference between elementary school and high school came down to one thing for me: you *went around* with girls in grade six and did things like play Truth or Dare? behind the school. If you were lucky, you got a closed-mouth kiss or maybe even caught a glimpse of a bra. In grade nine, you *went out* with girls and tried to hit a home run, one base at a time if need be.

Ali and I had been on the phone for a while, talking about music and movies mostly, when she asked if I wanted to swing by her school tomorrow. Dad was out at the time, which was good because there was no way I could talk to Ali with him in the same room.

"Yeah, sure." The phone cord had snaked itself around my forearm.

"Like, three-thirty or something?"

"That works for me."

"Great. Okay, so…"

"Right. I'll, ah…"

"See you tomorrow?"

"Yep."

I got to Ali's school at three-twenty-eight and watched her stroll out of the doors not long after that. I *might* have run from the subway station to make sure I got there in time. Ali broke the ice when she cruised up to me and said, "Hiya."

"Hey."

"How was your day?"

We walked down the street, close enough to hold hands, packs of teenagers all over the place.

"You know. Same as usual. You?"

"Ugh. I got two tests back today. I aced the one in math, but only got eighty-five on my geography mid-term."

Only eighty-five? Gulp.

"That stinks."

"Tell me about it. I mean, when am I ever going to have to know the difference between igneous, sedimentary and metamorphic rocks!"

"Never."

"Totally, right?"

When we got to Ali's place, which was just a couple of blocks away, my mind started racing. The only times I'd seen someone my age walk a girl home was in the movies and everyone knows that what happens in Hollywood never happens in real life. "So," I said, looking at her house and following that up with a completely useless question: "How long have the renovations been going on for?"

"It's disgusting, isn't it? I know. I hate it."

Scaffolding lined the three-story house, a structure from another era that Dad would've known the architectural term for, while a huge green lawn without any dandelions on it stretched all the way to the sidewalk.

"Aside from all the pipes and stuff, your place looks pretty amazing."

"Yeah, well, it's a major pain in my ass. They're working on it all hours of the day and sometimes even on weekends. *Daddy* wants them to finish everything by Christmas and it's driving me schizo. Anyway," she sighed and then turned. "I should get inside. My parents have me taking piano lessons once a week and it starts in five minutes." She looked at her watch. "Knowing Mrs. van der Meere, she's probably waiting inside already. She's always, like, twenty minutes early for our lessons."

"Right."

"Yeah."

"So, ah, maybe we can…Yeah, I should get home, too."

"Thanks for the walk."

"No sweat." I bit my lower lip. "Okay. So, ah, see you around?"

"You wanna maybe, I don't know, meet up after school on Thursday? I don't have any extra-*grooming* courses then, so we can actually hang out." Ali traced a circle with the toe of her shoe.

"Sure."

"Cool. Right, then. See you Thursday."

I refused to move as Ali put one long leg in front of the other (okay, I might have been checking out her butt as well), and got the reward I'd been hoping for at the last minute. As she disappeared inside her house, Ali looked back and waved.

Score one for the good guys!

On Thursday, Ali waited for me with one of her friends, Debbie Koteas, who, along with Rachel White and Vicki Hansen, was one of Ali's three best friends. She was a short girl with curly black hair, olive skin and a long, crooked nose. She had huge guns for a girl our age and legs too short for the jeans she wore, which bunched up around her shoes. Like Ali, she was really, really thin. "Debs here and me have known each other for*ever*," Ali said after introducing us.

"Hey."

"Hi."

Silence.

Then Debbie turned to Ali and said, eyes pointed up and into her head, "*Any*ways, like I was telling you, Brad Clarkson is way too immature for me. D'you know he still plays with action figures? How could I ever go out with someone who's still playing G.I. Joe at this age?" She lowered her voice and grabbed Ali's forearm. "I've heard he wets his bed and plays video games every night, too."

I had no idea what Brad looked like or what kind of guy he was, but based solely on my first impression of Debby, he was either the biggest loser on the planet or Debbie was throwing away the best thing to ever come her way, as she was as good a catch as a dead fish on the end of your pole.

The two of them hugged and said goodbye to each other. Instead of saying anything to me, Debbie just glanced in my direction, raised an arm and "waved" by scrunching her fingers up and down like one of those stupid cats you see in the window of Japanese restaurants.

Whatever.

"You hungry?" Ali asked when Debbie was gone.

"The better question is, am I ever full?"

"I'm pretty peckish myself."

"Want to head to McDick's?"

"You're going to get me very fat hanging out with you," she said, a pair of dimples forming on her cheeks.

The closest McDonald's was all of a block away. I got a Quarter Pounder with Cheese and fries. Ali ordered a cheeseburger made like a Mac.

"What's that?" I asked, pulling out my wallet to pay.

"You know, it's a cheeseburger with Big Mac sauce on it." We were standing off to the side and waiting for our food.

"So why not just get a Big Mac?"

"Do you know how many calories are in a Big Mac?" She punched my arm. "Like, a bazillion! There's way less in a cheeseburger. The least I can do is watch the number of calories I put into this bloated body of mine."

"But you're not..."

Think before you speak, Justin.

"I'm not what?" Ali took the tray from the woman behind the counter.

"You're not, you know…"

"Fat?"

"No!" I wanted to tell her she had a wicked-hot body. It was insane she could think of herself as "bloated," but I didn't trust how it would sound; she'd probably see me as slimy and only into her looks.

"Well, it's true," she said as we took a seat. "I'm Fatty McFatso these days and need to lose weight."

This was getting ridiculous. "Ali, I don't know what your friends are telling you, but I don't think you need to, you know, change anything about you."

"You're sweet."

I was about to recite a marvellously poetic poeticism (*You think I'm sweet, Honey-Comb? You're so sweet you make Lucky Charms look sugar-free!*) when some punk a year older than us that I recognized from the Toronto Marlies stopped at our table and said hi to Ali. He looked at me for a fraction of a half-fraction of a second, but didn't bother introducing himself. For a couple of minutes, Ali and what's-his-face then conversed/talked/chitchatted/spoke/chewed the fat (I tried to think of every word I could except "flirt").

When he eventually left, Ali apologized and said she would have introduced us, but could never remember his name. I smiled to myself as Ali swallowed one of my fries and leaned forward. I instinctively pulled back, as if dodging a punch.

"I'm not going to bite," she said, lifting herself from her seat and stretching across the table. "Here, you've got ketchup on your face." She dabbed at the corner of my mouth with a napkin and added, "Mister, I do believe you have an eating problem." Then she burst out laughing as she went to sit down and nearly fell off the stupid chair.

"And *you* may need a wheelchair," I said.

We made plans to see a movie on the weekend. Even though I still had some of Dale's gift left over, I needed a little extra coin just to be safe if I wanted to pay for Ali, too. Hunched over his desk, Dad was studying some documents when I guided the hair across my forehead with a steady hand and asked him for some money.

"What, may I ask, for?"

"Keith and I are going to a flick." There was no way I was telling him about my date.

"You'd best be served to go on a Tuesday when they charge two-fifty."

"But we have practices on Tuesday nights."

"Indeed." Dad took out his wallet and handed me five bucks.

"I was hoping to get some popcorn and a soft drink as well."

Dad lowered his pencil, turned around, and faced me. Up until now he'd been focused on his papers and hadn't bothered to take his attention away.

Uh-oh.

I may have sucked at math, but I did know one equation off by heart:

$$x + y = z$$

x: Removal of Dad's reading glasses
y: Speech that will teach me nothing and only make me more resentful
z: Hating myself for talking to Dad in the first place

"Justin, I don't know what kind of values your mother has inculcated in you when it comes to the almighty dollar, but it is not something to be taken lightly. If you don't learn a sense of responsibility with money at this age, you will go through life with a disrespect for the hard work needed to earn it. I've given you the means to see your movie tonight. Now, please, I'm busy working."

"Thanks," I said on my way out. His back turned to me, Dad raised a hand and waved.

At the Eaton Centre, there were eight different movies playing and still Ali and I couldn't agree on which one to see. In the end, it boiled down to two choices: *Beaches*, (hers) and *Die Hard* (mine). The answer, she said, was easy: "We'll see both of them."

"No, it's fine. Let's just see *Beaches*." We were looking up at the white signboard with all the showtimes. Buying four tickets would've wiped out the rest of Dale's gift and I couldn't let Ali pay for her own ticket.

"Tell you what. Get us two tickets for *Beaches* and leave the rest to me."

Ali wasn't doing so well halfway through the movie. By the end of the stupid thing, the scene where Bette Midler goes off with Barbara Hershey's daughter because her mom has kicked the bucket, Ali was bawling. That, of course, was awesome because it gave us our first excuse to get close when she sobbed onto my pipe cleaner of a bicep, her tears actually seeping through the fabric of my plaid button down. For my part, I'd spent most of those two hours trying to (unsuccessfully) work up the courage to reach out and hold her hand.

When the credits were done rolling, we stood up and Ali took my hand in hers as she led us across to a different theatre. We grabbed two seats at the back of Theatre 3 and watched a shoeless Bruce Willis dance his way around a building with a bunch of weapons, saving his wife and an office full of employees from terrorists while talking to a cop who loves eating Twinkies on the job. It was clear which of the movies we'd just seen was better.

"You can't even begin to tell me *Die Hard* was nearly as great as *Beaches*!" Ali howled ninety minutes later. We were at a hot dog stand on Dundas Street and had just been given our footlongs. "Oh my *gawd*, you're going to get me so fat on all this junk."

Ali put ketchup, relish and onions on hers. When I lathered mine in mustard and ketchup, she laughed and asked what I was doing.

"What do you mean?"

"Ketchup and mustard? That makes no sense."

"You put Big Mac sauce on your cheeseburger."

"You're weird."

"Whatever. They go great together."

"No one puts mustard and ketchup together on their hot dog."

"No one mixes sauces at McDonald's." I took a bite and asked Ali what her damage was because she'd stopped eating. Ali giggled, but the giggle quickly morphed into a fully-bent-over-holding-her-stomach laugh.

"What are you yukking it up about?" I said.

She wiped away the tears from her eyes and then leaned towards me with a napkin. "You really do have an eating problem." She started laughing to herself again. "This time you have ketchup *and* mustard on your face."

We began heading east. At first we talked about the movies, then gradually about things like our friends, school, and music. Turning south on Yonge Street, we walked lazily towards Lake Ontario when Ali asked if I'd heard the new Sonic Youth album.

"No. Is it any good?"

"You haven't heard any of the songs on *Daydream Nation*?"

"Nope."

"It's amazing. Best CD of the year. Hands down. What do you think about Jane's Addiction?" she asked a second later.

I told her I hadn't even heard of them."

"Justin! You haven't heard anything from *Nothing's Shocking*?" Ali gave me a punch on the arm.

"Ow!"

"How can you say you love music and know nothing about two of this year's best albums?"

She'd tongue-tied me.

"Anyway, don't worry. I'll make you a mixed tape. Just prepare to have your mind blown, okay?"

Nearing the lake, we hung a right and made our way towards a fountain full of coins. A light shining out from the bottom made the pennies and dimes and quarters sparkle. Ali asked if my brothers or sisters ever introduced me to new music as we sat down along a marble railing near the water. When I told her I was an only child, she howled, "So am I!"

As common enough as it was to hear that *Weren't you lonely when you were little?* question from adults growing up, I'd never actually met another only child. I guess that's why, when Ali said she didn't have any siblings, I wasn't prepared for what I'd feel, which was a strange sense of connectedness. It was almost like we shared a secret just by being kids who knew what it was like to do things on your own from a young age.

Each of us lost in thought, Ali turned and said, "What are you thinking at this very exact moment?" She had her fingers locked together in the shape of a gun and aimed at me, her hands pressed into her chest.

"Truthfully?"

"Nothing but the truth, so help you God."

"I dig that I don't have to explain anything to you about being an only child."

She cracked a smile. "I was thinking the same thing."

We were quiet again. I didn't realize how late it was until looking at my watch. While I didn't have a curfew, I assumed Ali must, so asked her what time she had to be home.

"Why? Do *you* want to go home?" she said, looking disappointed.

"No! I don't want you to get you into any trouble, though."

"It doesn't matter. They wouldn't notice anyway." Ali crossed her legs. She wasn't sad or on the verge of tears. She was, to borrow one of

Dad's sixty-four-thousand words, "reticent." After swinging her legs towards me, she kept her eyes focused on my lap. "We're three people all living separate lives under the same roof. We don't actually do anything together as a family. It's not as if me and my mom even do something normal and go shopping together or…or…like me and my dad go riding together. They're always sending me off to this or that place on my own because they both work *allll* the time. They wanted to send me to boarding school this year but I refused to go. It's almost as if I'm a pain in their ass. Seriously, we haven't taken a vacation as a family since I was, I don't know, five or six. My Dad goes golfing with his doctor buddies and my mom will take me to Florida or Martha's Vineyard, but we don't ever travel as a family. How wrong is that?

"And you know what the brutal thing is? They don't even love each other," she said, straightening her back. "They're in this *marriage*, but it's a contract, an arrangement. It has nothing to do with *love*." She paused and looked me in the eyes. "All my mom cares about is her billing hours and her *fabulous* waistline. All my dad cares about is his routine: work, sleep, work, sleep. It's got to be the same every single day. God forbid something in his life should change even slightly. But the worst *worst* part is that she cheats on him. She's gotten bad at keeping it a secret lately, but I'm pretty sure my dad knows. Maybe that's why they sleep in separate rooms now.

"I'm never going to use the word 'love', not in a bazillion years. I hate everything it represents. 'Love you', my mom will say to my dad over breakfast. 'Love you, too', my dad will say right back. And you know what? It's a lie. It's a big fat lie. They don't love each other, Justin. They don't."

Since sitting down at the movies, I'd been wondering if I'd have a chance to kiss Ali tonight. There were a bunch of good chances during *Beaches*, but whenever I'd lean even an inch closer, my arms would start vibrating and I'd chicken out. Now, though, the chillier weather was actually helping me because it didn't feel all that weird to be shaking a little bit.

"Anyway, thank you," she said in a small voice. "I've never told anyone most of that stuff. Not even the girls."

Now or never. Do or die. Man, this is harder than taking a penalty shot in front of a packed arena. Don't think!

I turned my head and, scared as all hell to put my hands on her in case she screamed, landed a tiny kiss on her delicious lips. She didn't scream and she didn't look freaked out. Then a couple of dimples appeared. I reached for her hand and squeezed it in a lame attempt to show I was here for her. She squeezed it two more times.

"Sorry," she explained. "It can't be just once. I'm obsessive compulsive about this stuff. I know, I know. Thank my mother for that wonderful trait in me, but everything needs to be done in threes. Six is fine, nine is great, but three is best."

We stayed out all night, walking along mostly empty streets and sitting on park benches in the middle of this concrete jungle otherwise known as Toronto. At times she'd lie down with her head in my lap and say nothing. Looking at the sky, I'd tell her useless facts Dad had taught me over the years: how Andromeda and the Milky Way were supposed to collide as galaxies in billions of years, our world being blown apart in the process; our sun would one day implode and take everything with it; the universe was expanding like an elastic but would one day contract on itself and create another Big Bang, life starting out all over again.

"Why are you so negative? About the fate of the world, I mean," she asked me at one point.

"I'm not negative. It's the truth."

"But you talk about the destruction of everything, the world coming to an end, the universe coming to an end. It's kind of depressing."

"Sorry."

Ali turned her head and buried it in the space between my neck and my shoulder. "You don't have to be sorry. Remember," she went on, snuggling up against me, "there's still a lot of time left before all that bad stuff happens. Like, a bazillion years."

I laughed. "Yeah, I guess there is."

"Tell me something happy, will you? Something that'll make me feel good?"

I racked my brain. "I don't know. All the stories I've learned about the stars end in fiery destruction."

"Not about the sky, dumb-dumb. Tell me something happy from your life, *one* thing that makes you smile."

Ali's head stayed pressed against my neck as I thought of something from my past that made me happy. "Four years ago," I started, "my mom fell off a chair. She'd been doing something with the curtains. My dad and I were watching hockey. The Leafs were playing the…I can't remember now. But it was a Saturday night. We were upstairs and there was this big crash. My dad said I should go and check what had happened. I rushed down the stairs and saw my mom on the floor, holding a hand against the side of her body, which kind of freaked me out.

"So, anyway, she got herself up and then tells me she thinks she's cracked a rib. What does a kid do when they've heard their mother's cracked a rib?" I looked at Ali, not expecting an answer. "So my mom sits down on a chair and keeps a hand on the side of her body, saying, 'It's fine. I'm okay. I'll be all right'. She reaches for her wine and then tells me to go back up to the hockey game. But you know what? I didn't move. You know what I did?"

This time I was looking for an answer.

"What?" Ali said.

"I got on my knees and put my head on her lap."

When I didn't go on, Ali pulled back and looked at me with glistening eyes. "That was your *happy* story?"

"Yeah."

We looked at each other as if strangers.

"What about that's happy?"

"My mom loved that I stayed with her."

"Oh, you," she said wrapping her arms around my neck. I was probably mangling the whole French kissing thing, but I hoped this moment would never end because here I was, making out with the hottest girl who'd ever talked to me, late at night, her hands rubbing my hair, the soapy smell to her skin driving me wild with pleasure. Nothing else was important right now. As long as we could stay kissing, everything would work itself out.

Winter

12

Mom was released from the detention centre on November 12. Jeff phoned me a few days before then and offered to drive me out to meet her. "No, thank you," I told him. He didn't say anything after that, no heroic speech about his own mother getting on without a husband who was in prison. He ended by saying he was always around if I needed anything.

She might not have been able to track down Dad's new address and write a letter, but his phone number hadn't changed. Mom had it. If she wanted to call, she knew how to reach out. I understood she might need a day or a week to get settled. That made sense to me. What didn't make sense was not phoning at all.

Nine days after she'd been released, when Mulroney and the PCs swept into power and NAFTA was all but a done deal, Dad doing what he calls a "jig" in the living room because this meant more business for him, Mom still hadn't called. Days before Christmas, when Pan Am flight 103 was blown up over Lockerbie, Scotland, I'd pretty much given up any hope of hearing from her.

Dad had grown quieter over the autumn. We didn't talk very much in the apartment anymore. Ever since the night he hadn't picked me up (the same night I'd met Ali, mind you), he hadn't missed a practice or game. Still, he was different; more withdrawn is maybe a better way of putting it. The passion was gone from his voice when he spoke about what needed to be improved upon—with our team and my game. While neither one of us brought it up, we both knew it. When two people don't have a whole lot to say, there aren't a lot of chances to argue. However, there was one time in December things got uncomfortable. Dad announced on the 23rd that we were going to Uncle Adam's for dinner the following night. I told him I already had plans.

"Excuse me?" he said.

"I've been seeing a girl." I paused and felt just as nervous as I was proud. Ali and I had been going out for more than a month before I found the courage to tell anyone besides Keith.

"How long?"

"About a month."

"So that would explain your lack of production on the ice of late."

We were eating grilled cheese sandwiches and tomato soup for dinner. I'd pulled Dad's desk out into the middle of the room earlier.

"What are you talking about?" I dipped a corner of the sandwich into my soup.

"You're down 0.8 points per game since mid-November and you have not had a hat trick since then either." He dipped his grilled cheese into some ketchup.

"But we're in first place."

Dad tapped a generous amount of salt into his soup. "That does nothing to negate the fact that your output is not what it was at the beginning of the season. I presume," he rolled on, "this girl you've been seeing will be graced with your presence on Christmas Eve?"

"Her name is Ali," I said resentfully, "and her family invited me over a couple of weeks ago, when I didn't know we were supposed to go to Uncle Adam's." He had no right to make me have dinner with a relative I hadn't seen in years. If Dale had been home for the holidays, I would've bailed on dinner at Ali's place, but as it stood

I wasn't interested in eating turkey with an uncle I barely knew, an "aunt" whose face I couldn't pick out from a police lineup, and two cousins who were total strangers to me.

"Yes, well, your girlfriend and her family will, I'm sure, relish your presence on the eve of our Saviour's birth."

"Dad…" I came up with a half-truth to make amends. "She really wants to meet you. I've told her a lot about you."

He took a sip of his drink and lit a cigarette, his meal half eaten. "I suppose she'll have to wait until the holidays are over now, won't she?"

I finished my soup and sandwich way before Dad and then got up to leave the table.

"That package on the sofa came for you today by the way," he said. It seems someone can remember the value of family even when sojourning on the other side of the planet."

The oversized envelope had some cool stamps on it. I moved over to my bed and ripped the top open. Inside was a cool card with samurais and snowy mountains and lots of fancy Oriental writing on it:

Justin,

Konichiwa from the Land of the Rising Sun! I won't be able to make it home this X-mas but wanted to pass along a little gift that I hope you'll be able to make use of.

Life is great here. I teach roughly ten hours a day (with privates) and go out for nearly as many hours every night. There's a good chance I'll still be out here when you graduate university! You should come join me. We can be brothers in arms!

Your father has told me you're still the best player in the league and that makes me so proud. I hope you have an enjoyable time *off school over the winter break and look forward to our next talk on the phone.*

Enclosed you'll find what Uncle Rick calls some Robert Bordens (which I happened to come across at the bank the other day), as well as a novel I think you should read by Murakami Ryū. He and his family name counterpart (Haruki) are causing quite a stir in the literary establishment here. I hope you enjoy the book.

It's a little screwed up, but so are the times, right?
Merry Christmas,
Cousin Dale

There was $500 inside the card. The book was called *Almost Transparent Blue*.

For Christmas Eve at Ali's place, I wore my school dress pants and a green long-sleeved Ralph Lauren dress shirt. The cuffs didn't quite reach the ends of my forearms. Mrs. Blake answered the door when I arrived and looked as done up as always, complete with all the jewellery. She wore a white silk top and a red skirt. "These are for you," I said, giving her the bundle of flowers I'd bought on the way over. Dad says you should always bring a gift when visiting a person's home for a special occasion, so I decided to be safe and get the one thing which always made Mom smile.

Mrs. Blake took the dozen long-stemmed roses in both hands and smiled. "You shouldn't have, Justin. Thank you. By the way, Alison will be right down. Come, let me introduce you to my husband while we wait." The smell of turkey hung thick in the air, whetting my appetite.

I took off my shoes and followed Mrs. Blake through a living room which could have been transported from the set of *Risky Business*. Nothing was out of place. There weren't any glasses left on the coffee table, no magazines or books on or under it. The couch and two chairs seemed not to have been sat in. Even the carpet, which spanned the entire length of the room, appeared new. They'd put up a Christmas tree, a huge thing that almost reached the ceiling, and decorated it with white lights, gold and red ornamental balls, and an angel on top. The space underneath the tree was filled with presents, all of which were wrapped up in the same gold-coloured paper and green ribbons.

In the den, a wood-paneled room lined with books on three of its walls, Dr. Blake was sitting on a black leather sofa, his feet up on a footrest. A large painting of a bowl of fruit hung on the wall behind him. I quickly scanned the titles of the medical texts and noticed the spines on most of them hadn't been cracked.

Dr. Blake had salt and pepper hair, a grey beard and half-rimmed glasses, making him look kind of Euro. He was wearing a tie and white dress shirt underneath a crimson sweater, with dark pants and slippers over his socks.

"Dear, this is Justin, Alison's friend. And look what he brought us," Mrs. Blake said through an amused laugh. "A dozen roses!"

Dr. Blake had the end of a pencil in his mouth as he worked away at something, the television on low. When he looked up at me, it took him a moment to make sense of his wife's comment. "A pleasure to meet you, Justin. Please," he went on in a dry voice, "have a seat," indicating the leather chair to his left.

"Thank you."

"I'll leave you two to share some boy time and check on what's taking our darling Alison so long."

"So," Dr. Blake said. Then nothing. Dead air. A canyon opening up between us. "My wife informs me that our Alison is quite smitten with you."

"Ahh…"

How's a guy supposed to respond to that one? Actually, sir, I think about her constantly when touching myself and would give my right arm to reach second base with her by next year?

"And you're at a private school, I'm told?" he went on.

"Yes. I've been there since grade seven."

"We tried to get our Alison into one this year, but…yes, well. Perhaps you could convince her to reconsider?"

I offered a dumb grin and hoped he didn't pursue the subject.

"So…" He put his book down and scratched his beard. "Do you have a favourite class?"

"English."

He frowned approvingly. "What are you reading these days?"

"Well, we don't have any assigned reading for the holidays, but I'm reading a book called *Almost Transparent Blue*." I could tell he'd never heard of it. "It's by a Japanese guy named Murakami, but I'm not sure how to pronounce his first name. It's R-Y-U."

"A Japanese author? Very impressive." He paused. "Have you heard of Sudoku by any chance?" He stroked his beard in a downward motion, then swung his squat legs off the footrest and angled his paunch towards me. "It's extremely popular in Japan, which is where I learned of it. I was in Tokyo for a medical conference some months ago and a fellow doctor, a Japanese man by the name of Akihiko Fukuhara—that's a wonderful name, isn't it?—he was the one to introduce me to it. Basically," he went on, a light forming in his dull brown eyes as he showed me the puzzle he'd been working on, "you're given a series of numbers in each column and row of a nine-by-nine grid, with nine three-by-three sub-grids making up the entire grid."

My head hurt. A week away from math and now this.

"The aim is to fill in the boxes so the numbers one to nine appear just once in each column and each grid, while each box has one to nine in it as well."

Before Dr. Blake had a chance to go on with the Sudoku 101 lesson, Ali walked in the den and said, "Hiya." I turned, with joy quickly turning to surprise—Ali's hair was dyed auburn. She still looked hot, wearing a pair of jeans and a white sweater with a high neck, but it took me a minute to get used to this new version of her.

When we'd met a few days ago to exchange Christmas presents, she hadn't mentioned anything about dyeing her hair. I got Ali a picture frame and put the best photo I had of the two of us in it. I included a letter I'd been working on for a while and said she had to open it later. Ali got me a brown leather wallet.

"What the devil's gotten into you, Alison?" Dr. Blake asked.

"Sorry I was late coming down," she said to me and only me. She then explained how she'd just finished dyeing it. "What do you think, *Daddy*?" Ali showed off her new hairdo in a variety of poses.

Mrs. Blake walked in and leaned a shoulder against the frame of the den's entrance. "Isn't this lovely? She'll be the toast of the town at the Ocean Reef Club next week. Was yet another act of rebellion necessary on Christmas Eve, Alison?"

"It wasn't an act of rebellion, *Mother*. It was an act of self-expression. I live in a free country and wanted to change my hair colour." Ali turned and left the room.

At the beginning of the meal, Mrs. Blake introduced the items on the table like they were guests. Standing up at one end of the long mahogany table, her husband directly opposite her, she described what was in each piece of fine china. As if numbers around a clock, the plates and bowls were placed around a short, round crystal vase holding a bouquet of flowers in a rainbow of colours. There were mashed potatoes, roasted garlic squash, lemon-herb-roasted beets, broccoli gratin, maple-ginger glazed carrots, stuffing, gravy and a sweet-tart cranberry sauce. The silverware was so polished that the light from the chandelier overhead reflected off of them.

When she was done describing the food, Mrs. Blake sat down and drank from a wine glass way bigger than the ones I was used to seeing Mom drink from. Dr. Blake cut the turkey with surgical precision, staring down at the bird and taking his time as he made each cut. The plates were passed around the table, starting with Mrs. Blake's, which had a microscopic amount of white meat on it. Mine was next. Dr. Blake gave me a generous portion of white meat and a drumstick. Ali's plate had a few slices of turkey breast on it, with only a small portion of vegetables on the side. I wasn't trying to be rude or stare, but Mrs. Blake ate nothing outside of her turkey and a spoonful of the squash and beets.

While Dr. Blake was quiet during the meal, Mrs. Blake was "in her element," as Dad likes to say, describing the ingredients that went into each dish, where she had bought the flowers, and the secret to her polishing. "And the *vase*," she went on, "I'm proud to say, is a Swarovski I scoured the city for relentlessly. I swear it was the last one of its kind in Toronto. And I found it!" Nodding now and again, I asked Mrs. Blake a few questions. Ali would look over at me once in a while and flash me a smile, but I could tell her mind was elsewhere.

For dessert, Mrs. Blake came out with hot apple pie and vanilla ice cream, though Dr. Blake and I were the only takers. Mrs. Blake had a cup of coffee and Ali had some herbal tea. With my last bite, I told the Blakes how incredible the meal had been. Ali scoffed. Mrs. Blake looked Ali's way, grimacing, then thanked me. "Good manners are always welcome in this home, Justin." Ali flicked the ends of her auburn hair. "I must say, it's been nice having one of Alison's friends over because she so rarely brings them by."

When Ali and her mom began clearing the dishes, I asked if I could help. "Nonsense," Mrs. Blake said. "You stay at the table and chat with Alison's father."

Dr. Blake had a glass of water in his right hand, which lay perfectly still on a coaster. "So…what are your plans for tomorrow, Justin?"

"Nothing special." *Now that he mentioned it, what were me and Dad going to do?* "How about you? Are you guys doing anything special?" I asked, even though I knew the answer.

"Oh, it's kind of a tradition around here that my brother, his wife and their three kids come over for lunch. It's great because the kids all get along and Fran—that's my brother's wife—and Deborah could go on talking for hours."

"That's great."

"Yes. Family is very important."

"I agree."

"Especially during the holidays."

"Absolutely."

"Now, Justin," Mrs. Blake said as she returned to the dining room, the dishes all cleared. "Can we offer you a lift home?"

"Thank you, but it's okay. I'm going to take the subway home. My place isn't too far away."

"And I'm going to walk Justin to Eglinton," Ali said as the four of us gathered at the front door.

"Very nice to meet you, Justin," Dr. Blake said, shaking my hand.

"Are you sure you'll be warm enough?" Mrs. Blake asked uncertainly, looking at Ali's jean jacket.

"Would you stop it? It's not even cold out tonight. I'll be fine."

I thanked the Blakes for everything, then Ali and I left and made our way down a street blanketed in fresh snow.

"You're probably wondering about the hair, huh?" Ali asked when we reached the first corner and turned right.

"The thought may have crossed my mind."

She looked at me and smirked. "I had a *maaasssive* blowout with my parents yesterday. My mom's making me go to Florida with her on Tuesday. I've been trying to get out of it for a couple of weeks but she's put her foot down. Ugh. I hate it down there. Anyway, I only dyed it to irritate her. I wanted to stay here and celebrate New Year's with you," she went on, taking my hand in hers, "and now my mom's totally ruined it all."

"That stinks."

"I know. I'm dying a thousand deaths."

We turned left on Yonge Street and I asked Ali what she was going to do with her hair.

"Why? You don't want to be with me if I have 'crazy woman' red hair?" We laughed. "Honestly, I don't even know what my original hair colour is anymore. But, yeah, you'll probably recognize me when I get back."

"It's going to suck not having you around for New Year's."

"Tell me about it. Now I have to hang out with a bunch of geri-atrics. Ugh. Anyway, it meant a lot that you came over for dinner tonight."

"It was good to finally meet your dad."

"You are *sooo* not a good liar."

"I mean it. He was really, you know—"

"Boring?"

"No! He's got a certain—"

"Annoying habit?"

"No!" I said. We were laughing again. "It was an amazing meal. Thanks for having me over."

We walked a few more steps and then Ali said, "Well, this is where I get off."

"Right."

We turned and faced each other. Ali grabbed my right hand and pulled me to a staircase between two huge signs, then up a few steps off the street. No one else was around.

"I'm going to miss you next week. You know that, right?"

I nodded.

She brought herself closer and added, in a whisper, "I'll call you lots, okay?"

"Sure."

"And Merry Christmas." Before I had a chance to say it back, Ali's lips were on mine.

13

Although January meant the beginning of the winter term, it also meant Ali was home and the hockey season would be starting again. We won the first three games of the new year by a combined total of twenty-seven to four, including one shutout. Keith and I were also playing for our school's Under-16 hockey team. As awesome as it was to have even more hockey in my life, it did mean an extra game and practice a week. Put another way, I would be playing hockey seven times a week until late March. This made winter the toughest time of year because I was just as exhausted when waking up every morning as I was going to bed.

Dad wasn't helping things either because my allowance had all but vanished. Forget about Slushies and movies on Saturday nights. I had to beg just to get hockey sticks replaced and TTC fare. If not for Dale's gift, I would've been, as Dad says, "up a creek without a paddle."

Ali and I had plans to meet at three-thirty on the first Monday of the winter term, but she wasn't outside the front entrance like she usually was. A freezing cold, miserable January day, I gave up waiting after half an hour, my cheeks raw and red. While a little miffed, I knew something most have come up because this wasn't like her to bail on me.

Unless she just happened to meet a guy our age in Florida and he just happened to live in Toronto and he just happened to be with her right now, of course...

I spent the subway ride nearing the end of the book Dale had given me, and made myself a sandwich when I got back to the apartment. I'd just taken my first bite when there was a knock at the door. With a mouthful of turkey, I went to see who it was (Jung-ho wasn't supposed to here for another half hour) and froze as soon as I opened the door. Ali stood there, a look of sadness/disappointment on her wickedly tanned face.

"Can I come in?"

"Of course."

Ali asked if she could sit on the bed. I nodded and sat down beside her, both of us staring at the floor.

"I just want to know why you haven't told me where you live. You know, why you've never invited me over. You said your Dad works from home and is always here but ..." Ali trailed off as she crossed her legs.

"He does work from home. That wasn't BS. I swear." Ali waited for me to go on. "Look at this," I said, standing up. "I live in a room with my father and a...a...a plant dividing our 'bedrooms'. You think I'm proud of this?"

"It's where you live, Justin. It is what it is. Who cares?"

"That's easy for you to say."

"What's that supposed to mean?"

"It means you live in a mansion." I said, staring over at an empty bottle on Dad's desk and hating myself for saying that.

"Justin, I understand you may not be proud of this, but do you think I care? Have you not met me?" She got up and came towards me.

I told her it was impossible not to think that way when almost all of my friends had big homes and nice cars. Ali was less than impressed.

"Yeah, well, you know what? I hate my parents most of the time and I still invited you over for dinner on Christmas Eve, didn't I? I

146

mean, what's worse, that you live in a small apartment or that my parents are totally fake? You know what?" Ali pressed on, "my Mom didn't even cook the turkey we had for dinner when you came over. She made none of it. Not even the stupid apple pie. She had the entire thing catered because she wanted to fit in just a few more hours that she could bill her corporate clients! I'm going out with you because you're real; because you actually listen to me; because you actually give a shit about me and let me pick the food off your face." Ali smiled a sad smile and then fell onto the bed. "I had to follow you home today like some kind of stalker just to find out where you lived."

"I'm sorry. I should have told you."

Ali looked down and asking me about Mom. "You never talk about her. All this time we've been going out and not once have you brought her up."

"Okay, here's the deal," I said, joining her on the bed again. I slipped my hand into hers. In the month Mom had been a free woman and not phoned, I'd fought every day to forget about her. "The reason you haven't met my mom is because I don't know where she is."

"What do you mean?"

"I mean, ever since she was arrested and let out of the *detention centre*, she hasn't contacted me. I have no idea where she is, or even if she's still in Toronto."

"What was she arrested for?" Ali asked in a quiet voice.

"Cheque kiting and drunk driving."

"Shit."

"Yeah."

"How many people have you told?"

"Nobody."

"No one?"

"Not even Keith. Listen," I said, "do you mind if I grab my sandwich from the kitchen? I'm kind of starving."

"No. Go ahead."

When I was on the bed again beside her, Ali lifted a chip from my plate and looked at it like she'd never seen one before. "You know it's funny, but whenever I'm with you I'm hungry. Like, *hungry* hungry. Do you remember the first time we talked, on that bench in the park?"

"Yeah."

"And you fed me salt and vinegar chips?"

I laughed.

"Or how about our first date, when we went to Mickey D's? You made me get a cheeseburger."

"Made like a Mac."

"Exactly! But the thing is, I hadn't had fast food in something like two years before that afternoon. This is going to sound *terribly* romantic, but that was the day I knew I liked you." I waited for her to say something like *You were so good-looking* or *You made me laugh like Chevy Chase in all his movies*. Instead, she followed that up with, "You made me feel comfortable eating with you."

"Ah...okay," I said, not sure this was a real compliment.

"Usually—fine, all of the time—I hate eating in front of anyone."

"How come?"

Ali tucked some of her (once again) blonde hair behind an ear. "Okay. Here it goes. Basically," she said and took a deep breath, "I was anorexic and bulimic when I was twelve." All those years highlighting words in a dictionary and Ali had just pulled out two whose definitions were lost on me. "It started right around my twelfth birthday. I'm pretty sure my mom had been going through the same thing for at least a couple of years. This was when she was at the peak of her thinness and everyone always commented on how "gorgeous" and "amazing" she looked. Even my friends were jealous of how skinny she was. At school the boys would make fun of the fat girls and in grade six I started becoming paranoid about how I looked. This was around February, I think."

"What happened?" I said, desperate to figure out what on earth anorexic and bulimic meant.

"I stopped eating. Actually, that's not true. The bulimia came first, but it became too hard to keep up with. It got to the point where just thinking about putting a finger into my throat would make my stomach turn. Besides, I was tired of chewing gum all the time to make my breath smell better. Even today, the smell of Trident makes me think back to that time because I'd be chewing on it day and night.

"Anyway, not eating just seemed to be easier than purging myself after every meal. And it worked. I was losing weight, constantly, to the point it became obsessive. I'd weigh myself every morning when I woke up, then again when I got home and once more before bed. I'd throw out my bagged lunch and instead walk around the school when it was cold out or the track when the weather was warmer. More exercise and less eating meant burning more calories, and burning more calories was the key to being as thin and pretty as my mom.

"By spring I dipped below a hundred pounds. That wasn't enough, though. Nobody at school was complimenting me on how skinny I was. Or at least as much as people did with my mom." Ali paused and ate a chip. "This went on till May, I guess. That's when things got bad. Like *bad* bad. I was doing a show and tell presentation in class and just blacked out, crumpled right to the floor. I still have no memory of that day. All I remember was my mom showing up at school and driving me home, with friends filling in the gaps later on.

"My parents checked me into a hospital the next day. I'll never forget the doctor when he weighed me and the look on his face. I was seventy-three pounds, Justin. *Seventy-three!* You know how much a girl my height is supposed to weigh?"

I shook my head.

"A hundred and ten pounds."

"Holy..."

"Holy shitballs is right. And I had to stay in that stupid hospital for two months before they'd let me go, only to have Dr. and Mrs. Blake ship me to a loony camp for screwed-up girls who were all recovering from anorexia." Ali looked at me and added, "That's where I met the girls, Rachel, Debs and Vickers, and now it's our dirty little secret."

"You know, to this day, I'm not sure who I hate more, my mother for planting the seed in my head or my dad for turning a blind eye to the whole thing. I mean, here's a doctor who saves lives every day, doing nothing as his wife and daughter slowly starve themselves to death." Ali sighed and had another chip. "Like I said, it's not terribly romantic, but I still struggle with the whole eating thing, especially when out with strangers. When I'm with you, though, I want to be, I don't know—what's the word—*healthy*? Something like that. So, thank you," she went on, leaning my way and giving me a kiss, "for making this crazy girl want to put food into her bloated body."

"Ali, you're not—"

"*Kid*ding! Anyway," she went on, "although I've gotten *waaaay* better about eating since meeting you, I still weigh myself every morning. Bad habit, I guess, but there it is."

A knock interrupted our conversation. When I didn't move, Ali smiled. "It's okay. Answer it. I'll still be here when you get back."

Jung-ho was waiting in the hallway with her swimming gear on.

"You're early," I said.

"But you're home."

Ali got up and joined me at the door. I made the introductions.

"You're very pretty," Jung-ho told Ali.

"You're very pretty, too."

"I'm teaching Jung-ho here how to swim," I explained.

"Do you want to come swimming with us?" Jung-ho asked. Ali and I laughed.

"I didn't bring my bathing suit," Ali said. "But I'd love to watch if that's okay with you guys." Jung-ho shook her head up and down like she'd just been asked if she wanted a tour of Willy Wonka's chocolate factory.

"Nah, we can do this another time."

"What other time?" Ali asked.

"But I want to show her my swimming! And you photocopied your promise, Justin!"

Two against one. No fair.

When the doors opened on the top floor and we stepped out, Ali was blown away. "Ah! The view up here is *schmazing*!" She walked around the pool, which offered a pretty good view of the city, before taking a seat on one of the bucket chairs lining the windows. She watched Jung-ho thrash around the shallow end as two people did laps on the left-hand side. There were none of those dividing lane thingies they have in Olympic pools, so I was careful to guide Jung-ho around and steer her clear of the traffic as water kept flowing in and out of her mouth.

It was a short lesson; I didn't even get my hair wet. As we left the pool area, Ali came up to me and whispered, "That was very cute," then gave me a peck on the cheek. When we got back to Dad's place, Ali was still giggling behind me about my new role as a "teacher."

Smoke…golden liquid…classical music…oh, man…

"And who might this be?" Dad asked, rising from the couch and finishing his drink. He stubbed out his cigarette and walked towards us.

"Hi, Mr. Maloney. I'm Ali."

"*Ali, Ali, Ali,*" Dad repeated like a nutbar. "Such a pretty name for an even more attractive young lady. It is an honour and a privilege to finally meet you."

"You, too."

"My son has not deigned to open up about you with very much forthrightness. I'm afraid he's a tad negligent in matters of the heart with his father," he went on, looking at me.

I flashed him my *you're-a-weirdo-and-don't-you-dare-embarrass-me* look

"Are you familiar with the poet William Butler Yeats, Ali?"

"No."

"He was an Irish poet, one of the founders of the Irish Literary Revival, in fact."

"Was he?" Ali stole a quick glance at me and smiled.

"Indeed, he was. And he once wrote a poem called 'Dream of a Blessed Spirit'."

"Dad," I cut him off, "will you stop it? You're going to make her think you're off your rocker."

"Maybe I think *you're* off your rocker," Ali fired back, looking right at me.

Dad ignored me and continued down Poetry Road: "In it he wrote, 'With white feet of angels seven/Her white feet go glimmering;/ And above the deep of heaven,/Flame on flame, and wing on wing'. I believe Mr. Yeats may well have had someone like you in mind when he penned those words, Ali."

I craned my head back and groaned. Ali put her arms over her heart, one hand on top of the other. "That's beautiful, Mr. Maloney. Thank you so much."

"Now, may I have the pleasure of inviting you to sit down in our humble abode?"

Ali looked at me, then at Dad, and said, "I'd love to, Mr. Maloney, but I should be getting home. My mom is probably wondering where I am."

"Ah, yes. I see."

"But it's been really great meeting you. Justin's said so many amazing things about you."

"Dear, the pleasure is convincingly unrequited in this matter, but thank you."

"Okay, then," Ali said, lowering her arms to her side and bouncing on the balls of her feet. "I should get going."

"Oh, Ali?" Dad said, locking his hands together in front of him. "May I have the pleasure of taking you and my esteemed son out to lunch next weekend?"

"Sure," Ali answered uncertainly, as if waiting for me to say something. "That would be…" Ali looked briefly at me and just a corner of her mouth turned up. "That would be really nice, Mr. Maloney."

"Excellent. I'll have Mercury here relay the details *tout de suite*."

"Okay. Now go back to your book," I said flustered, flurried and frustrated. "I'm taking Ali out."

On the way down, I thanked Ali for putting up with Dad.

"I imagine he'd say the same about you," she said.

The snow was really coming down when we got outside. The streets were wet and you could see the flakes hanging in the air with the lights of each car that drove by. Small white mountains lined both sides of the road. "You don't want me to walk you to the subway?" I asked as she stopped at the corner.

"No, I'll catch a cab."

"Right."

"Listen, you. Nobody's perfect. We're all screwed up, me especially. But there's nothing to feel weird about with your place or your mom or whatever. I don't care how big or small your apartment is. And if your mom is demented enough to disappear like she has, there's nothing you can do about it." Her hand glided into mine, fingers locking themselves around each other. "Okay?"

"Okay."

When a taxi pulled up, she went to open the door. I didn't let go of her, though, and Ali was given a tug towards me.

"What?"

I squeezed her hand three times. "Your tan looks awesome by the way."

153

She smiled. "Oh, you."

For a change, Dad was listening to something on his record player not entirely depressing when I was upstairs once again. I'd heard the song a few times over the years, one of those classics you hear when watching movies from World War II. Dad was shuffling around the room like a fruitcake.

"Did I ever tell you I learned to tap dance when I was your age?" he asked me. There was no glass or cigarette in his hand. "Every child needed a skill when I was young, and many parents sent their children to tap dancing lessons. Of course, Irving Berlin is not the type of music to tap dance to, but every time I hear a song from that era it reminds me of my..." and here Dad clicked his dress shoes together "...lessons all those years ago."

The song ended and another one came on that was just as old and flowery. "She's lovely, Justin," Dad went on, falling onto the couch and sighing. He reached for his glass and lit a smoke. "More than lovely. She's celestial. And those eyes! My goodness. They contain enough warmth to hush a crying baby."

"Dad, what's going on?"

"Whatever do you mean, Justin? I'm telling you I find your girlfriend delightful. What more is there to say?" He took a big sip and then looked at me like I was the one dancing around the apartment. "Most teenage sons would be happy that their father approves of their *catch*."

"Their *catch*?"

"I'm trying to use the lingo of your generation, Justin. Don't fault an old man for trying. In short," he continued, clearing his throat, "I think she's perfect. And perfect for you."

"Thanks." I looked into the kitchen out of the corner of an eye and saw an empty bottle. There was another one, half empty, on his desk. I asked him how the day went, still unsure what was going on.

"My day was empyreal. How was yours?"

"Fine."

"How was work?" Something was definitely off; Dad was in la-la land.

"Shouldn't we get going to practice?" he said at once. I looked at my watch and realized he was probably right.

My hockey bag, which I'd left open to air out, had been on the balcony all day and was now full of snow.

Crap.

The snowstorm had now turned into a full-on blizzard. You could see maybe ten feet ahead and cars were sliding all over the road. Dad was driving pretty carefree, coming to rolling stops and not bothering to indicate when he turned. We were a couple of blocks from the arena when he tried to gun a red light. We must have hit some black ice because the car started spinning in the middle of the intersection. The Volare slammed into a traffic pole on Dad's side of the car, smashing the side mirror and doing some serious damage to his door.

We were quiet a second. I looked sideways and made sure Dad wasn't hurt. His gaze was motionless. Fortunately, there weren't any other cars or pedestrians around.

"Are you okay?" I asked, undoing my seatbelt.

No reply.

"Dad? *Dad?*"

"Stop it, Justin," he said, annoyed. He opened and closed his eyes. "I'm fine," he went on as I fell back into my seat. "You should get going. The arena's just up ahead. I'll handle this debacle and hopefully see you at practice. If for some reason I don't make it, find a lift home with Keith."

Practice was grueling. Apparently Mr. Wainwright had the same philosophy as Dad: train harder when your team's doing well and winning games than when you're sucking the joint out. He was particularly upset with the amount of heart we were playing with lately.

"I have more passion in my pinkie than all of you put together," he said, standing at the hash marks in his funny-looking goalie skates and toque with a ridiculously massive pompom. "I'm sick and tired of you sending the puck to the net game after game like you don't give a rat's ass if it goes in or not. This half-ass shooting ends tonight. Timmy," he went on, turning to our goalie. "Give me your blocker, glove and stick." Timmy looked like a kid who's been told Santa doesn't exist and couldn't really process what was happening. "Come on, Timmy. Glove, blocker and stick. Hand them over."

Reluctantly, I'm sure, Timmy gave our coach what he asked for and then, like the rest of us, probably wondered what he'd do next. Mr. Wainwright skated to the net and turned to face us. "Here's what we're going to do. You're all going to get one chance to take your best shot at me from the blue line." Guys giggled and punched each other on the arm. "I'm not fucking around here. If anyone doesn't put a hundred percent behind their slapshot they're going to be watching the next game from the stands." No one was laughing anymore. "Now let's go. Dean," he said, singling out the guy on our team with the hardest shot, "start us out."

I made a mental note to look up the definition of "insanity" later on. I was pretty sure I'd see a picture of a balding five-foot-nothing middle-aged man standing in a goal crease with no pads and no equipment, save a trapper and blocker. Guys made some space for Dean to take his shot. Talk about being stuck between a skunk and a sewer. If Dean truly let one rip, he could potentially kill our head coach, but if he didn't put everything he had into it, he'd be riding the pine next game.

Dean fiddled with the puck on his stick, almost as if wondering which was the less crappier of the two options. Then he got set, took a single stride, and blasted the puck towards the top corner of the net.

Like taking candy from a baby, Mr. Wainwright snatched the puck out of the air, threw it aside with a look of disgust, and yelled, "Next!"

I was star-struck. There'd been legendary stories of Mr. Wainwright playing goal in junior with some pretty famous players. Maybe I'd just thought they were exaggerations because it never dawned on me that our coach could have been that good when he was younger. In all, Mr. Wainwright faced seventeen slapshots from the point. He made seventeen saves.

After putting on an impressive goaltending clinic nobody was sure to forget, there was no scrimmage, no shootouts or penalty shot contests to close out the night. We skated those heinous drills where you go from the goal line to the blue line; the goal line to the centre line and back; the goal line to the far blue line and around again; then one goal line to the other. When that was done, we did a couple of skills drills with puck handling and then the chase drill where you have to catch the skater ahead of you as you do laps around the ice surface. By the end, everyone was ready to puke, including me.

"We're in first place, gentlemen, but it's ours to lose," Mr. Wainwright said in the dressing room later. Guys were bent over and dry heaving. "If we don't keep up the hard work, we'll fall behind and have no one but ourselves to blame. Good job out there tonight. I'll see you all on Thursday."

With our two assistant coaches in tow, Mr. Wainwright left the dressing room.

"You mind if I grab a lift with you?" I asked Keith when the coaches were gone. I'd noticed Dad wasn't in the stands by the end of practice, so figured he was still dealing with the car.

"Sure."

"You okay?"

"I might just barf up my guts," Keith said, bent over and holding his stomach with two hands.

For once, I was out of the dressing room before my best friend. "Is Keith on his way out?" Lorraine asked as I walked up to her. She was waiting in the heated section of the arena, the snack bar behind her closed.

"Yeah. He had a tough practice."

"I didn't see your father. Is he outside in the car?"

"Actually, he dropped me off but had to take care of a few things. Would you mind giving me a lift?"

"Of course not." There was a pause. Then, "Everything okay?" It was an innocent enough question, but I knew Lorraine. And she knew me. Her BS radar was as good as any parent, so when she said something like "Everything okay?" I knew she was onto me.

"Yeah. He had to go to my uncle's house and wasn't sure if he could make it back in time."

"How are you enjoying being with your father again? It's been a while since you two last lived together, hasn't it?"

"It's fine."

Lorraine didn't respond, choosing instead to move her head up and down a fraction. Her silence told me she *definitely* knew something was up.

Keith was slumped over in the car on the way home. I was happy to watch the city lights go by under a curtain of tiny white dots. At Dad's apartment, Lorraine got out with me. As I lifted my bag and sticks out of the trunk, she said, "We're always around."

"Thanks."

"Day or night."

"I know."

"Good," she said, not standing around to make it feel all fake, but hopping right back into her car and driving away. I walked into the apartment building and, while waiting for the elevator, Jung-ho came strolling through the entrance.

"What are you doing out this late?" I asked.

She looked exhausted and said she was coming home from art class.

"Huh?"

"I take private lessons once a week. It's fun." She said this last word with as much enthusiasm as Keith would have when describing tonight's practice.

"Right."

"How was your game?"

The doors to the elevator opened.

"It wasn't a game. It was a practice."

"Did you make a lot of goals?"

"Yeah."

"I like Ali."

"Thanks." I knew my bad mood was coming through so I tried to say something nice. "She liked you as well. Said you were a good swimmer."

Jung-ho looked up. "Really? She really said that?"

I nodded as the doors to our floor opened and we got out.

"Justin? Do you think I'll ever be able to swim? On my own, I mean?"

"No doubt."

"Promise?"

"Promise." I extended an arm and we slid our hands together, the photocopy complete.

I expected to see Dad reading on the couch when I got home, but instead found him pacing around, talking to himself and slamming a fist into his palm.

"Hey," I said, passing him on the way to the balcony. I unzipped my bag outside and then came in again, sliding the door closed. "Everything all right?" An empty bottle stood beside the stove.

"Your Uncle Adam is a lecherous…conniving…*bastard!*"

"How's the car?" I asked.

"In the shop and in need of twelve hundred dollars in repairs to fix the front axle."

"How long do they say it's going to take?"

"They will only fix it once they receive at least fifty percent up front. And, unlike certain people I know, I'm not in the business of writing cheques I'm not good for."

"Dad?"

"What Justin?"

The anger is his voice was unmistakable. He drained his glass and went for a refill.

"Nothing. I'm going to wash up now."

When I was done my shower, I sat on the bed and reached for my dictionary. The first word was easy enough to find and led me to yet another term.

an·o·rex·i·a

noun

1. loss of appetite and inability to eat

anorex·ia ner·vo·sa

noun **Psychiatry**

an eating disorder primarily affecting adolescent girls and young women, characterized by pathological fear of becoming fat, distorted body image, excessive dieting, and emaciation.

The second word was harder to find because I had no idea how to spell it. I suppose I could've asked Dad, but he was simmering on the sofa, chain smoking and talking to himself now and again. Only after looking for words starting with *ba* and then *be* did I stumble on what I'd been trying to find.

bu·lim·i·a

noun

2. Also called binge-purge syndrome, bulim·ia ner·vo·sa
Psychiatry a habitual disturbance in eating behaviour mostly affect-ing young women of normal weight, characterized by frequent episodes of grossly excessive food intake followed by self-induced vomiting to avert weight gain. Compare anorexia nervosa.

14

Dad chose an Italian place that was crazy expensive for our lunch with Ali. He was in a good mood as he got dressed, whistling to one of those songs that made him tap dance. Although the Volare had been fixed and was now sitting in the apartment complex's parking lot, Dad said we were taking a cab to the restaurant.

"How come?" I asked.

"Today, we arrive in style."

While in the taxi on the way up to College Street, I told him Dale had phoned last night. Dad asked a couple of simple questions—how he was doing, what was new—but didn't seem very interested in his nephew's news. He wore a confident grin and was taking in everything outside the window as if he'd just arrived in Toronto from the sticks.

When we got to the restaurant, a young babe in her twenties said they were still preparing our table. I gave Dad the once-over and had to admit he looked pretty sharp. He had on a blue suit, a white dress shirt and a paisley tie. Even his shoes were shined. I had on a pair of khakis and a sky-blue Polo shirt with a twisty brown belt Mom got me at Roots last year.

After we were led to our seats, a waiter asked if we'd like something to drink. Dad scanned the smaller of two menus and said, "Indeed. I'll have a bottle of…the Pertimali Brunello di Montalcino, 1986. And a ginger ale for my son." When the guy returned, he poured Dad a little of the red wine into his glass. Dad swirled it around, held it up to his nose, and then took a sip. "Excellent," he said. The waiter filled the rest of his glass and then left our table.

Dad and I talked about the Leafs, who were not only last in the Norris Division but dead freaking last in the entire NHL. Ed Olczyk and Gary Leeman were having okay seasons, we agreed, but the rest of the team was stinking the joint out. When Ali arrived, Dad had already gone through half the wine. A different waiter led her to our table. As she approached, Dad got up and I did the same. Ali had on a red coat, a black dress, black tights and black flats. She'd curled the bottom of her hair into big, loopy rings. For the first time since we'd met she was wearing makeup as well, which made her look *at least* seventeen.

Ali flashed me a smile and said "Hiya" quietly. "How are you, Mr. Maloney?" she then asked, the waiter standing over her and pouring a glass of water with a slice of lemon in it.

"Ali, I wish I could say there has been a happier day in my storied life, but in truth there has not. You look radiant."

"Thank you."

"Yeah, you look amazing," I added. "Like, seriously amazing."

"Oh, you."

"Ali, I have brought you here today for two reasons. Aside from giving us the Colosseum, no one can cook like the Italians. This restaurant is among the best I have dined at in this fine city of ours."

"I love Italian food!" Ali took a sip of water and brushed some of those wicked-hot locks off her shoulders.

"Second, it holds a very fond place in my heart, as this is where I proposed to Justin's mother."

"Really?" She lit up. "That's so romantic!"

"Really?" I echoed. No one had told me this.

"Indeed. It was at this very establishment that I got down on a knee and proposed. In those days, you could hire a violin player to serenade you at the table and that's precisely what I did. As he played Tchaikovsky's "Serenade Melancolique," I asked Justin's mother to be my wife."

"That's so beautiful, Mr. Maloney."

I was still trying to figure out how neither one of my parents thought to tell me this before.

"Yes, well, love is a many-splendored flower. Do you know what the Romans said of love, Ali?"

"No."

"Dad, can we go one meal without a history—"

"Justin, let your father continue," Ali cut me off, giving me an evil glare.

"You can't blame my son, Ali. He has to put up with my ramblings on a daily basis."

"Well, *I'm* interested."

I let out a *pff* through closed lips and flipped my bangs gently to the side.

They said '*amor est magis cognitivus quam cognito*'." Dad played this out dramatically.

"What does that mean?" Ali was sitting up perfectly straight in her chair.

"*We know things better through love than through knowledge.*"

Ali tilted her head slightly, like Mom does sometimes. "That's perfect."

"Indeed." Dad looked down and finished his glass of wine. Our waiter came over immediately to refill it. "They were the same words I uttered to Justin's mother that night." Ali had to catch herself. Her mouth was open, as if to say something, but she stopped short. "In any event, we should order some antipasto before the house staff revolt."

Dad put on his reading glasses and began studying the menu.

"Mr. Maloney?" Ali said timidly.

"Yes, my dear?"

"Would you mind ordering for me?" Ali had a shy look on her face. "I really don't know anything about fancy restaurants or fancy food."

I wanted to throw my head back in frustration. Dad looked like he was going to start crying.

"It would be an honour to order for you."

"And you, too, right?" Ali went on, giving my leg a tap below the table.

"Yeah. I mean, right. It would be splendido...or whatever the Italians say."

The two of them ignored my sarcasm. Although I was pissed off Dad was playing the role of hero at the meal, I probably would've gotten spaghetti if I'd had to order on my own. Instead, Dad ordered crostini and bruschetta to start, with risotto for our *primo*. Then he ordered a rabbit dish as his *secondo*, a chicken dish for Ali and a meat pasta dish for me. When the waiter left our table, I told Dad that his Italian accent wasn't nearly as crappy as his French one.

"What do you mean? His Italian sounded perfect!" Ali seemed more insulted than Dad.

"Well, not perfect, but three months in San Gimignano certainly helps the cause."

"Where's that?" Ali asked. "Hook, line and sinker," as Dad says. My hair could've caught on fire at that very moment and Ali wouldn't have noticed.

"It's in Tuscany, a couple of hours outside Florence, in a land so resplendent that it inspired the great painters of the Renaissance to create some of the world's most beautiful art."

"Wait," I said. "You were where and for how long?"

Dad explained how he'd taken a ship over to Europe from Montreal after graduating from university. He went with his best friend, Bill Lafayette, who now lived in Milton and someone I hadn't seen in forever. The two of them spent a year wandering around Europe. As I listened to Dad recount part of his youth, I found it kind of hard to believe how different Ali was with Dad compared to her own family—and the effect she had on him. He was opening up to her in ways even I wasn't used to. Elbows on the table, Ali's chin rested on top of her hands, which formed a bridge.

"Anyway, Bill and I ended up staying in San Gimignano for three months, picking grapes at a winery and doing odd jobs. That's also where we started learning the language because Italians, dear, speak English about as well as people like Napoleon and Hitler do at invading Russia in winter." Dad laughed, a real laugh, not one of those "chuckles" he usually gave me. Ali laughed her ass off, too. I was just trying to understand the joke.

He was on his second bottle of wine by then and looking—there was no other way to put this—blissful. For the nearly two-hour meal, Dad had Ali fascinated at one turn, in stitches the next. She was spellbound by his life and his knowledge of the world, asking him question upon question. When his rabbit dish arrived and he offered us some, Ali touched her chest with one hand and said, "I'm not a vegetarian or anything, but I have a tough time eating anything as cute and cuddly as rabbits. I'm sorry. Thank you for offering, though, Mr. Maloney." All of a sudden a successful car salesman, Dad went off on how great rabbit was in Italian dishes. Ali looked squeamish at first but eventually gave in, that whole "they're so cute and cuddly" comment now a distant memory.

In place of dessert, Dad ordered something called grappa. "What's that?" I asked as Ali and I ate our tartufo, which, even though it had a gay name, was pretty good.

"It's a *digestivo*."

"Dad, you are truly the funniest person sitting on your side of the table right now." For once, Dad laughed at my sarcasm.

"That was very clever."

"What *is* it, though!"

He explained it was an after-dinner drink that helped the digestion process, sliding the glass over towards us to smell. "Gross!" I said, my nose hairs tingling. I couldn't even find the words to describe it.

While Ali and I finished off our Italian-style ice cream, Dad said he wanted to tell one last story about me.

"Seriously? You're going to go down this road?"

"Why not?"

"No, I want to hear it," Ali protested.

"When Justin was seven, he played his first AAA game. He was with kids a year and two above him. The coach had approached me earlier and asked Justin to try out for the team. I was reluctant at first because I worried about any number of things: the challenge of playing at such an advanced level, the age gap, the physical size difference. But the coach convinced me to give Justin a shot. I acquiesced and in his first game, he…" Here, Dad had to stop himself he was laughing so hard. He finished off his drink and tapped the rim twice. "Justin played his first game on October 4, 1981 and scored…" Ali was about to fall over. I was just trying to remember what had happened that day. "… eight goals."

"What?" Ali said, her jaw dropping to the table.

Dad was cracking up and slapping a knee, which was crossed over the other leg. "Unbelievable, isn't it?"

"Totally!"

"Mr. Davies, the coach, came up to me after the game and said he'd never seen a player of Justin's calibre before. He commented on how Justin had the gift. And he was right. Justin *does* have the gift. However, I didn't want my son playing above his age group until he reached Junior A, so from the following season I had him stay back with kids his own age. It was an unacceptable risk to move him up with boys who were older than Justin when bodychecking was involved."

With the meal over, Ali excused herself and said she needed to use the restroom. Dad stayed behind to pay the bill and I told him I'd wait on the sidewalk. On my way out, the waiter from our meal stopped me.

"Oh, my dad's paying the bill right now," I explained.

"It's not that," he said. "Is she your girlfriend?"

It took me a second to realize he was talking about Ali. "Umm… yeah."

"She's stunning."

"Thanks," I said and hurried towards the door, embarrassed by the compliment but proud as hell at the same time.

Only while waiting for Ali outside, Dad inhaling a cigarette like it was the last one on Earth, did I realize he hadn't smoked through lunch. This made me wonder what was more mind-boggling, that Dad had gone an entire meal without smoking, or that Ali had finished a three-course meal (not to mention a bit of Dad's rabbit dish) without blinking.

When Ali joined us on the street, Dad said we'd share a taxi and drop her off at home.

"Mr. Maloney, you don't have to—"

"Nonsense."

"Dad, let's just—"

"And you, my friend, should be supporting this endeavour. Someone as ethereal as this needs to be kept watch over."

Dad had called me many things over the years, but never "my friend."

We hailed a cab and when we got to Ali's house, I got out and tried to find a blind spot where Dad wouldn't be watching us. "I love your dad. He's *schmazing!*" she said, laughing. "Really. Thank you so, so, so much for lunch today. It was perfect."

On the ride back, Dad recounted his favourite moments from lunch, telling me how much he loved Ali's company. He slapped my knee at one point and said, "I always knew you'd find someone like her. *Vir fortis natus.*"

"Dad, you know that means nothing to me." He didn't say anything in response, a big, goofy smile glued to his face as he kept his gaze fixed on the passing scenery outside. I waited a few seconds and then added, "Thanks for today. It was really awesome of you."

"She's an angel, Justin. Someone fashioned in the heavens. Women will continue to enter your life for as long as you live, but few will turn heads like Ali does. Fewer still will have her *spiritus.* Take it from someone who has been down this path many times, seen a great deal, and failed more often than not. Hold on to what is precious in your life with the strength needed to resist a gale-force wind. And never, ever let go."

15

I was listening to a mixed tape on my Walkman that Ali had made me when Dad tried to get my attention from the couch. She'd put together a bunch of them for me, but this one, which started with U2's "Bad" and ended with "With or Without You," was my favourite. I took off my earphones and asked him what was up.

"What is it you propose we do about dinner?"

"Whatever."

"Then perhaps you could run downstairs and pick us up something before the supermarket closes at six."

"Mr. Grocer closes at seven."

"Regardless, you have practice in two hours."

This had become more of a regular thing recently. When Dad started asking me to buy our food, he'd give me a bit of money and say to pick up as much as I could with it. Most times I'd grab something from the frozen food section and he'd heat it up. By the middle of January, however, I was doing both the grocery shopping and the cooking. Dad didn't offer me as much as a loonie anymore, so it was Dale's Christmas fund to the rescue again. Something had happened to Dad, professionally, but he wouldn't talk about it. Not only was he sleeping in later these days, but he wasn't working with the same thick pile of papers I'd seen him looking over when he landed the big corporate client in the fall.

Downstairs, I cruised the aisles of the supermarket attached to the apartment building while keeping an eye out for specials. It was all about saving money, which meant No Name products and anything on sale. I had zero skills in the kitchen, everything I did know having come from watching Lorraine make lunches and dinners over the years. Aside from her tilapia, Mom's staples were hot dogs, hamburgers, canned soup and sandwiches.

Guessing I'd be cooking tonight's meal, I kept it simple and picked up a box of pasta, some ground beef, garlic, an onion, and a jar of spaghetti sauce. I'd seen Lorraine make this a bunch of times and figured I could handle it on my own. It would also be a step up from last time, when I'd made Sloppy Joe Hamburger Helper with Wonder Bread.

The total came to $6.78, which was pretty good because I could probably stretch this into two meals for each of us. I did okay cutting up the garlic but made a mess of the onion and nearly sliced a finger open on the glass cutting board. My plan was to fry them in olive oil, but we were all out and so I used water as a substitute. As the pot came to a boil on the second burner, smoke began rising from the frying pan.

"Everything under control in there, Hestia?" Dad asked from the couch. If he was worried, he certainly didn't sound it.

"Uh-huh." I was trying to push the smoke out the kitchen's half window with a dinky little dish rag the size of a face cloth.

"No need to alert the fire department of an impending disaster?"

"Nope!"

"As you were, then."

I threw the beef on top of the smoldering vegetables and the smoke disappeared. *Phew.* Cooking beef was easy enough; the noodles were a different story. Each time I'd followed the instructions on the box they'd come out crunchy and gross.

When I put Dad's dinner on the desk, he looked up at me, his glasses halfway down his nose, and said, "Bowls?"

"What? Is there a rule about how you have to serve this stuff?" Dad didn't look impressed. "Eat, would you! It's getting cold."

"Indeed, I will. Will you fetch us the salt and pepper?"

"Hey, Stevie Wonder. This not good enough for you?" I lifted the white and black shakers.

Dad grinned. "Very clever."

"Well, we're not getting any younger here, Shakespeare, and I have practice in an hour."

Dad shook his head. "Not as clever. Shakespeare died young, at 52, in fact."

"Right."

Swallowing his first mouthful of pasta, Dad looked at me and said, as if in shock, "On top of being palatable, I dare say this is excellent. And the spaghetti is done *al dente*. The Italians would be proud of your accomplishment, Justin."

On the way to practice, I was on my guard every second we were in the car. Those two full rotations a couple of weeks ago when we'd spun out of control had shaken me. My eyes darted back and forth as we drove, looking for jaywalkers, upcoming stoplights, unexpected road conditions—anything, basically, that might get us in another fender-bender.

He asked me a couple of questions about Ali on the way over and I answered them more honestly than I would've before our lunch together because I got that he wanted to know more about her. I also got that he was trying to be nice. And I got that he wanted to be a part of my life in some way outside of hockey. The fact was, talking to Dad about Ali sucked. As we neared the arena, he asked if Ali and I were "going steady."

"Dad, this isn't the 1950s."

"Then what do you kids call it nowadays?"

"First of all, we're not kids. And second, we call it going out."

"So you and Ali are merely *going out*?" he asked, the Volare's hood rising as it limped over a speed bump and into the parking lot.

"Yes. We're going out. Are you satisfied?"

Dad slid the car into PARK. "Justin, I am simply trying to be polite and ask after your girlfriend."

Hearing Dad say the word "girlfriend" gave me goose bumps. "Yeah, well, don't try so hard," I said, sliding off the vinyl seat and grabbing my bag from the trunk.

Mr. Wainwright pulled me aside when I got to the dressing and said he wanted to have a talk with me. This generally means one thing, like when Mom wanted to "have a talk" about her and Dad getting a divorce and Dad wanting to "have a talk" about me moving in with Mom last spring. Mr. Wainwright paced as I leaned up against the wall for support.

"Justin, I sense a problem brewing. Not today, not tomorrow, but it's festering. We've been doing great since the start of the year, but there's been a shift in our attitude. I can feel it. I've been coaching for years and I know what I know. We're easing up on the gas and we can't afford to do that at this time of year."

This made no sense. We were playing awesome, winning games and outscoring opponents by crazy amounts. It almost felt like he was trying to find a problem for the sake of finding a problem.

"I need you to go in there tonight and talk to the team, put some sense in their heads, tell them the score, so to speak. If we go into February in cruise control, we risk losing our place at the top of the standings." He paused for a moment. "Can you do that, Justin?"

"Ah, yeah, I guess."

"Good."

"I'll wait out here with Mr. Hervey and Mr. Bird. Give you some time to talk to them on your own terms." He said this last part with a wink and then gave me two pats on the shoulder. The thought of public speaking scared the bejesus out of me. The last time I'd tried something like this I'd sworn and got a few laughs. This time I wasn't so sure things would turn out so good. Sorry, so *well*.

Lead by example, Dad says, which is what I've always tried to do. This was different. Mr. Wainwright might as well have asked me to do this in Russian. I walked into the dressing room on eggshells. A chorus of "Hey, Baloney!" and "Yo, Baloney!" rang out. I was racking my brain for what to say, something that would be cool and inspirational. I started taking out equipment and laying each piece beside my bag.

"Hey, J.R. Who got your panties all in a bunch?" Keith asked me from a couple of guys away. "What's the deal?"

A Bon Jovi song was playing on the ghetto blaster. Everyone looked relaxed. Who was I to go and ruin this with some *speech* about keeping our play up, or whatever Mr. Wainwright wanted from me?

"Boys," I said, rising from the bench, "we've been doing really good—really well—lately, but we've got to step up the pressure and keep the pressure on. Pressure, pressure, pressure," I went on, clapping my hands together. The guys were looking at me as if I were on crack. "We're in first place and we need to stay there. No letting up on the gas. Let's go out there tonight and skate as hard...and as fast...as we would in the Provincials."

I sat down and got dressed. "Living on a Prayer" was playing. Nobody was saying a word. Ryan broke the silence. "What was that all about, Baloney? You practicing for a speech contest or—"

"Oh, you should talk about giving speeches, Delaquack," Michael Bolton cut him off. "Maybe you could give one on your newest hero, Brian Orser."

"Whatever." Equipment flew across the room and jokes followed. Guys were talking so loud they drowned out the music. On any other night, I would've said we were going into practice on the right note, full of energy. Now, though, I'd let the guys down. Mr. Wainwright had asked me to do one simple thing as captain and I couldn't even do that much.

"You weren't yourself in practice," Dad commented on the drive back to the apartment later that night.

"I was distracted."

"By whom or by what?"

"Nothing. Forget about it." Dad looked over. "There's nothing going on. It was a bad practice. End of story."

I showered and crawled into bed with my novel soon after returning to the apartment. Dad was sitting on the couch with his favourite "triumvirate," a full glass, a cigarette and a book. We were reading *Lord of the Flies* in English and Mr. Robertson had told us this was one of the "great works of...*blah blah blah*...to examine...*blah blah blah*... whether man was inherently good or evil." We'd just learned the definitions of "metaphor" and "simile" in class, and while I could never remember which one was which, reading *Lord of the Flies* felt to me like a metaphor (simile?) of Dad's childhood.

While he never told me much about himself, Mom would fill in gaps here and there, leaving me to piece together a pretty messy puzzle. Dad was originally the youngest of three kids. He and Uncle Adam had a middle sister, Nancy, who killed herself when she was sixteen. Dad, who was nine at the time, found his sister's body hanging from the ceiling in her bedroom. I don't know if she left a note like they do all the time in the movies, but Mom believed Nancy's blood was on Grandpa Robert's hands.

She called Grandpa a bully, saying he constantly made people feel stupid, "even someone as immensely bright as your dad," Mom explained to me one time. "Everyone was a 'useless tit' or a 'waste of space'. Your grandfather was especially cruel with Grandma Ellie and the kids, and it only became worse as he got older. The ridiculing, the belittling—he was an awful, awful man."

The next thing I knew, I was struggling to open my eyes and wiping at my nose. There was a smell in the air that wasn't going away. The lamp beside Dad's couch was on, I noticed, as I picked the sand out of each eye with my thumbs. A haze clouded the light, making me think I was still asleep. Only when the coughing started did I know for sure this wasn't a dream.

Then there was a *poof*, like what happens with Mr. Fraser's propane barbecue when he lights it. A shadow danced against the wall and the room grew brighter. I scrambled out of bed and ran to the sofa. Dad was on the right-hand side, sitting upright and asleep, the cushion beside him in flames.

"Dad! Dad! Get up!"

He shook his head both ways, unaware of the danger. I raced to the kitchen, grabbed the bigger of the two pots we had and starting filling it with water. It took forever and as I stood there waiting, the flames only got bigger as the fire alarm went off inside the apartment.

Dad lifted himself off the couch unsteadily. With the big pot in one hand and the smaller one under the kitchen faucet, I hurried over and doused the flames. Some of the cushion fabric was still smoldering. I put that out with the second pot of water a moment later, while Dad sat on his chair at the desk, speechless. I opened the balcony door and took off my T-shirt, using it to fan the smoke so the damn alarm would stop ringing.

The silence in the apartment came suddenly. All you could hear now was the sound of traffic eight stories below. I was worried the fire department had been called.

Ugh…No whammies, no whammies, no whammies…

"Quick thinking," Dad mumbled.

"What happened?" I asked, adrenaline flowing through me like electricity. Dad frowned and said he didn't know. "Was it your cigarette?"

"It would seem so."

He went to the kitchen and returned with another pot full of water, explaining how fires "can reignite even when you don't see any flames," then dumped it on top of the blackened cushion. The couch hissed. Dad poured himself a drink and said thank you, unable to stop shaking his head from side to side.

"Dad…are you okay?"

"I'm fine, Justin. I was just caught unawares."

Dad took out a record and put the volume on low. I got into bed again. He dimmed the light to near blackness as classical music started playing, a piece I'd heard a bunch of times by Beethoven that sounded like raindrops falling.

In the morning, I woke up and saw Dad sleeping on the floor, a pillow under his head and a blanket covering his body. He was turned over on his side and facing the sofa.

16

We split the next eight games, the losses coming all in a row. Michael Bolton was also injured in our season's worst skid when Dean blasted a rip-roaring slapshot into his ankle. Doctors said he'd be back for the playoffs if he was lucky. Mr. Wainwright had been right. We'd "let up on the gas" and thought we could sail into the play-offs free and easy.

I got a Social Insurance Number when Dale's Christmas fund began disappearing faster than Dad went through packs of smokes. There was no such thing as an allowance anymore either. I knew things were really bad for Dad and that I'd have to find a part-time job when he stopped buying me new hockey sticks. The week I got my SIN card, I applied to a few places around the area. A coffee shop down the street ended up hiring me for six dollars an hour and offered me two shifts a week: Tuesdays and Thursdays, from five-thirty to eight a.m. Dad says irony is like the characters in *Romeo and Juliet* thinking Juliet is dead, when all she did was drink some sleeping potion. For me, the irony was I'd never had a cup of coffee in my life.

My new schedule had me up at five a.m. and meeting one of the coffee shop's owners, Mr. or Mrs. Thompson, so they could open up the place for me. Mr. T was a short, quiet white guy with glasses. His

Japanese wife was a serious looking woman with no sense of humour. There were no questions about school or hockey like other adults asked me. It was all about today's special and ensuring I could make the drinks "properly and with efficiency." After taking thirty minutes to set up the place each morning, I'd spend two hours pouring foreign-sounding blends and getting weird stares when people asked me what such-and-such a coffee tasted like, with my highly detailed answers varying from "amazing" to "great" to "you won't be disappointed." When my shift was over, I'd run to Dad's apartment, grab my school bag, and wait outside for Lorraine.

On Valentine's Day, I went over to Ali's house. Her parents were out and we had at least a couple of hours to ourselves, maybe more if Cupid was in a good mood. I'd barely made it a foot into her place when Ali gasped and said I look exhausted.

"I *am* exhausted," I said, collapsing onto the sofa in her den. Ali disappeared into the kitchen. "This job is kicking my you know what." When Ali got back, she handed me a glass of ginger ale with three ice cubes and a straw in it. She took a sip from her Diet Coke as she flipped through the channels until reaching MuchMusic. Ah-ha's "Take on Me" was playing.

"*Ugh*," she said, lowering the volume. "This song is *sooo* amazing but the video is so brutal!"

"Not nearly as gay as Toto's 'Africa'."

She laughed. "You know you're a crazy person to be working in the mornings, right?"

"What else can I do? They wouldn't give me a weekend shift, and between hockey and school—and playing hockey *for* the school—I have no free time during the week except to, you know, do things like…" I lowered my hand into my knapsack and pulled out a square black box with a card "…Happy Valentine's Day."

Dimples.

She put her drink down on the coffee table and asked which she should open first, the card or the present.

"Whatever you want." Mom says you should always open a card first, but I don't think she meant between a girlfriend and boyfriend. I'm pretty sure that was more when getting something from a stranger or your grandmother.

Ali took the card out from the envelope and read it as much to herself as she did for me: *To My One and Only Sweetheart* the card said on the front. Okay, it was cheesy, but Hallmark didn't leave a lot of options between "A Friend in Need Is a Friend Indeed" and "You're the Love of My Life." Ali read on. *Dear Ali, You've made the last four months the most amazing of my life.* "Ooooh," she said as she imitated Mom's pouty face. *I ~~love~~ really like our time together.* "You took out the word 'love'!" she said, glowing. *I just wanted to tell you how much you mean to me and give you a special present. Happy Valentine's Day. Justin xo*

"Oh, you..." She wrapped her arms around my neck and we kissed—the real good kind of kiss. "I can't wait to see what you got me!" she said with the excitement of a kid on Christmas morning. She tore off the wrapping paper and stared at the box as if it were radioactive. "What is it?"

"Well, I could tell you. Then again, you could open it yourself and find out."

She clapped her hands together and took off the box's lid, pulling out a thin silver chain which she held between her fingers. "Is this an anklet?"

"Yeah," I said, growing nervous. Mom had always worn one and I figured it was a good first step in the jewellery category because it was simple and inexpensive.

"Oh."

"You don't like it?"

"No, it's not that. I guess...I don't know anyone who wears an anklet."

"I'm sorry. It's just that my Mom..." I couldn't finish my sentence.

"Your mom what?"

Now I was knee deep in it, but didn't want to say Mom wore one because clearly Ali hated it and then she'd think Mom was tacky. "Nothing. She's into all kinds of jewellery. I thought you'd...anyway... it's fine. Sorry."

"Justin, you don't have to be sorry. It's lovely. It is. Just not on me, you know?"

"That's cool."

Ali put her gift away and took a few moments to think. I was kicking myself, wondering how I'd bought such a bad present when she asked me about Mom. "You know, I've been wondering for a while now," she said, fiddling with the box lid. "I've been thinking a lot about what you told me at your place a couple of weeks ago. I know you don't have any idea where she is, but didn't you say that cop was able to help you in the past?"

"Who, Jeff? He drove me out to see her, Ali. That's all."

"No, I know. It's...Look, I don't mean to pretend I know anything about what you're going through. I guess I thought, well, maybe Jeff could help you find her. I've wanted to tell you this for a long time now, but was scared you'd take it too personally or too...I don't know."

I took a sip of my drink, more upset at myself about the dumb anklet than Ali bringing up Mom. Still, I wasn't in the mood to talk about something as heavy as Mom's whereabouts on Valentine's Day and Ali could sense that.

"Tell you what," she said, jumping off the couch. "Why don't I go and get your present from upstairs?"

"You got me something?" I was genuinely surprised, partly because we hadn't talked about exchanging gifts, but mostly because of Ali's whole "I'm never going to use the word 'love', not in a *bazillion* years" speech on our first date.

When she returned to the den, she folded her legs underneath her on the sofa while hiding something behind her back. "Okay, so I've been reading this book about origami my dad got on his trip to Japan, and I wanted to give you something special today. *Sooo...* I've been making this over the last few weeks and...*ta-da!*" she said, passing me a see-through cylinder of miniature red, yellow, blue and orange cranes. "What do you think?" Ali was beaming, her arms raised in the air like she'd just won a race. I bit my lip. The origami were beautiful and must have taken a really, really, *really* long time to make. All I'd done was use part of Dale's Christmas fund to get something my girl-friend didn't even like. Ali could sense something was up. "What's the matter? I thought it would be nice for your apartment. You know, give it a little colour."

"It's not that. It's amazing. I just, you know, can't believe you spent so much time working on this."

"Seriously. Have you met me? What do I do at home except pro-crastinate? It was nothing." She leaned forward, put her lips to mine and fell on top of my body.

By the time I left Ali's house that night, I'd finally reached third base.

Dad asked me to pick up some things from the supermarket when I got home, including Clamato Juice, salt and a can of Scotch Broth soup. I also bought some pork chops and a box of Uncle Ben's rice for dinner. Every time I'd made rice in the past I'd destroyed it. Tonight I was determined to nail it and do a side other than potatoes. Although I didn't love pork, Lorraine had scared the pants off me with chicken, which was way better than pork, because she said you could get salmo-nella poisoning if you didn't cook or handle it properly. I didn't know what salmonella was, but if it got paired up with the word "poisoning" that probably wasn't such a good thing.

I hadn't seen Lorraine or Mom make pork, so had nothing to go on. I put some salt and pepper on it because that's what moms seemed to do with every piece of meat. I hovered over the plate as I thought about what to do from there. Dad was on the sofa and asked how things were going in the kitchen.

"Fine."

"Any azzanze required?"

"Nope."

"Az you were, 'den."

The water had come to a boil in the pot so I threw in some salt, figuring if you did that for pasta then you did it for rice, too. I put the lid on and went to the fridge, where I took out the French's mustard and one of those round green lime juice bottles, wondering if they'd go well together. I squeezed some mustard over the two pork chops and spread it around with a fork, spraying a little lime juice on top of that. The pork went straight into the frying pan, which was lined in olive oil, before I turned the heat up to maximum.

I flipped the pork from time to time so it wouldn't burn and when it looked done, I poured the oil down the sink drain and lifted the cover off the pot. Most of the rice was sticking to the bottom.

Crap!

"So here it is," I said, lowering our plates onto the desk when everything was all done.

"T'lookz zenzational."

Now that I was sitting across from him, I could tell Dad's eyes were more screwed up than usual.

"Well, I killed the rice and the pork probably tastes like a used hockey glove. But aside from that," I went on with a smile, "dinner should be great!"

"Juzin, iz a meal fit fer a king." The pork wasn't bad, I have to admit, but the rice was too crunchy. Back to potatoes, I thought.

"Thanks."

"And the rize is *al dente!*"

"How was work today?" I asked, curious about the cause of tonight's over-the-top booze fest.

"Juz'in, today was Val'ntine's Day. D'you know dat?"

"Yeah."

"D'you zee Ali?"

"Uh-huh."

"And?" Dad took a forkful of rice and chewed with his mouth open, something he usually never did.

"We exchanged gifts."

"Wha'd'ye get'er?"

I swallowed and told him I'd got her a stupid anklet, wanting to end that with *which she's never going to wear.*

"Egzelent."

"Right."

"She'z a keeper."

"Yeah."

"Girlz like 'dat don't come'long e'ry day."

"Right."

"Hol'on to'er," Dad started. He burped and tapped his stomach. "Wiz…wiz…da ferce of…of…a…"

"Gale-force wind?"

"Yez!" Dad said, clapping his hands together. "And n'ver, n'ver," Dad went on, shaking his whole body, "le'go!"

"Okay."

Dad poked at his meal with a tired hand. With less than half of his food eaten, he lit a cigarette and said he was going to The Last Resort.

"You don't want to hang out here and do some reading?" I said casually.

"Alicia'z waitin' fer me with openin' arms and a thersty throt."

Dad staggered out soon after this and I turned on the TV while doing some homework. When that stupid "It's 11 o'clock. Do you know where your children are?" PSA came on the Buffalo channel, I'd had enough and went to wash up. I'd been to Buffalo once to play in a tournament there. It was a depressing place, but as I brushed my teeth and lifted my bangs up, checking to see how the Himalayas on my forehead were doing, I wondered if parents there had a hard time tracking down their kids when it got dark out. I crawled into bed and read a couple of chapters, then dozed off, the book still open on my blanket and the lights on. The sound of the phone ringing woke me up. "Hello?" I said, groggy and running a hand through my hair. The clock on the desk said it was one-oh-nine a.m.

"Justin, it's Alicia, over at The Last Resort."

"Oh, hey."

"Darlin'," she went on, "your dad, he's not doin' so hot tonight." Alicia explained that Dad was in rough shape and needed some help getting home. "I hate to put this on ya, darlin', but he's not doin' good at all. Would you mind runnin' over and, maybe, givin' him a little help?"

I got to The Last Resort so fast my shoelaces were still untied, my hair, I'm sure, looking as put together as a bird's nest. Alicia came out from around the bar and hugged me.

"Thanks for comin' over so quick."

"It's okay. I was up doing some homework anyway."

"I'm both bartender and legal guardian here sometimes, and with your dad, I'm cuttin' him off because he's had a little too much tonight. Thing is, when I tried to get him to leave he said he didn't remember where he lived. I'm really sorry for puttin' this on you."

Dad was slumped over the bar. When he lifted his head, he looked around the same way he had the night of the fire. "Juzzzn," he said. "L'a ma live!" Alicia looked at me and raised her eyebrows. "Aliza her'z be'n kind 'nough to..." *burp* ... "fill me up a few timez en..." *burp*... "to'me up to boot!"

"Dad, we need to go."

"No'yet!" he said, raising a finger. "*Ze Germanz* still need to be *zealt wiz...*"

"Listen, darlin'," Alicia said to me. "You tell your dad to settle up the tab tomorrow, K? Let's not worry 'bout that tonight."

"All right." I turned to Dad and said it was time to go.

"But *ze Germanz!*"

Somehow I managed to drag him out in one piece, his arm around my neck. Upstairs, he stumbled through the door and fell flat on his stomach. "Dad," I said in a concerned voice, lifting him to his feet. "Let's just make it to the sofa." We walked together, shoulder to shoulder, until we made it to the couch. I tried to lower him down slowly, but he fell backwards, against the balcony window. As he tumbled, he reached for something to stop his fall, which happened to be the curtains. He tore them down in one fell swoop, the rod crash landing to the floor as the curtains came to settle over his body.

"I'm o-kay!" he cried, throwing the curtains off. "Ev'rythinz o-kay! Juz' time to hi' the hay," he went on. It took all his strength, but he got himself up and began taking off his clothes. He was okay getting his button down off, then struggled with his pants. I moved closer to help him. "I can do'is on my own, young man," he said. When he tried pulling the second pant leg off, though, he collapsed again.

"Dad, it's okay. We can do this together."

"No, no, no, no, no, no...I can..."

Then he stopped in mid-sentence. He had a look on his face like movie actors get in those seconds before they realize they've been stabbed. When he didn't move, I reached down and helped him to his feet and onto the couch, the floor stained brown where he'd just been lying. With Dad in nothing but his briefs now, I realized what had happened when he rolled over a second later.

Sighing, I spread a blanket on top of him and then made my way to the bathroom to get a towel.

Dad wasn't home after school the next day. I put my knapsack on the bed, grabbed a banana from the kitchen, then sat on the floor and watched TV. I channel surfed for a while before my thoughts drifted to what Ali had said about Mom.

Cartoons, reruns of crappy shows, home shopping, cartoons, more reruns of dumb shows...

This was pointless. I turned the stupid thing off and went through my notebook as I made a plan of attack for my homework. I removed the math test I'd been given back earlier and smiled while looking at the "71%" written at the top. I'd passed three tests in a row and this was my highest mark all year in math. My overall grade was still pretty sad, but Mr. Ingersoll had helped me understand a little more by working with me one-on-one after class a few times. Although most of the stuff we did, especially geometry, still mystified me like the Bermuda Triangle, he'd at least been able to make me understand integers better.

Antsy and in no mood to do any homework, I threw out the banana peel and walked to Dad's desk. While looking outside, I started to day-dream...about Ali...about me and Ali...about me and Ali and rounding the final base...which is when I noticed the curtains were gone.

Last night.

Dad.

Pulling them down.

While searching all around for something to clean the windows with, I found an ancient bottle of Windex under the bathroom sink. I grabbed some toilet paper and headed to the living room again. The big glass panes were disgusting. There were cobwebs in all four corners and dirt-brown lines on the glass itself. I wiped them clean, top to bottom, side to side, then stood back and admired the view. Still the same grey concrete building directly ahead of us, the same depressing scenery, but at least it was clearer. I threw the toilet paper out and heard Ali's voice urging me to have Jeff help find Mom.

I took out a phone number from my wallet.

One ring, two rings…

"Hello?" came a soft voice from the other end.

"Hi, is Jeff there, please?"

"I'm sorry. He's at work right now. Can I ask who's calling?"

"No. That's okay. I'll just—"

"Is this Justin by any chance?"

What is she, telepathic?

"Yes."

"Hi, Justin. My name's Jasmine. I'm Jeff's wife. How are you?"

"Good, ah, thank you."

"I'll tell Jeff you phoned as soon as he gets home. Is that all right?"

"Sure. Great. Thanks."

"And it was really wonderful getting a chance to talk to you. Jeff's said so many nice things about you."

"Thanks."

"My pleasure. I'll pass along the message."

Jeff phoned me after dinner. Dad was still out and I was watching John Tesh and Mary Hart go on about how *Rainman* was the odds-on favourite to win the Oscar for best film at the Academy Awards. Jeff did a decent job of trying to hide the concern in his voice, but I could tell it was there. It kind of felt like he thought something bad might be going down. "I was wondering if I could ask for another favour," I said, the receiver already sweaty in my hand.

"Of course. What is it?"

"I ah, I was just, you know…" Jeff said nothing. "My mom, well, you know how she got let out a couple of months ago?"

"Yes."

I asked if there was any way he could track down her phone number. There was a pause.

"You have no other way of getting in contact with her?"

"No."

"I'm not sure I can get that information for you, Justin." I hadn't heard Jeff sound this uncertain in the past. "Can you give me a little time?"

"Okay," I said before thanking him and hanging up.

And by "a little time," Jeff meant less than 24 hours. I was working on an English essay as Dad talked out loud about the Soviets leaving Afghanistan today. "They've been there nearly a decade," he said, "sinking in a quagmire of their own Leninist incompetence." Dad called it their Vietnam and grumbled, more to himself than to me. "When will the world learn? No one can take over that land. The world's greatest armies have tried, each and every one of them coming away with their tail between their legs. You know what you call a historian who doesn't learn from his past mistakes?"

"What?" I said, not caring about the conversation but not wanting to give Dad the silent treatment.

"A politician. Ha!" Hands clapping could be heard a second later.

That's when the phone rang. I assumed it was Ali because she was the only person calling here anymore. "Good one," I said to Dad, striding over to the desk. It wasn't Ali calling, though. It was Jeff and he said he was downstairs, which made no sense. "I'm at a payphone in the shopping complex," he explained. "I've got what you need. Can you come down and meet me?"

I said yes and hung up, telling Dad I had to go over to Jung-ho's apartment. He was lost in his own world, rambling about the Soviets and their "descent into darkness."

Jeff was sitting on a bench and wearing a big blue parka, blue jeans, and a pair of construction boots. His elbows were pressed against the inside of his thighs as he waited for me.

"Hey," I said.

Jeff stood up, raised his arm and slipped a piece of paper into my hand, as if we were spies and he was passing me state secrets.

"Now it's my turn to ask you a favour, Justin."

"Sure."

"You can't tell anyone where you got this. It has your Mom's phone number and current address, okay? But under *no* circumstances can you tell *anyone* where you got this because I could get in serious trouble if this comes back to me."

"Yeah. No. Absolutely. I won't say a thing."

He gave me a nod. "Great. I hope you two can reconnect, big guy."

17

The zodiac sign for someone born between February nineteenth and March twentieth is Pisces. February's birthstone is the amethyst. The reason I looked this up was because of Ali. Her birthday was February twenty-second. I wanted to get her something special and make up for my crash-landing on Valentine's Day. Mom says if you want to impress a girl, buy her a nice piece of jewellery. If you really want to impress her, it's got to come in a blue box with the Birks logo on it.

I *really* wanted to impress Ali.

The Birks I went to many blocks west on Bloor Street was pretty swank, with plush carpets and well-dressed salespeople. Glass cases lined the floor area in a U-shape, a security guard with a gun standing by the entrance. When I bought the anklet, I'd gone to a store in the Eaton Centre with lots of shiny things at super low prices. The purchase took me all of two minutes to make. This time around I'd do it right.

A decent-looking woman around Mom's age with ginger hair came up to me, her hands wrapped around each other. She was kind of hunched over, even though I was taller, and asked if she could help me.

"I'm looking for a present."

"Is this for a special someone in your life?"

"Uh, yeah. It's for a...yeah, you know, it's for a girl."

"Is her birthday coming up by any chance?"

"Yeah."

"And did you have anything in mind?"

I shook my head.

"Okay, then. Why don't we start over here?" she said, guiding me to the left-hand side of the store with a hand at the bottom of my back.

I'd seen a picture of an amethyst in the book with all the zodiac information. It was purple. Nothing under the glass here was purple. Most of it was gold and silver, with rows and rows of diamonds. There were necklaces and rings and funky-shaped things I didn't know the names of. The woman asked how much I wanted to spend while describing some of these glittery objects.

"Maybe around seventy or eighty buc...dollars."

Although that was probably chump change at a place like Birks, the saleslady smiled and said they had lots to choose from in that price range.

"And you said you weren't looking for anything in particular?" She led me to the other side of the room, again, a hand at the bottom of my back.

"Well, her birthday's this Thursday so I was thinking of maybe getting something with an amethyst in it or on it or, you know, just an amethyst....or whatever."

She smiled. "I think we have just the thing for you." She asked my name as we walked up a couple of showcases.

"Justin."

"And may I ask what her name is?"

"Ali."

"What a pretty name."

"Yeah," I said, fighting hard not to smile and come across as a lovesick doorknob.

"Justin, if you want something spectacular with an amethyst, you don't need to look any further than this," she explained, pointing down to a necklace that had a small purple stone in the middle.

Hello, beautiful.

"The necklace itself is eighteen carat white gold and you won't find a purer amethyst anywhere. It's Deep Siberian grade, so it's got a primary purple hue upwards of eighty percent, with secondary hues of blue and red." She could have been talking about the Soviets leaving Afghanistan. All I saw were Ali's dimples coming out when she opened the blue box and had this waiting for her. "Now, it's a *touch* pricier than what you'd told me you wanted to spend. *However,* I wanted to begin by showing you the finest we had in this type of jewellery and something, quite frankly, Ali is bound to love." I blinked and a second later she added, "It's one hundred and twenty-five dollars." I might have blinked a few more times. Or not. My mind was racing through numbers, which, given my talent for math, took me a bit before I realized this would 1) pretty much empty my wallet; 2) wipe out the last of Dale's Christmas fund; and 3) obliterate my first paycheque from work.

I asked for a moment to think about it.

"Of course. Take all the time you need. I'll be over here." She motioned towards another part of the store. "Come and get me if you want to continue looking or if you have any other questions."

I thanked her and looked into the showcase once again. There were rings and other things with purple stones on them, amethysts, I guessed, but the one I'd been shown was perfect. I reached for my wallet and flipped through the bills to make sure I had enough to cover it.

Six twenties (thank you, Cousin Dale) and four tens (thank you, part-time job).

I lifted a hand to my chin and did the same thing Dr. Blake had done on Christmas Eve, except I didn't have any facial hair to pick at or stroke. I just had a nice new zit coming up on the side of my mouth, which I avoided touching. The internal debate lasted approximately one-point-three seconds.

"Okay," I said, walking up to the woman. "I'll take it."

"Ali's going to love it. Now, would you like that giftwrapped as well?"

"Yeah. That'd be great."

With tax, the total came to a hundred and thirty-three dollars and fifty cents. I left the store with a bag so small it made me feel a little light in the loafers, and I had barely enough money left over to get me through the next two weeks.

But I had a blue box from Birks for Ali.

Debbie's parents were out of town the weekend after Ali's birthday and she'd offered to throw a party for her on Saturday night. Ali told me to invite three or four of my buddies over, so I called Keith, Dean, Ryan, and Michael Bolton. They'd seen Ali at the arena snack bar and knew one of the most important equations guys learn when they hit puberty: hot girl = hot friends.

Keith and I had talked on the phone that afternoon. He told me to meet him at Summerhill Station at seven o'clock. When I said Debbie lived three subway stops north, Keith said he had a plan.

"What's the plan?"

"Don't worry about it."

"But it makes more sense to meet up at Eglinton," I explained. "She lives, like, two blocks from Ali's place."

"Listen, Corky, will you just meet me outside Summerhill at seven?"

"Fine."

Keith got there fifteen minutes late. There was no *Sorry for keeping you waiting, pal* or *Get a load of my latest crackpot plan*. We simply headed towards Yonge Street from the subway exit just up the road. For a January night, the temperature wasn't too bad, though the wind was stinging. Keith was still all hush-hush about why we had to meet here and didn't talk to me while we hung around the corner. He kept poking his head this way and that, as if he was expecting to see someone he knew.

"Are you seriously not going to tell me what we're doing here?"

"How much money do you have on you?"

"Why?" I asked, instinctively putting a hand into my pocket to cover my wallet.

"Forget it. Hey there," Keith said as he blew by me. He went up to a guy walking our way who was in his early twenties and had on a cool leather jacket with a white wool collar. "Would you mind helping us out?"

"What do you need?" The guy took a drag off his cigarette and looked as cool as Kiefer Sutherland in *Stand by Me*.

"Do you think there's any way you could grab my buddy and me here," Keith said, bending his neck in my direction, "a two-four? We'll throw in a little something for the effort, of course." Keith had a bunch of bills in his hand.

"I like your style, lads," he said, grinning. "Maybe next time. But right now I'm headed the other way."

After he took off, Keith came my way again and I asked him what the F he was doing, keeping my voice low even though nobody else was near us.

"Would you chill? A little shoulder tapping never hurt anyone. We're going to a party tonight, right? And parties are all about good times. Therefore, we need beer."

"What if we get caught, moron?"

"Think about the alternative, J.R. 'Hey, girls.'," Keith said in a sarcastic voice. "'Thanks for inviting us to your party. Ali, me and your boyfriend here will just sit in the corner, drinking Shirley Temples and slapping our salami around.' Anyway, it's fine," he went on, the dramatics over with. "I've done this before."

"What? You have? When?"

"Well, not in real life. But I've heard lots of stories about how it's done. All you need's a little confidence and some extra coin, both of which I have."

"You're demented."

"And you're chicken shit."

This was going to play out badly. We'd be arrested on the night of my girlfriend's birthday party. Officer Jeff Brady would pick us up and shake his head as he drove us to 53 Division. He'd call Dad, who would then tell Jeff to lock us up and throw away the key. It goes without saying Ali would be so embarrassed she'd dump me as soon as she learned she was going out with a criminal.

"Take a chill pill, would you?" Keith nudged me. "Let me do the talking. What've you got in that gay bag of yours by the way?"

Keith wasn't looking at me anymore. He was rubbing his hands together to stay warm and searching around, trying to find someone else to land us a case of beer.

"It's Ali's gift."

"What'd you get her, a paperclip?"

"Yeah. I got her a paperclip for her paperclip collection."

"What? It's a fruity little bag."

"You're a fruity little bag."

Okay, not my strongest comeback.

"You don't think she's going to figure out what you got her when she sees the Birks bag?" Once in a while, Keith actually said something intelligent. "Isn't part of the reason you wrap up a gift so it stays a surprise till the last minute?

Twice in one night!

I took the present out and stuffed it inside my jacket, then threw the bag into the trash can on the corner as a middle-aged dude zigzagged his way down the road towards us. He had on a pair of ripped jeans, with a huge gut filling his open black leather jacket and black Harley Davidson shirt. Keith went up to him far enough away so I couldn't hear them and handed over a wad of bills. All those scenes I'd played through in my mind about getting arrested came rushing back. Thankfully, they were just as quickly erased when the fat guy came rumbling our way like a streetcar, one case of beer on each shoulder.

"Thanks, fellas. Been a pleasure doing business with you gents of good intent."

When we got to her house, Debbie let us in and gave me a quick "hey" before I introduced her to Keith, who had the case of beer on his shoulder like the Harley Davidson guy.

"You ordered a two-four?" Keith said. "I'm the delivery guy."

"We totally did! Come on in." Easily the first time I'd seen Debbie smile, she focused all her attention on Keith—and Keith alone—as we walked through the hallway to the back of the house. Ali, Rachel, and Vicki were sitting around a red table in an area off to the side of the kitchen.

"What do we have here?" Ali got up from her seat and gave me a hug.

"You can thank your boyfriend," Keith told her. "He did all the hard work. Say, any of you guys want a beer?" he asked, taking off his jacket and revealing a Hawaiian shirt underneath.

"We're okay," Ali said. "We got into Debbie's parents' collection of liquors and *liqueurs*." The girls giggled. Keith headed over to the fridge, where he put the bottles in, one clang after another.

"What do you guys want to listen to?" Debbie asked. She was crouched down in front of a CD tower practically as tall as her.

Keith put a beer in my hand and swung a chair around the other way. He took a swig from his beer and requested some Van Halen.

"No way!" Rachel said. "They're *so* 1984."

199

"Whatever. They're totally better now that they've got Sammy Hagar! He'd kick David Lee Roth's ass any day of the week."

George Michael's "Faith" started playing.

"So what did you get Ali for her birthday?" Rachel asked me. "Something shiny and expensive?"

I rubbed the back of my neck, told her it wasn't much, and could give it to her later.

"Later! Give it to her now!" Rachel said.

"I don't know. It's not much and, ah—"

"Yeah. No shit, Sherlock. You already said that."

Thanks, Keith, you fartface.

"—but here it is anyway," I went on, putting the box on the table. Ali, who'd made a triangle with her hands over her nose and mouth, was careful to remove the giftwrapping paper. When she got to the blue box, she looked at me and beamed. The case didn't open up nearly as easily as that stupid anklet one. She gasped when she finally lifted up the necklace and twirled it around her fingers so the light in the room bounced off the amethyst. Rachel and Vicki said it was gorgeous. Debbie mentioned "how nice" it was. Ali was shell-shocked.

Score one for the good guys.

"Oh my *gawd*, Justin! Thank you, thank you, thank you! I love it," she said, planting one square on my lips.

"Get a room!" Keith moaned as he polished off his beer. I had yet to take my first sip.

Ali asked me to clip the necklace on for her. Tremors ran along my arms as I fastened it in place, her hair falling down to her shoulders with a whoosh. She put her hands across her chest and showed off her present as the girls went gaga. When the doorbell rang a second later, Debbie went to get it and returned with Ryan.

"Fraze," he said, slapping hands with Keith.

"What's up, Dealacrutch?"

"Baloney," he went on, locking hands with me.

"How's it going?"

"Good. Very good. Couldn't be better. I snagged some hooch from my dad's private collection, I'm pleased to report." Ryan took out a jam jar from his coat pocket that had its label peeled off.

"What, so you're bringing water to parties now?" Keith looked Rachel's way as he said this and earned himself a laugh.

"Actually, tough guy, it's vodka. Well, mostly vodka. There's a little gin as well. At least, I think it's gin. It's the bottle with the wolf on a hockey skate or whatever that thing is, right?"

Rachel pulled out a pack of cigarettes and asked if anybody wanted one. Ali and Keith each readily accepted one. While I'd never seen my best friend smoke, the bigger shock was seeing Ali light up.

"I didn't know you smoked," I kind of half-muttered, half-gasped.

"Only when I drink," she said with a scoff. "Besides, they're just menthols."

When Dean and Michael Bolton got there, Dean asked if we should play a drinking game. The girls hollered "ABSOLUTELY!" over top a Cyndi Lauper song. Unfortunately for them, they didn't have the skills to pay the bills when it came to bouncing a quarter into a glass. This meant one of them was downing their drink at the end of every turn. Many-a-round later, the girls were singing at the top of their lungs and dancing around the kitchen as me and the guys sat around the table and talked about the City Championships next month.

By the time Dean had to leave because of his heinous curfew, Keith and Rachel were nowhere to be seen. Ali and I also disappeared and headed to one of the bedrooms upstairs, where I spun her around and asked if she really liked the necklace.

"I love it," she said, lifting herself on her toes and giving me a kiss. "You couldn't've gotten anything more beautiful. Now come here, you." We collapsed onto the bed like felled trees, our shoes still on. As we made out, I took off Ali's shirt and started kissing her bra, a white thing with purple flowers on it. Too paranoid to even attempt unclipping it myself, I slipped the cups over her breasts. Ali pulled it back down and undid it with one hand through a giggle. My hands and mouth were at centre ice, though every time I went below her blue line, she pulled me back up. This made no sense because I'd gotten to third base last time. Ali might've been my first girlfriend, but I was pretty sure you ran around the bases one way, as in, *not* running backwards.

When Ali went to turn off the lamp on the nightstand, she swivelled her hips and I saw something—or two "somethings," actually—at the bottom of her back. On one side was a picture of a screwed up leaf; on the other side was a butterfly. "Hold on," I said. Don't turn it off yet."

"But I don't like doing this with the lights on."

"It's not that. It's just…Are those tattoos on you?"

Ali turned over so we were facing each other, then reached for her shirt and covered her chest. "Yeah. I got them last summer. What do you think? Do you like them?" she asked, snuggling into my chest.

"Uh…yeah. I guess so."

Jeez, the next thing Ali would tell me is that she'd gone around all the bases with someone else before.

"The tattoo on the left is the Chinese character for beauty; the other one's a butterfly."

Ali wasn't in the mood to talk about her tattoos and I was too turned on by her half-naked body, so we fooled around for a bit more even though she kept denying me access south of the border. At the end of the night, I walked her home. It took a little longer than expected because we stumbled our way past her house and then took a wrong turn a block later. When we finally got to her place, she gave me a slow, wet kiss and whispered, "Thanks again for the necklace, babe. It's the nicest thing anyone's ever bought me."

"Second base, pal." Keith said with a sly grin. We were playing our own version of Around the World in his driveway, taking slapshots with real pucks, not the stupid little plastic ones you play floor hockey with. We were aiming for a net twenty feet away with a thick white piece of wood covering it. There were four holes, one in each corner of the net. The rules were pretty simple: you started in the upper left-hand corner and moved clockwise from there, but only after shooting a puck through the correct hole.

When I'd woken up a couple of hours ago, my brain was still swimming in a pool of beer. The sides of my head shook like speakers on full blast, and my mouth was pretty much a rusty old sink. I took a long hard look at myself in the bathroom mirror.

Crap. Another zit.

Someone had folded over my face in the middle of the night. There were lines running over my cheeks and neck like a map of Canada's rivers. I brushed my teeth and got in the shower, hoping the hot water would make me feel better. When that didn't work, I searched the medicine cabinet for some Tylenol, which Dad had a good supply of. I popped a couple of those bad boys, went back to bed and reached for my dictionary.

hang·o·ver

noun

1. the disagreeable physical aftereffects of drunkenness, such as a headache or stomach disorder, usually felt several hours after cessation of drinking.

Disagreeable physical aftereffects? *Check.*
Headache? *Uh-huh.*
Stomach disorder? *Or several.*

"It's for you, Dionysus. I believe it's your esteemed partner in crime," Dad said. He was standing by his desk and holding the phone in one hand as he puffed away on a cigarette. I was out of it and had no clue how much time had passed since I'd fallen asleep again. I rolled out of bed and took the call.

"Hello?"

"Hey."

"How are you feeling?" Dad was maybe two feet away from me, so I told Keith everything was great. "Congratulations. Because I feel like a dirty piece of ass right now."

"Nice image," I said, faking a smile.

"Your Dad's in the room, isn't he?"

"Yeah. I guess so. They say it's supposed to be okay weather today, though."

"Right. Listen. Head over here and let's drill some pucks at a net and lose this hangover, okay?"

"Sure thing. Be there in an hour or so."

Keith didn't waste any time asking about the personal stuff when I got to his place. "So how far did *you* get last night?" He was leaning on the butt end of his stick off to the side of me.

I took a shot and nailed the upper left corner.

"Asswipe!" Keith took two more shots before he got one in the net. "So," he went on, "were you swinging for the fences last night à la Kirk Gibson?"

"You're a douche." I nailed the upper right-hand corner with a wrist shot.

"Well?" He reached for a puck with the blade of his stick. "Tell me you at least hit a single!" He missed his shot, the puck singing into the open garage.

I was still frustrated about running in reverse on the bases last night. "We did what we always do, you know." I missed my next shot.

"What's that supposed to mean?" Keith asked as he lifted a slap-shot over the net and sent another puck into the garage.

"It means we, you know, we did the dirty."

"You guys did it? You popped her cherry!"

"Would you drop it, man? We did what we did. Whatever. Let it go."

We finished up Around the World and then headed inside to play video games. When I got back to the apartment hours later, Dad was reading on the sofa. I asked him if he'd had anything to eat today.

"No," he answered, "but I'm still quite satiated from my meal last night."

"Do you want me to make us some hot dogs?"

"Don't worry about me."

"No, seriously. I haven't had much since lunch and we've got a pack of Oscar Mayers in the fridge. Why don't I just boil up a few?"

"Splendid."

I made four beef franks, but Dad barely finished one. He ate his with a sliver of relish and some Cheez Whiz; I dumped tons of mustard and ketchup on mine. When he was done, Dad lit a cigarette and asked how Ali was doing.

"Fine."

"You were out late last night."

"Yeah. Ali's birthday."

"Enjoy yourself?"

"Sure."

"You passed on my best, I hope."

"Yep."

"Okay."

"Okay, then."

I cleared the dishes as Dad shuffled to the couch and opened up his book, Erwin Rommel's *Infantry Attacks*.

18

February stinks in Toronto. March pretty much sucks, too. The weather's crappy. It's cold. No one's nice to each other. At the coffee shop, customers were flat-out mean. They didn't say please or thank you when they got their stupid drinks. We had a tip jar beside the cash register and we'd be lucky if anyone left a dime or a quarter. To be honest, those early morning shifts were wearing me down. I was napping after school most days. Between hooking up with Ali once or twice a week, Jung-ho's swim lessons, homework, Nats and school hockey, and making dinner every night, I was getting my butt whooped. Swimming with Jung-ho was probably the one thing I could've cut out of my life, but that wouldn't do anything except hurt someone I sort of/maybe/kind of had a soft spot for.

Ali and I had our first fight in March, which didn't exactly help things. As with a lot of the fights Mom and Dad used to get into, ours seemed to start from nothing very important. It happened one day when I'd forgotten Ali and I were supposed to meet up. She'd invited me to her house and I was so dazed by three o'clock that it slipped my mind. After yawning pretty much the whole subway ride to the apartment, Ali called a couple of hours later.

"I thought you were going to swing by my place today," she said. She wasn't angry, at least not yet she wasn't, but she sounded peeved.

"Sorry. I totally forgot. I was so zonked after—"

"You know, you haven't been yourself lately, Justin. It's like you're always thinking of something else whenever we talk."

"I'm wiped out." Just having this conversation was hard. All I wanted to do was crawl into bed and close my eyes. "I can't even concentrate in school anymore."

"It's more than that."

I tried to blame it on the lack of sleep and the stress at home, but Ali wasn't buying it. She thought it had something to do with us. "It has nothing to do with us. I swear. I'm not hiding anything from you. There are no secrets or…or conspiracies here."

"I don't think there's any *conspiracy* here, Justin. I'm only saying you're different."

"Nothing's changed with me, Ali!" I was pissed off she wasn't dropping this and let that affect me in a bad way. "It's you who's changed. I mean, what happened on the night of your birthday? You getting all cuddly and then brushing me off? It's you who's got a problem with us apparently."

"Whoa, whoa. Simmer down, Charlie Brown. See! You've been pissed about that for days now, haven't you? Well, for your information, it was that time of the month for me, dumb-dumb. You clearly don't want to talk about this and instead just want to bottle everything up. Tell you what."

"Ali, hold your water."

"No. No, it's fine. Tell you what. Let's forget about it. This is getting us nowhere right now. I'll talk to you later, Justin."

Click.

As Dad saw it, my games were suffering because of whatever was going on within me. I'd gone through the fall with all but one penalty, a bum call I got when fighting for the puck in the corner. Now I was getting a penalty a game, it seemed, sometimes two. I was taking stupid tripping and hooking and elbowing minors. Dad knew they were stupid. Mr. Wainwright knew they were stupid. Even I knew they were stupid.

Things were getting more serious by the beginning of March. I was dozing off in class and barely paying attention even when awake, which is why I asked Dad to call the school one morning and tell them I was sick, something I hadn't done all year.

"What, may I ask, is your ailment?" he asked from the couch. I was still lying in bed, my eyes as heavy as dumbbells.

"I'm dying."

"I see. Any other symptoms?"

"I truly can't get out of bed. I need to sleep for the next twenty-four hours. Will you please just phone the school?"

Dad walked to the desk and picked up the phone. "This is Justin Maloney's father. I'm calling on behalf of my son, Justin, who is *gravely* ill. I'm afraid he won't be able to make it to school today…Yes…Yes…I will, of course…All right…Thank you very much."

I crawled out of bed around ten and made myself some chicken noodle soup. Dad was still sleeping. When he eventually got up, around noon, he showered and said he was going out "for a tootle" as he polished off a drink. I watched TV for a bit, but daytime shows stink the joint out unless you're into soap operas. After getting through some homework, I got under the covers again and cracked open our latest book for English, *Great Expectations*. While the story was about as exciting as watching paint dry on a wall, it did manage to put me to sleep. When I woke up, the sun was starting to set, the apartment mostly dark. I rubbed the sand out of my eyes, looked at my watch, and saw it was nearing six o'clock. Dad still wasn't back.

In the bathroom, I took down my swimming trunks from the shower rail, where they'd been drying since Jung-ho's lesson yesterday. I grabbed a towel and went upstairs to do some easy laps. The swim was refreshing and exactly what the doctor ordered. My grogginess was gone and I felt full of energy going into tonight's game.

"How was the swim, Poseidon?" Dad asked me when I came downstairs again. A cigarette burned away in his hand under shade of the lamp.

"Good."

"How many laps today?"

"Twenty."

"Feeling better?"

"Yeah."

"Going to be okay for tonight?"

"Yep."

"I trust you won't ask me to commit any other acts of subterfuge with the school tomorrow."

"Nope."

"Excellent. As you were, then."

When I was done my shift the next day, I told Mr. Thompson I had to quit, saying the schedule was hurting my grades and my health. I'd heard of something called "giving two weeks' notice" in the movies, but I was giving him two and a half weeks' notice and so figured that would work in my favour. Mr. Thompson was disappointed in me, he claimed, because he'd spent time and money training me, and now all for nothing. "A job is not a joke. Neither is it a hobby. The next time you fill out an application, keep in mind that you should work more than six to eight weeks, Justin. My wife and I operate more than one of these cafes. This might have been fun for you, but it's hard work for us to hire and re-hire, train and re-train."

I'd wanted to ask him about getting some extra shifts during March Break, which started on Saturday, but talking him to just then had sapped that desire away in a heartbeat. The guy was an A-hole, pure and simple.

I called Ali as soon as I got home, saying sorry for yesterday and telling her that I was going to stop working at the coffee shop. She thanked me for the apology, but didn't say much else until I told her about quitting my job; that made her feel better than me fessing up for being an idiot.

"I'm proud of you, Justin," she said. "It was hurting you and, I don't know, warping your personality in some weird way. It was better to leave now than keep letting that place drain your soul."

Math was our last class before March Break. Fifty minutes of Mr. Ingersoll's going on about numbers and angles and degrees was all that stood between me and a fourteen-day holiday. Freedom was so close I could smell it. He started things off by cracking a joke: "Yesterday, a student whom I will not name sauntered by the Teachers' Lounge and asked for me. When I got to the door, you know what he asked me?" Mr. Ingersoll's mouth twitched. Nobody moved. Not even Mitchell looked interested. "He asked...is General Calculus a Roman war hero?"

Blank stares.

Keith yawned.

"Yes, well, we should get started. I have your latest tests marked," he continued, pulling out a stack of papers. Most teachers kept our stuff neatly arranged in binders and folders. Not Mr. Ingersoll. He just threw everything in together and read out the name on each test paper in a monotone voice.

I was hoping against hope here. *No whammies...no whammies...no whammies,* I said to myself. I'd passed four math tests in a row and...

...the streak was over. Forty-eight percent.

Stop.

Ugh.

Not exactly the best way to end off the day. Not exactly the ideal way to end the term either, especially as we headed into our final game of the regular season that night. Call it a feeling, but I knew before getting to the arena that my head wasn't into it. More importantly, my heart wasn't into it. We were playing the last place team in our division and we'd already locked up first place. On paper, it was a meaningless game. Still, Mr. Wainwright told us to think of it as the opening round of the playoffs, which started next week, and to play with the same level of intensity.

By the third period I was frustrated and banging my stick against the boards after a bad shift and slamming it against the ice when I missed a scoring chance, like the breakaway I didn't even put on net. Our line had been held scoreless the whole game, which hadn't happened all season. We were losing three-one with five minutes left in the game when everything fell apart. I'd taken a bang-on pass from Keith at the top of the hash marks and sent a laser beam to the low far corner. Their goalie saved it and quickly covered the puck with his glove. I drove the net and tried to sneak my lumber underneath to get the puck free. Admittedly, it was a pretty dumb move, but I was desperate and would do anything to score.

The goalie didn't waste any time giving me a Ron Hextall whack to the back of a leg. Without thinking, I slashed his pads. A thug from the other team lost his marbles and punched me square in the face mask. I threw down my stick and went at him even though he was way bigger and stronger than me. He fended me off easily, dropped his stick and then started punching me—*boom, boom, boom*—with his gloves still on. Although I still had my helmet and cage on, the pummeling hurt and I soon went down.

I don't know exactly how it all unfolded after that and have to rely on the stories I was told in the dressing room later to fill in the gaps, but apparently Keith came in, lifted the goon off me and made short work of punching the guy out. The defenceman sailed off his skates with one punch and landed on his back. When their goalie got into the mix, Timmy Atkinson skated the length of the ice to even the numbers up. That's also when Ryan was the first guy on our team over the boards. Seconds later it was a full-on bench-clearing brawl. Things got so out of control that the referees gave up trying to stop the madness. They ordered the game forfeited and had the lights turned off inside the arena. Only then, with almost forty guys on the ice, everyone paired up with an opposing player, did the fights die down and we made our way off the ice.

Mr. Wainwright tore a new you-know-what out of us in the dressing room, aiming the brunt of his attack on me. He called me selfish and unsportsmanlike. I'd cost us the game, he said. Ali wasn't working that night at the snack bar and I had no desire to stick around, so when I got undressed, Dad and I went straight home, no Slush Puppy in hand.

"Anything on your mind?" he asked casually in the car.

My chin was resting in the palm of my hand as I stared vacantly out the window. "Not.........a.........thing."

"Quite the ending to tonight's game." I said nothing in response. "You know I'm here if you need to talk." I lifted my head off my hand and turned to face him. *You're about as here for me as Mom is*, I wanted to yell. Dad kept his eyes focused on the road. Sleet was coming down hard. "If something's bothering you," he continued, "feel free to get it off your chest. I might not be a model father for the ages, Justin, but I do care about you." He paused. "Everything all right with Ali?"

That set me off.

"Yeah. Ali's fine and I'm fine and life is effing fine, Dad. Everything's just a walk in the park, just perfect. Couldn't be better! Actually, you know what? I'm not okay. I quit my job yesterday and now have no way of buying our food or replacing sticks or going out with Ali. How's that sound?" Dad kept his crap together. "Because you know what? I'd love it if something could go my way right about now. That would be fan-*freaking*-tastic."

"You're feeling sorry for yourself, Justin. That's all this is."

I flipped through a Rolodex of vocabulary Dad had introduced me to over the years—*audacity, blitheness, impudence*—thinking these would be the words to insult him most. But I was seething and couldn't string together a sentence that would describe how upset I was with him. He had no right to say I was feeling sorry for myself when I was taking care of him. As I lowered my window, I breathed in the cool night air, which helped calm me down, if only a little.

"You have a great deal going for you, Justin," Dad said a minute later. "You're a remarkably gifted hockey player and you're *going out* with someone whose face could launch a thousand ships. People should be so lucky to have that much."

He has no right to say that I'm feeling sorry for myself. Absolutely no right.

When we got home and Dad slid the car into PARK, he told me he was going to The Last Resort for a nightcap. I slung my bag over a shoulder and walked away without looking back as he called out after me. "You're better than this, Justin," he said. There was no bitterness or disappointment in his voice. "You come from better stock than the way you're behaving."

I got on the elevator and hit the stupid DOOR CLOSE button with my finger like a machine gun. Upstairs, I threw my hockey bag onto the balcony as pain screamed up the back of my leg where the goalie had slashed me. Limping into the apartment, I poured myself a glass of water and downed it as quickly as Dad can make his golden liquid disappear. Before showering, I called Ali and told her what had happened.

"Hiya," she answered.

"Hey. How was dinner?" Ali had to miss our last game of the regular season so she could go out with her stinking uncle and aunt and cousins.

"Not bad. We went to a new restaurant not far from us, an Italian place that wasn't nearly as deluxe as the one your Dad took us to."

"Great."

"How'd the game go?" Ali was tense as she asked this. She knew I was in a pissy mood.

"I think it fair to say I had the worst game of my life."

"What? What happened?"

"I started a bench-clearing brawl."

"You *what?*"

"I took a cheap shot at the other team's goalie and started World War III." Silence on the other end. "Ali?"

"Yeah, I'm here."

"I got hit hard by one of their players after that and then got ranged out by Mr. Wainwright." More silence. "My leg's in serious pain now because the turdball tried to machete me with his stick."

Dead air. "What were you thinking?"

"I wasn't thinking. That's the point. But," I went on, annoyed at Ali's lack of sympathy, "I was hoping my girlfriend might be a little more understanding. On top of the game being forfeited, the back of my calf now has a massive line across it. I think there's something wrong with my jaw, too."

I could see it all in my mind's eye right now, Ali pacing around her bedroom with the cordless phone, shaking her head in disbelief. "What's gotten into you?"

"Nothing's gotten into me. What's gotten into *you?* What's happened to the Ali who supported me when things—"

"Justin, this isn't you. I thought it was the job at the coffee shop, but there's obviously more than that eating away at you."

"This *is* me, Ali! I haven't changed. You have."

A heavy sigh on her end. "I hope you feel better, Justin, but I've got to go now. Let's talk later on, maybe tomorrow or Sunday."

"Ali, wait. Hold on."

Get a grip, Justin.

"I'm sorry. I'm still riled up from the game and I shouldn't have been so quick to—"

"Just take some time to calm down. We'll talk again in a day or two." When I didn't say anything, Ali added, "Okay?"

"Fine."

"Okay, then. Good night, Justin."

"Right."

Click.

Spring

19

Both teams were fined three grand by the MTHL for the bench-clearing brawl, but there were no suspensions. In the dressing room before our next practice, Mr. Wainwright was pretty pissed with us. "As it stands, we dodged a bullet and we'll start the first round of playoffs next Wednesday with a full squad. But if I ever—and I mean *ever*—see anything like that again, rest assured you won't be playing for the Young Nationals any longer. You'll be kicked off the team faster than you can say Jack Robinson."

After practice, Mr. Wainwright took all the parents aside and told them they needed to write the organization a cheque for a hundred and fifty dollars, the sooner the better. Of course, Dad didn't tell me this. It was Keith who mentioned it later on. When I asked Dad if he'd already paid, he said, "I will most certainly not pay for your ungainly transgression. This is part of growing up, young man: taking responsibility for your actions."

"I don't have that much, though."

"You'll have to find a way to get it now, won't you?"

I'd just made us two bowls of Kraft Dinner and toast for dinner. Dad was eating his with a fork. I had a spoon. Even if I put my last two paycheques together, I'd have less than ninety dollars, and I needed every cent of that to get home from school, replace sticks, and go out with friends.

The thought weighed on me. Would Mr. Wainwright ask me for the money himself? Would he bench me because Dad hadn't paid? If I wasn't so paranoid, I'd have realized Mr. Wainwright would do neither of those things because his focus was on nothing but the playoffs. You'd actually think he wanted to win more than us as we swept that first round. Michael Bolton was healthy again, and he, Keith and I combined for twelve goals and twenty-one assists over those four games. Timmy Atkinson got a few lucky breaks but was otherwise solid in goal. When school started up again at the end of March, we were waiting to see who won the other series in our division.

Going back to school after a day off sucks the big one; after two full weeks at home, you might as well punch a guy in the gut. I'd finished my last shift at Mr. Jerkface's Emporium of Crappy Coffee during March Break and spent the rest of my time off hanging out with Ali, as well as Keith and Rachel, who were now going out, swimming with Jung-ho, and slogging my way through *Great Expectations*.

On Monday morning, Mr. Papadopoulos was making us do push-ups, sit-ups, burpees and every other heinous exercise part of the Canada Fitness Testing program in phys. ed. Guys were dropping like flies, Mr. Papadopoulos shouting, "Come on, *ba-bees*! Push it!" He was overweight and nearly bald, with thin, greasy grey strands dangling from the side of his head. He had a handlebar moustache and was the only teacher to walk around school in sweatpants and a T-shirt all day.

"Do you mind if I grab a drink of water?" I asked. We were in the middle of doing wind sprints and I had to wait for my next heat.

Mr. Papadopoulos was looking at the guys panting up and down the floor. "Hurry back. No loafing."

The water couldn't get into my mouth fast enough. With several litres of H_2O swishing around my belly, I spun around and threw my drenched bangs off my forehead. As my breathing slowed, I looked into the change room. My thoughts wandered while staring through the glass. Pants and blazers and dress shirts were hanging off pegs, which made me think of Ron Cuthbert, the guy whose only mistake had been in keeping the evidence lying around…

…a school of rich kids…

…tons of money just sitting there…

…the bench-clearing brawl fine…

One look left, then right. Not a soul in sight. I was in a trance, like the night I'd woken up and saw the couch on fire. One more peek down the hallway before I popped in the room and rifled through pockets, my heart beating so fast it was making my eardrums ring. Twenties, tens, and fives all got stuffed into the pockets of my shorts. No loose change. Loose change meant rattling, and rattling was evidence.

I was about to return to the gym when I thought it would be smarter to leave the money in my dress pants. Then I considered the fact they might search us in our uniforms on the way out. Panicky, I turned towards the shower stall area. There were a bunch of plastic white cases on each of the chrome soap holders. I grabbed one and stuffed the money inside. After poking my head out into the hallway, I made sure the coast was still clear, then lifted the back of a toilet in the bathroom and dropped the container inside, convinced I'd have a heart attack by lunchtime.

shame

noun

1. the painful feeling arising from the consciousness of something dishonourable, improper, ridiculous, etc.

Sleep didn't come on Monday night. I just lay in bed, eyes open, ears sensitive to the slightest sound. Dad read on the sofa until really late. I went through a mental shopping list of words that described how I felt. It had started with shame, which I'd looked up and seen highlighted, and continued on with guilt, self-loathing, and disgust. When the phone had rung during dinner, I didn't answer it. Dad wasn't in the habit of picking it up anymore, so when it went silent he asked, "Something rotten in the state of Denmark?"

"Nope. All's good, Hamlet." I took a bite of the pizza I'd bought in the frozen food section earlier.

Dad grinned. "You're getting much better at this, though it was Marcellus, and not our mentally frail Danish prince, who deserves credit for the quip." I shoveled a piece of the cardboard-tasting pizza into my mouth. Dad put his knife and fork down and lit a smoke. He exhaled through his nose and used a fingernail to get at something in his teeth. I was working my way through slice number four when Dad asked if something had happened at school today.

The hairs on the back of my neck stood on end. "No. Why? Did the school phone here?"

"Should they have?"

"No." My mind scrambled to say something that would get Dad off this topic. "That was probably Ali calling and I didn't really feel like talking to her."

"Trouble in paradise?"

"Nope."

"How is the lovely Ali by the way?"

"Fine and dandy."

"Pass on my regards next time you speak with her, will you?"

"Yep."

Dad stubbed out his cigarette and said he was off to The Last Resort. On his way out the door, he turned towards me and said, "Justin?"

"Yeah?" I was sitting on the bed and looking over my notes from a worm dissection we'd done in science class.

"Guilt…" he said, holding the door open a fraction as the pencil fell out of my hand. "Guilt takes many forms in people. What most fail to realize is that it can serve a higher purpose, a greater function, than merely impeding us as the weight of the heavens bear down upon our shoulders. I just want you to know that I am trying to be a better father to you, even if it appears I sometimes lose my way."

"Sure."

"We all have the power and the ability to do the right thing, and that's precisely what I want to do with you. We all need a helping hand from time to time, and as François-Marie Arouet once opined, 'Appreciation is a wonderful thing: it makes what is excellent in others belong to us as well'."

The phone rang.

"That's probably Ali," I said, getting up and walking over to the desk.

"Don't forget to pass on my best."

"Right."

The lights were off when Dad got home. I was in bed, alert, one part of my brain absorbing the guilt of what I'd done in phys. ed., the other part working through how the hell to fix it. All told, I'd taken two hundred and five dollars, more than I needed for the fine. Obviously I wanted to keep it, but knowing it was sitting in my knapsack made me feel sick to my stomach.

My eyes may have been shut when the alarm went off at seven-thirty, but I wasn't sleeping. After taking a quick shower and wolfing down a bowl of Rice Krispies, I went downstairs. On the ride to school, I kept to myself. Keith said I was acting like a freak. Lorraine told him to leave me alone.

Before heading to homeroom, I went down to the basement and left the soap container, all two hundred and five dollars inside it, at the foot of Mr. Papadopoulos's door.

When my birthday rolled around two days later, everyone was still going on about the Revenge of Ronnie C. Mr. Jenkins asked us to come forward if we knew anything about the theft. So far, no one had said a thing. Later that night I asked Mr. Wainwright if we could speak in private before the opening game of our second round playoff series.

"Sure. What's up, Justin?"

"I was wondering, ah, is there any way I could pay the fine in, like, installments or something?"

"What are you talking about?"

"For the fight. The brawl. The hundred and fifty dollars."

"Justin, it's already been dealt with. All the parents have paid." I had a blank look on my face. "Mrs. Fraser wrote the organization a cheque for three hundred dollars."

"Oh."

"I thought she told you."

"Yeah. No, I'm sure I forgot. No big deal."

"Good. Now, can we focus on tonight?"

"Yeah, of course."

"Give 'em hell out there, all right?"

"Okay."

I started walking to the dressing room when Mr. Wainwright called out to me. He'd craned his neck halfway around without turning his body. "Give the boys something to fight for tonight. Make sure they know what's at stake."

Guys were a lot more serious while getting dressed than they'd been all season. I didn't feel the same pressure as the last time Mr. Wainwright had asked me to give a "pep talk." I knew exactly what I wanted to say. Skid Row's newest single was playing on Ryan's ghetto blaster. Feeling relaxed and at ease with myself, I slid my socks and shin pads on, telling everyone that tonight was game seven. Yes, it was technically the first one in a best-of-seven series, but we needed to treat it like the end of the world. "If we lose tonight," I said, "our season's over. We can call it a day right here, not bother coming to the rest of the games. Personally, I'd like to stick around and show these punks what they're up against." There weren't any cheers or laughs or punching of pads. My teammates—my friends—finally got it. "And no stupid penalties," I added. "Let's just do what we do best: put the puck in the net, don't let it in our own, and keep our sticks on the ice all the time."

By the end of first period, it was three-two for the good guys; four-two by the end of the second period; and five-two when the final buzzer went at the end of the game.

"Your five assists tonight were flawless," Dad said on our way back to the apartment. "Perhaps the best of your season."

I had an orange Slushie in one hand, though Ali hadn't served it to me; she'd been in the stands watching with Dad. She'd quit her job a couple of weeks ago because it wasn't only cutting into time with us but time with the girls. We'd made up since our fight on the weekend. As I was quickly learning, being in a relationship was hard. In between the highs of spending time together, sharing laughs, kissing, rounding bases, and holding hands was a whole minefield of arguments and fights and disagreements. There were apologies done in person and over the phone. Occasionally there were tears and frustration and annoyance. It was kind of overwhelming when you thought about it, but then I'd do something as simple as see Ali in the stands and be reminded why it was all worth it. Even though I didn't get a goal that night, she cheered harder for me than anyone else there.

After the game, Ali was waiting with Dad, Rachel, and Lorraine. Ali had on a blue beret and matching blue jacket, and in my opinion looked pretty damn hot. "Hiya," she said when I came through the door of the dressing room hallway and stepped into a lobby swimming in cigarette smoke.

"Hey."

"Terrific game, Justin," Lorraine said.

"Thanks."

"Yeah. You played really good," Rachel added.

"Whatever. They shouldn't have got those two goals." It was one thing to be complimented by Lorraine. There was no way I was taking any of that from one of Ali's best friends.

"Do you know if my adorable son will be joining us anytime soon?"

"Yeah. He'll be here shortly."

Outside, the girls hugged as they said goodbye. Lorraine was giving Rachel a lift home and Ali was coming with Dad and me. Even though it was a short drive to her place, you could tell Dad was out-of-his-mind happy to have this much time with my girlfriend. They talked the whole ride as I kept quiet in the front seat and didn't involve myself with the conversation. Even when we'd dropped Ali off, I was still zoned out and staring at the passing scenery.

"The Great One would have been envious of your performance tonight," Dad said as he blew out a cloud of smoke.

"Thanks."

"Ali's quite your cheerleader, you know."

"Yeah."

"I was thinking we might go out for a bite to eat again. Not right away, of course. No rush. It doesn't have to be this weekend." Dad was trying hard not to push my buttons and it wasn't lost on me. "Perhaps before summer looms her sepulchral shadow?"

"Okay." I wasn't exactly dying to go out for a meal and watch Dad put on the Rick Maloney Show again, but knew it would mean a lot to him and to Ali.

"By the way, Bill invited me out to Milton this Saturday. Apparently Portuguese bullfighting is quite *du jour* out there these days. From what I gather, it's the same as the Spanish version, except they don't kill the bull. Rather civilized, I'd say. Whatever the case, we will have the opportunity to watch Iberian *hombres* in boleros and bicome hats dance around thousand-pound beasts."

"Huh? Bill who?"

"You remember Bill Lafayette, don't you?"

"The guy you did Europe with?"

"Indeed, and he's asked me to come and spend some time on his pastoral estate. We'll take in the *obra espectacular* on Saturday afternoon and then, I'm sure, retire to his farm and excavate memories old enough to be housed in a museum. I'm going to stay there for the night and return Sunday. Do you think you can hold down the fort for the duration of your father's absence?"

"When exactly are you leaving?" The wheels were spinning in my mind and coming up with ideas about how I could take advantage of a whole night with the apartment to myself.

"Well, I need to be out there by two o'clock," Dad said as we pulled into the apartment's parking lot. Upstairs, I hopped in the shower, but when I came out of the washroom to change into some fresh clothes the lights were off in the apartment.

"Oh, man. What gives? Did the power go out?"

A single candle was burning at the other end of the room, on top of the desk. It took me a second to figure out it was planted in the centre of a cake.

"Happy birthday, Justin," Dad said from across the room.

I slipped a T-shirt over my head that was missing its old three-sheets-of-Bounce smell to it and walked towards him. "Dad, you didn't have to do this."

"'Tis true, but then what kind of father would I be if I forgot my son's birthday?"

"Thanks," I said in a quiet voice. "What kind of cake is it?"

"Chocolate with vanilla icing."

My favourite as a kid.

Dad was breaking my heart, but the truth was that I'd lost my sweet tooth a while ago and now rarely ate chocolate. Potato chips were *obviously* a superior food group, most definitely when they were salt & vinegar or ketchup, but chocolate just didn't do it for me anymore.

"I also went downstairs while you were in the shower and picked up some milk. Two percent is what you always drink, is it not?"

"It is."

On each side of the desk was a paper towel folded over, a fork on top, and a small plate beside it. Dad cut two slices, a ginormous one for me and a small piece for himself. We sat down and he proposed a toast, raising his glass as he said, "Pride is a curious thing. The Church calls it a sin, a Deadly Sin, which, I suppose, is all the more reason to discredit those Luddites. But I digress. There is nothing in this world as breathtakingly miraculous and poignant as a father's pride in and of his son. Despite my shortcomings as a parent, Justin, not a day goes by that I don't acknowledge my good fortune, and feel eternally grateful for being the luckiest father in the world."

We clinked glasses and the two of us ate as Dad entertained me with stories about past birthdays of mine: hiring a magician who ended up making some of Mom's jewellery mysteriously "disappear" by the time he left our house on my fifth birthday; taking me and my friends to Canada's Wonderland for my eighth birthday, Mom so scared she refused to go on a single ride; and Mom making a "money cake" for my tenth birthday. He actually smiled at the last story when he got to the part about Keith chomping down on a quarter wrapped in aluminum foil and chipping a tooth. "Lorraine certainly had words for your mother that afternoon!" Dad laughed, clapping his hands before lighting a cigarette, half of his cake still uneaten. I remembered parts of each story he told, but I wasn't exactly hanging on his every word. What surprised me, and captured more of my attention, was that he was mentioning Mom without tearing her down or making fun of her.

As Dad went on, every bite became a real effort, the sugar killing my teeth. All I knew was I had to get through it. When I'd finally grinded my way through the last of the slice, I rubbed my belly and said, "That was amazing. Thanks a lot." Dad looked *almost* as happy at that moment as he did when he was with Ali. He leaned back in his chair, a cigarette and drink balancing his centre of gravity while the light from the candle made our profiles dance, glitter almost, against the balcony windows.

"Close your mouth, McFly. You're catching flies. Hel*lo*? Ali stood at the door of the apartment with a sizeable bag in her hand. "Can I come inside?"

"Oh, yeah. Sure."

She glided in, as if on skates. Although she didn't have any makeup on, she looked as amazing as she had the day we went out for lunch with Dad. She'd even done that thing with her hair where she curled the ends.

"What?" she said, taking a seat on the bed.

"You look hot."

"Will you stop it! I look like I do every day. Anyway, we have lots to do tonight, the first of which is to order some food. Is there anything you want, because it's my treat."

"Ali, we can split it. It's fine."

"Nope. This one's a done deal. Now out with it. What do you feel like?"

In the kitchen, I went searching through a couple of drawers before finding what I was looking for. Whenever restaurants would leave one of their menu flyers in the crack of the door, Dad would put it with the rest of them and not give it a second thought. After pulling out a handful of them, Ali and I sat on the bed, cross-legged and facing each other. We went through them and told each other what each one delivered: pizza, chicken, ribs, pizza, pizza, shawarmas and falafels (whatever those were), pizza, Chinese, pizza...

"Oh, man. It's been, like, forever since I've had Chinese food," I commented.

"Chinese it is, then. Here," Ali said, patting the bed with a hand. "Come sit beside me so we can look at the menu together. What have you usually gotten in the past?"

"I don't know. A spicy beef dish maybe? Some chicken, not like the kind we have but, you know, with a crusty outside. I'm not sure, really. My mom always ordered for us in the past."

"Don't worry. One advantage about having a mom who doesn't cook is all the delivery and take-out experience you get."

We decided on hot and sour soup, Szechuan beef, almond soo guy, and some vegetable fried rice. I called the order in and painstakingly repeated the phone number and address to the woman on the phone, Ali giggling away in the background. They said it would take forty-five minutes.

"Now that we have that done," Ali said excitedly, "you have to open your gift." Ali put her legs underneath her and slid over, tapping the bed in the spot where she wanted me to sit.

"What did you get me?"

"*Well, I could tell you. Then again, you could open it yourself and find out.*"

I flipped my hair over. "Nice."

"Thought you'd like that one. Keep in mind," she went on, "this is only the first of two presents."

"What's the second one?" I asked as I tore the wrapping paper off.

"All in good time."

Inside a small white rectangular box was a miniature photo album. Every page held a single picture, each one a shot from my hockey games. I recognized the first one, a breakaway I'd had near the beginning of the season. There were more after that, mostly of me, but some of other players like Keith and Michael Bolton. Cover to cover, the album was filled with a highlight reel from the year.

"Do you like it?" she asked in a doubtful voice.

I put my hands on her cheeks and kissed her, slowly. "I love it. You're going to kill me with these presents of yours, though. They're too much."

"Hold on," she said, grabbing me by the arm. She kissed me on the lips again, woodpecker style, then once more. "Gotta be three," she said and smiled.

"How did you ever track down all these pictures?"

"I can't tell you that!"

"Seriously, when were you ever at one of our games with a camera?"

"A girl's got to have her secrets." Unable to figure out how she'd pulled this off, I shook my head. "Listen, why don't you find us a show or a movie to watch on TV while I poke around the kitchen and get us something to munch on?"

"There's not much in there, but go ahead."

"Boy, you weren't kidding," Ali said a minute later as I heard a cupboard door being shut.

"Nope."

Twenty-eight channels into my search, I found *Ferris Bueller's Day Off*.

"Hey, can we have some of your Dad's stash?"

"Uhh…I think he'd notice if any of it was missing."

"Justin, it's your birthday! Replace it with water later on and he won't know the difference."

"Ahh…"

She came back to the bed.

Dimples. Pouty face. A kiss on the lips.

Done and *done*.

Ali went back to the kitchen and returned with two glasses full of golden liquid and ice. "Do you mind if I do a crossword while we watch TV?" she asked, taking a seat beside me on the bed.

"Of course not."

Ali didn't really like doing one thing at a time, whether watching television or doing homework. We were lucky because we'd caught the movie right near the beginning. Ferris was outside the school, standing in front of Cameron's Ferrari and waiting for a very cute Mia Sara to cruise down the school steps and plant one on "Daddy's" lips when Ali said, "Cheers, by the way."

"Cheers."

"Happy birthday, babe."

We clinked glasses and I was still coughing from the rocket fuel burning my throat when Ali asked if I knew a four-letter word for "snob." It took me a minute to answer because my throat had seized up. When I trusted myself to speak again, a warm sensation ran through my body. "Does 'prig' work?"

Ali went across the spaces in the puzzle with her pen. "That totally works! Look at you! Okay, one more I can't get. Sorry," she said all of a sudden. "Am I taking you away from the movie?"

"No, it's fine. I've already seen it. Fire away."

"Not that you'd know this one because this is a totally brutal clue, but three down is a ten-letter word for Hitler's plan to invade Russia."

A smile cropped up on my face and I laughed.

"I know. Brutal, right?"

"Barbarossa," I said, not believing Dad's love of talking about World War II had actually proven useful for once.

Ali traced the letters over the squares and then exclaimed, "Ahh! You're so right! You're officially my new crossword hero."

We were on our second drink by the time the food arrived, not forty-five minutes later but closer to ninety minutes after I'd placed the order. Ali paid the guy while I took out all the cardboard boxes from the bags in the kitchen. Over dinner we put the TV on low and talked about Keith and Rachel. Although it was cool to have our best friends going out, it was also kind of like having your twin brother going out with your girlfriend's twin sister. When I asked Ali if she thought they made a good couple, she gave it a moment's thought, then said they got along fine most of the time but that Keith's temper worried her.

"He's harmless," I told her, feeling the need to defend my best friend. "He's like a baby tiger."

"Maybe with your friends, but girls don't like aggressive guys, especially overly aggressive ones."

It kind of irritated me she thought that way about Keith, but we'd had too many fights in the last few weeks to make a big deal of it so I dropped the subject. I think both of us could sense it wasn't the best conversation to get into as we made our way through the never-ending beef and chicken and rice.

At the end of the meal (with more than half the food left over), Ali pulled out the two fortune cookies included in our meal, put one in each hand, and asked me "Left or right?"

"Right."

"Why right?"

"I don't know. It's my default answer. I scored my very first goal in the upper right-hand corner and that was how I learned the difference between left and right. You know how some people have a go-to number? Well, I have a go-to side."

"You're weird," she said handing me a fortune cookie. "Okay, you open yours first," she went on, giddy.

I cracked the stale cookie in half and reached inside for a piece of paper. Maybe it was a girl thing, but Mom always got excited about this part of Chinese meals as well. "All right. Are you ready?" I announced, clearing my throat.

"Absolutely."

"*It is better to make mistakes in kindness than work miracles in unkindness.*"

"That's beautiful!"

"Yeah." I guess the place we used to order from had a different bakery they used because our fortunes used to give lame advice like *Life is a puzzle which must be solved* and *The early bird catches the biggest worms.*

"Okay. My turn. Yay for me!" Ali exclaimed, raising an arm in the air. She carefully split the cookie in the middle and removed her fortune: "*Now is the time to make circles with mints, do not haste any longer.*"

"What the?"

Ali broke out laughing so hard she fell over on her side. "Quick! Where are the mints?" she asked me, sitting up again.

"I don't have any mints."

"Kidding! That is the best fortune ever. The next time I'm in trouble I'll remember to have mints on me so I can make circles with them."

I got up to put away the leftovers when Ali asked if we could listen to some music.

"I don't have a tape deck, though."

"On the record player, dummy."

"Oh. Sure. The records are—"

"—below the desk. I'm not blind, you know." She took her time scanning the titles of the albums. "Everything in your Dad's collection is from the Stone Ages," she said a minute later.

"He's kind of old-fashioned." I was in the kitchen, washing our greasy orange dishes in lukewarm water.

By the time all the plates and cutlery were clean and put away, Ali had finally found something. We took a seat on the floor together, the TV on mute, as we listened to "Whole Lotta Love."

"Nice choice," I said.

"Thanks."

"That's got to be my dad's most recent record by at least a hundred years."

We were on our third drinks and I was definitely feeling the effects, my body a little numb all over.

"Say, do you think we could finish the crossword we started before dinner?" It was a Monday *New York Times* puzzle we were doing, Ali explained, and she'd never finished one. "Without cheating, that is," she added.

As "What Is and What Should Never Be" came on, Ali filled in the last squares and shrieked. "Ah! You totally made this happen." She leaned over and gave me a really sexy kiss, her mouth warm with alcohol. "Have I ever told you how cute you are by the way?"

"Who, me?"

Laughing, we fell to the floor, her warm skin pressed up against mine. "Oh, wait," she said, her face directly above mine. "Do you want your second present now?"

"Sure."

"It's not very big, and it cost, like, a dollar. Is that okay?"

"Ali, I don't care how much it cost or how big it is." She reached for her bag and pulled it closer. When I saw what she was holding in her hand, my heart stood still for a moment.

Oh…my…freaking…God…

Tremors began racing up my arms. "I wanted our first time to be special," she whispered, kissing me again. "Hey, are you okay?"

"Yep."

"I just thought this was what you wanted."

"Totally."

Dimples.

"Should we maybe move over to the bed?"

"Uh-huh."

We got under the covers and peeled off our clothing, one layer at a time, until Ali was in her bra and panties, the condom on the floor beside us. Ali unclipped her bra and guided my hand to her panties, which I took off while holding my breath. All that was left between us were my boxers.

"Hold on," I said. "Give me a second."

"Where are you going?"

"I've gotta take a leak."

I grabbed the domer off the floor. Inside the washroom, which I'd locked, I took the vial of propranolol and tried to shake out a pill. Three popped into my unsteady hand. Even though I wasn't supposed to take more than two at a time, this was an exception if ever there was one. After a nervous pee (almost nothing came out), I tore open the condom and looked at it like a piece of moon rock. I'd never put one on and couldn't figure out how you did it. Was it supposed to go down to up or up to down? The thing was flat and there were no instructions on the stupid thing.

If I put it on the wrong way, would Ali get pregnant?

"Are you coming back, babe?" Ali asked from the bed.

"Yep. Give me two secs." I could hear "The Lemon Song" playing from the living room.

Although the ring at the top was dry, the inside was smooth and wet. My boner wasn't the problem; it was sliding the dumb thing on that proved, well, hard. When I finally walked out of the bathroom, I turned out the lights and slid under the sheets beside Ali.

"Are you okay?"

"Yeah."

"You're shaking, babe. Are you okay?"

"Just a little chilly."

"This is what you want, right?"

"Absolutely."

I placed a hand on her cheeks and could feel an indentation beside her lips. Only when on top of Ali did I realize the condom wasn't as smooth on the outside as it was on the inside, and so had trouble getting my thing in. Ali must have thought I was having a seizure because my body wouldn't stop shaking.

"Ow," she said, moving her hips against my trembling legs.

Now my stiffy wasn't as stiff and this freaked me out.

Would I even be hard enough to do this?

That messed with my confidence. Then I got self-conscious about the tremors and about pleasing Ali and about coming across as a total failure in the sack. Planting my hands on either side of her head, I raised myself up, and tried entering her again. "Does it hurt? Should I stop?"

Ali moaned, but not in the good way you hear girls do it in porns. "No, it's okay. Just go slow."

"Okay. Tell me if it hurts, though, okay" I went on as "Thank You" started playing on the record player.

When I eventually got inside her, I was blown away with pleasure and fear and tremors and excitement. I was doing it! *We* were doing it! And then, just like that, it was over. I'd watched pornos with Keith and saw guys go forever and in a hundred positions. We'd done it missionary style and I'd lasted all of a few seconds. Ali disappeared into the bathroom afterwards, water running the whole time. I flew into the kitchen, took off the condom and buried it deep in the trash. I used some Sunlight to wash my hands and the gross crap from the domer still on me down there. Before getting back in bed, I flipped the album over and "Heartbreaker" started playing. When we were under the covers again, I asked Ali if everything was all right. She said yes and then rolled over on her side as she slid against me. My mouth resting on her ear, I asked her how long she could stay out for tonight.

"I told my mom I was sleeping over at Debbie's."

"So..."

"Exactly."

We talked a bit before we fell asleep, though neither one of us brought up what we'd just done. I was still kicking myself for how bad I'd been and how much my girlfriend must think she was with a loser. As we both started fading—Ali in my arms, her hair on my face, my hands on her chest, her legs wrapped around mine, her breathing one with mine—she said, "Justin?"

"Yeah?"

"Can I tell you something?"

"Of course."

In a sleepy voice, she whispered, "I adore you."

20

This must be why people get married.

When I opened my eyes on Sunday, Ali's body was warm against mine. We were like Lego pieces fit perfectly together, just as we'd gone to sleep, her back to my chest. I didn't move a muscle, scared it would wake Ali and this moment would be over. With an arm under her neck, pins and needles shooting up and down it, I had the other one on her shoulder. Her eyes were puffy and trying hard to stay open when she did wake up and turn to face me.

"Morning," I said.

She kept her eyes lowered as she brought her arms together and put them on my chest. Then the snuggling began.

"Morning."

Her head between my shoulder and neck, she rubbed up against it a few times.

"Good sleep?"

"Uh-huh."

It wasn't long before we were asleep again. The next time we woke up it was almost noon. I asked Ali if she was hungry.

"Just a little."

"Well, we have cereal, cereal and cereal here." I was about to climb out of bed when she said, "Hold on, Justin. Can I ask you something about last night first?" Her back was to my chest, her face towards the wall.

Gulp.

"Sure."

"You were shaking so much. Did you really…did you really enjoy it?"

"That had nothing to do with you."

"What do you mean?"

Only Mom and Dad knew about my essential tremor. Like my vocabulary, it was something I was too embarrassed to tell anyone. "Have you ever heard of something called ET?" I said.

"The movie?"

"No!" I said, laughing. "But I guess you're right. Spielberg has ruined my chances of ever saying 'ET' again without people thinking I'm from another planet."

Ali wasn't laughing. She just lay there, waiting for an explanation, which I gave her a second later. When I was done telling her about my condition, she asked if that's what had caused me to shake so much in bed last night.

"Basically, yeah."

"So it wasn't me? I didn't gross you out?"

"No! My God, no! You were…you were…perfect. It was me who was a total spaz."

There it is, Ali, your window, you're opportunity to tell me I wasn't a complete and utter dweeb with you; that I didn't let you down; that you got some tiny pleasure from it; that you wouldn't make fun of me to your friends tomorrow at school.

"Okay." A moment later she added, "So what kind of cereal do you have?"

Deflated, I said, "Rice Krispies and Frosted Flakes."

"I'll take some Rice Krispies."

Over bowls of Snap, Crackle and Pop!, we went over our plans for the day, the homework we had to get done, and how much it sucked we had to go to school tomorrow. She asked what time Dad would be back and I told her it probably wouldn't be until the afternoon. Our conversation was almost like one of those she'd described to me that her parents had on a daily basis, where nothing was actually *talked* about.

On her way out the door later, something felt off. Ali had her hair in a ponytail and looked as if she were somewhere else, kind of like how she was on Christmas Eve. She kissed me once at the door and told me I didn't need to walk her down.

"But I want to walk you down."

"It's okay. Really. Go back inside."

"Sure," I said, uncertain what was going on.

Tell me I wasn't a total dipstick last night. Tell me I didn't let you down.

"Ali?"

"Yeah?"

There was a blank look on her face.

"Nothing. Have a good day. Call me later, okay?"

"Sure."

No dimples. A forced smile.

Frustrated and confused, I threw myself on the bed and tried to make sense of why Ali was acting this way. I had tons of homework to catch up on, but I didn't have the energy or the desire to start it. I watched a movie on TV instead. Halfway through, I lay down for a nap. It was only the sound of keys rattling at the door that woke me up.

"A midafternoon's dream, Eris?" Dad asked as he put his bag down and struggled to get his keys out of the lock. I rolled over and faced him. "A siesta, as it were?"

I rubbed the sand out of my eyes. "How was the bullfight?"

"None of the matadors had to be taken to the hospital and the bulls lived to see another day. All in all, a successful outing for everyone involved."

Dad walked to the kitchen, animated and in good spirits. A second later, he came my way, a nearly empty bottle in his hand. "Would you care to explain this?"

"What do you mean?" I asked stupidly.

"This!" Dad said, raising the bottle higher. "What gives you the right to think you can do this?" He was getting angrier as he went on. "Aside from the fact that you are a minor, you had no business going into my personal belongings."

"Sorry."

"Don't be sorry. Get out of bed and face your father." I got up and stood in my boxers and a T-shirt. "The liquor store is closed on Sundays, Justin." A purple vein on the side of his neck was throbbing. I didn't say anything. He shook his head and came closer. "I'm extremely disappointed in you."

I was about to apologize again when he slapped me hard across the face. "What the hell was that for?" I stammered.

"For being an insolent and ungracious son."

Dad had never hit me. Although my cheek stung, I wasn't going to show him it hurt. For some reason, it was more upsetting that I'd disappointed him. He was always proud of me. Even when I showed him a pathetic report card, he'd point out how happy he was at my English and history marks, ignoring the less-than-stellar numbers beside math, science and French.

Fighting hard not to let any tears fall, I raised a trembling finger. "Don't you ever touch me again."

Dad turned, headed for the kitchen and poured himself a drink. I got dressed and left the apartment, not saying where I was going; he didn't bother asking either. It must have been one or two degrees out. Rain fell lazily, with puddles all over the stupid streets and sidewalks.

Lorraine answered the door when I got to Keith's and threw an arm around one of my shoulders, telling me to take a hot shower downstairs. She didn't kick up a fuss and make the situation awkward. She just said, "I'll have Keith bring down some things for you to change into."

"Thanks." I didn't have the heart to look at her.

Downstairs, I was shivering after removing the last of my clothes. The steaming hot water fixed that soon enough. Lorraine bought shower gels like the ones Mom did, which, although a little fruity, did smell amazing. I must've been in there a while because all of a sudden Keith was pounding on the door.

"You almost done in there, dirtbag?"

I turned off the water, wrapped a thick red towel around my waist, and unlocked the door.

"What, were you parking a trout in there or something?"

"You're gross."

"Yeah, well, you ever thought of working on your pecs? You look like that faggy little dude in *Mike Tyson's Punch-Out!!*"

"It's called being lanky," I said, closing the door in Keith's face.

While Keith and I played Ping-Pong, my clothes were tumbling away in the dryer. Lorraine had offered to do them for me, but something about Keith's mom handling my wet boxers made me want to upchuck. So, just before we hit the Ping-Pong table, I threw my crap in her high-tech machine (the ones in Dad's apartment building were probably built when that May Tag guy was still a kid) and added three sheets of Bounce for good measure.

Keith and I were rallying for serve, neither one of us saying much, when I slammed a shot into his body.

"What the hell!"

"Sorry," I said, not doing anything to hide my grin. "I'm sure *your* pecs can handle it, though."

It was my serve to begin the game, with Keith taking the first point. We had totally different styles of play. I sliced and spun every ball I could. Occasionally, I'd hit a top-spin if I had an easy shot sent my way. Keith, however, was all about the power. He literally stood behind the table, arms down by his side, waiting to slug the ball. After I won the second point, he asked if everything was cool. I sliced a backhand down the right-hand side of the table and told him things were fine.

"How was your date last night?" he asked, returning my shot like he was swinging for the fences.

"You know..." I missed the ball and felt my cheeks flush.

"Yeah? What *exactly* do I know? Hey," he said suddenly, "it's three-two. My serve, J.R."

I tossed him the ball.

"You know, like, we had, you know, a good time."

"Like you had a good time getting up her shirt or like you had a good time trying to fix your broken balls?"

I landed a sweet topspin. Keith swung and missed.

"Nice shot, dick. Anyway," he continued, serving into the net. "Did Ali put out or what?"

"First of all, Ali doesn't 'put out'. Second of all, she's my girlfriend. Have a little class. Now, are you going to serve again and double fault for me, please?" I took the point and when he served again I added, "and, yes, to answer your question, we, you know, we...got...you know..."

Crap. Keith could see right through me.

My best friend didn't bother returning the shot when it hit his side. He grabbed the ball out of the air, laid his paddle on the table and walked over to me. Putting one of his hands on the side of my neck, he tried to look me in the eye. My face burned a shade of fire-engine red.

"Are you telling me you guys did it? Holy shit! You guys actually did it!"

"Boys!" Lorraine yelled from upstairs. "Dinner's ready."

"You're unbelievable."

Lorraine made spaghetti and meatballs with homemade garlic bread. A simple dish by her standards, it was Victoria's favourite so she was all smiles. Put another way, Keith's sister didn't complain once during the meal. Afterwards, Lorraine offered to drive me back. On the ride to Dad's apartment, Lorraine asked me a few questions about life at home with Dad these days. She knew firsthand how bad he looked, physically at least, because they saw each other at every game. When we pulled up to the apartment, it was still raining. Budding leaves were being blown off the trees and swept down the street towards the gutter, where a bunch of them had already started to clog it up.

"I know how much you love books, Justin, and, ah…Anyway, I was at the bookstore the other day and thought you might like this."

She handed me a copy of *The Apprenticeship of Duddy Kravitz*, explaining how she'd loved it as a teenager. "Have you read it by any chance?"

"No."

"Well, let me know what you think of it when you're done."

"Sure."

While riding the elevator up, panic set in. Dad had been pretty crooked when I'd left and I couldn't imagine what was waiting for me. To my shock, he was actually in a good mood, jazz music playing in the background.

"How was the evening?" he asked when I walked in. He looked at me as he put his book down, took a haul from his cigarette and stubbed it out.

"Good. I went over to Keith's and played a little Ping-Pong. How was your night? Did you have dinner yet?"

"No, I had a very filling lunch at Peter's. However, the night has been extraordinary. I've been reposing here on the sofa for the last few hours, working through a delightful account of how Japan lost the war. Fascinating, really. This author is doing a magnificent job of showing how Emperor Hirohito's inner circle of military advisors manipulated information coming in from the front to then manipulate the emperor himself." He lit another cigarette. "Did you know that the Japanese navy and army couldn't agree on a shared secret code or even what to tell each other? The same armed forces and they couldn't agree on how to help each other as the entire country was being decimated!"

This was like being told you had to go to detention and the teacher says how happy they are to see you. *Please, have a seat. Let's reminisce about the good times!*

"What do you have in your hands there?" Dad said, changing gears.

"This? Just a book."

"Indeed. Does it have a title?"

I told him what Lorraine had given me.

"Ah, yes! Mr. Richler is a literary auteur whom I'm sure you'll enjoy."

"Anyway, I should do some homework. Oh, hey," I said, struck with a thought. "Did Ali phone?"

"I'm afraid not."

"Right. Well, I guess I'll, you know, get down to studying."

Dad raised his feet on the chair and took a swig from his drink. The strangest part is that it wasn't golden in colour. It was see-through, almost like…water.

21

Jung-ho had finally learned how to get around the shallow end without her inflatable arm thingies and not touch the bottom with her toes. What she did was a mix between the doggy paddle and treading water. One minute her legs were near the surface, the next they were almost touching the bottom. Her arms would be going side to side, then just as suddenly they were pawing at the water as she tried to get her legs up higher.

Later, while drying off, I told her she'd already come a long way and should be super proud of herself.

"But I want to *really* swim, Justin. All by myself in the deep end," she said matter-of-factly.

"You will one day. I promise."

Jung-ho stuck out her hand. "Fine," I said, exhaling loudly, our palms making the photocopy.

On the way down in the elevator, she asked me how Dad had liked his present. "What present?"

"Daddy gave him a gift on Sunday. He visited our apartment." I asked Jung-ho what she was talking about. "Your father asked for alcohol from Daddy." Now things began making sense as I put together a chain of events that had Dad so happy when I got home from Keith's on Sunday night. "Daddy gave him a *biiiiig* bottle of soju," Jung-ho went on.

"Soju?" The elevator doors opened and we got off.

"Yes."

On the way to the arena that night, I asked Dad about Mr. Kim's gift. Somehow it felt like he'd taken advantage of my relationship with Jung-ho and her parents to get ahold of booze. As we drove up the ramp to the Gardiner Expressway and headed west, I tried sounding all casual when I asked how the soju was.

"Very powerful. Unlike anything I've tried."

"Really?"

Dad looked over at me, a cigarette in one hand, the steering wheel in the other. "Yes. It was, dare I say, a little like moonshine."

"I guess I'm just wondering, you know, where you might have got that soju if all the liquor stores are closed on Sundays."

Dad rolled down his window. "I visited your little friend's parents. The Kims are very nice people, as it turns out. They invited me into their apartment and we had a drink together. Mrs. Kim heated up some dried squid over a portable burner." Dad chuckled. "With mayonnaise and a fiery red paste on the side!" Grinning, he shook his head and took a drag from his smoke. "Your little friend's mother doesn't speak much English, but Mr. Kim was wonderful. He's very funny and quite engaging. He's also grateful for all the time you've spent with his daughter teaching her how to swim."

"Dad, what gave you the right to use Jung-ho to get what you wanted?"

"I'm not sure I like your tone of voice, Justin. But if you really must know, it's called being neighbourly; neighbours assist one another in times of distress."

"What was your distress?"

Dad kept his eyes on the road, but he knew what I was up to. "Might I remind you, Justin, that you are the reason I had to do this in the first place? If it were not for you and your lovely girlfriend, I would have been content to stay at home all night and not bother a soul."

"Yeah, right."

"And please wipe that smirk off your face, young man. I'm still your father and deserve the respect accorded one's birth parent. In any event, this is neither the time nor the place for such a conversation."

Because you'll get in another car accident?

"I promise you we'll discuss this at a more appropriate time in the future."

"Sure."

"Good, then."

"Right."

Although we won the game seven-three, with Keith, Michael Bolton and I combining for five goals, the mood around the dressing room quickly turned dark when we learned what all the brew-ha-ha had been about towards the end of the third period. Dad had collapsed, Lorraine explained to me on the way to the hospital. He'd been on his feet and giving the refs a hard time when he complained of losing part of the vision in his left eye. Then, without warning, he collapsed and lost consciousness. An ambulance had arrived on the scene and taken Dad to a nearby hospital.

It was my second time in a hospital waiting room, the first time being when Mom had to get stitches to her mouth because she'd been slapped hard by her boyfriend, Ned Payne, the jerkface she'd started seeing after Dad moved out. When the doctor finally came to see us, he introduced himself as Dr. Singh. "I believe your father has suffered a transient ischemic attack, or TIA for short," he explained in his softly accented Indian voice.

"What exactly is that, Doctor?" Lorraine asked.

"In layman's terms, it's akin to a mini-stroke, Mrs. Maloney." Lorraine didn't flinch at the title. "Based on what he's told me, I think he had something called a 'drop attack' and that this TIA occurred at the base of his brain. Now, this could have been more serious and with lifelong damage, but fortunately for him, at this stage I believe he will have little to no long-term problems. He's conscious and reports no irregularities with his vision or any blurriness, which was one of my primary concerns. He also claims to have full sensation in and control over his limbs, which, again, is a very positive sign. That said, I would like to keep him here overnight for observation."

As he said this last part, the look on Dr. Singh's turned to wonder/ awe/jaw-dropping disbelief. Dad was walking in our direction.

"Mr. Maloney, what in heaven's name are you doing?"

"Thank you very much for your assistance, Doctor, but I have no interest spending the night in the hospital and further burdening John Q. Taxpayer."

You could tell Dr. Singh was throttled by Dad's decision. "Mr. Maloney, I cannot stress enough how potentially damaging what you've suffered could be."

"But you yourself said it was a minor TIA, Doctor."

Lorraine jumped into the mix and tried to make Dad see Dr. Singh's point of view. "Rick, it couldn't hurt to spend the night here and just have the doctors one hundred percent sure it was nothing more serious, could it? I'd be happy to drive Justin home. In fact, he could stay over at our place and—"

"Lorraine, thank you for your kind offer, but I really must get home. Work, among other things, beckons."

"Mr. Maloney—"

"Dr. Singh, thank you for everything. You've been nothing short of wonderful. However, my son and I will now be leaving."

Lorraine dropped Dad and me off at the arena. After asking one more time if he was sure she couldn't drive us home and return tomorrow to get the car, Dad said he wouldn't dare impose on her like that.

Back at the apartment, I waited to see if Dad would go out to The Last Resort and I could phone Ali in private. No luck. Dad poured himself a drink, propped his feet up on a chair and opened his book.

"I'm going out for a walk," I told him. "You know, clear my head and all."

"It is lovely outside, isn't it?"

"Yeah. I'll see you in a bit."

I called Ali from a payphone in the mall downstairs. She gasped when I told her the news about Dad. I explained it was something called TIA (I'd already forgotten what the initials stood for), like a mini-stroke, but that the doctor had said Dad should be fine.

"And how are you doing? You must have been pretty shook up."

"Ah, you know," I said, flipping my bangs. The mountains on my forehead had gotten worse lately so I was growing my hair longer. "Same as usual."

"Seriously. Are you dealing with this okay?"

That made me think. "It's hard, you know? He looks so weak and frail these days." I stopped and had a random thought come to me. "I did this project when I was in grade two. It was on leaves. We had to collect a bunch of different ones, find out what kind of tree they came from. That sort of thing. At the end, we had to do a presentation on the stupid things.

"My mom and I went all over the neighbourhood, picking up freaking leaves one Saturday in late October. Or maybe it was early November. Anyway, I taped them all on a huge piece of cardboard. After the presentation, I put the dumb thing away and forgot all about it until Christmas, when I came across it by accident in my bedroom closet. I was going to throw it out, but noticed the leaves looked a lot different from when I'd found them.

"So I peel off the Scotch Tape and the leaves fall to the floor. Thing is, when I went to pick them up, they all disintegrated in my hands.

They were like ashes." I paused, realizing how retarded the story was. "Sorry, I shouldn't be allowed to open my mouth anymore."

"No! Justin, I see what you're saying and I feel awful for you. Honestly."

"You're only trying to make me feel better because I went on and on about frigging leaves."

"No. It's the truth. Cross my heart and hope to die, stick a needle in my eye. You never tell me anything about yourself, from your past, I mean. It's always me talking your ear off about how crazy my parents are, or my stories from camp which, may I point out, I know you hate."

"I don't hate them. Anyway, I guess you think your parents are going to live forever, you know?"

"Yeah."

"Or I did, at least. And then something like this happens and you get scared. It's, like, what would I do if something really bad happened to him? Something that kept him in the hospital for a long time? Or worse, what if—"

"Stop it, Justin. You yourself said he's going to be fine, right?"

"This time, yeah. That's what the doctor said. But I'm thinking… forget it."

"What?"

"It's nothing. I'm just messed up in the head."

"That's totally understandable. And you know I'm here for you no matter what."

"I know."

"Good."

"Listen. I meant to ask you," I went on, hoping to talk about something else. "Are you able to come to the game on Saturday night? We're back at home for the next two games."

"What time's it start?"

"Seven or seven-fifteen. I'll have to check." Saturday was also the ISAA championship tournament for our school team. It was taking place all day in St. Catherines, and assuming we made it to at least the semis (though we'd gone undefeated all season, so it was a good bet we'd make the finals), there was no way Keith and I would make it back to Toronto in time for our game with the Nats. It was going to suck to do, but Keith and I had to tell the coach that we had to skip the tournament.

There was a sigh on Ali's end. "I have plans Saturday night, babe."

"With who?"

"It's Debbie's parents' 25th anniversary and me and all the girls were invited to it. They're having a big to-do at the King Eddy starting at six o'clock. I'll probably be there most of the night."

"So let me get this straight. You're choosing *Debbie* over *me*?"

"I'm not choosing Debbie over anyone, Justin. She's my best friend and her parents really want me and the girls to be there."

"So…Debbie? Really? Debbie of all people?"

"Would you stop it? It's about her parents, not Debbie, and I've been really close with them since forever."

"Right."

"Justin, don't be like this. I know you're going through a lot right now and you're worried about your Dad."

"Really? You know what I'm going through?"

"Justin!"

"Forget it. That's fine. We can talk tomorrow."

"Justin, please—"

Click.

I lifted the phone from its cradle as soon as I'd hung up, inserting a quarter and punching the digits with trembling fingers. The call rang on and on until the stupid answering machine picked up and Mrs. Blake began her monologue: *Hi, you've reached the Blakes. We're not home right now. Please leave a message at the sound of the beep and we'll get back to you as soon as we can. Thank you.*

"Hey, Ali. It's me. Can you call me when you get this?" I was about to apologize, but thought better of it after realizing Mrs. Blake might listen to the message first. "Okay. Great. Thanks. Talk soon. Take care. All right. I'll, ah, you know, I'll be around. Okay. Bye."

Only when I hung up yet again did I put two and two together and realize that if she returned my call right now I wouldn't be home. *Smooth move, Ex-Lax.*

I raced upstairs, but when I asked Dad if anyone had phoned, he said, "All quiet on the Western Front."

"So that's a no?"

Dad didn't look up from his book. "That it is."

I mindlessly watched a TV show until it was time to go to bed. I brushed my teeth and washed up, taking extra time to lather soap all over my forehead. I got under the covers and reached for the novel Lorraine had given me, which made me think of something she'd said while we were in the emergency waiting room. We were told a doctor would be with us soon (Dr. Singh hadn't come out yet) to update us on Dad's condition, when she leaned over and said quietly, "You know, my own father used to tell me that when life gives you lemons, you should make lemonade. Sounds corny, doesn't it?" She laughed and looked down at her fingernails, which had red nail polish on them. "Over the years I've learned that's not always true, though. My father was a hardworking man, but extremely stubborn." She placed both hands on her lap. "Sometimes life takes a wrong turn and all you can do is watch the scenery go by. There aren't any lemons or lemonade or lemonade stands. There's just this snippet of your life that goes by and all you can do is protect yourself and be strong." Lorraine smiled in a way that made her look sad. "I know this is a tough time for you, Justin, but it's going to pass. There are greener meadows on the other side. It's all about peaks and valleys. When you get to be my age, you learn to accept the ups and downs of life as a natural part of the cycle.

You're a very special young man and your dad is going to get better and things will be just as they were before you know it."

I opened the novel to the first page, not of the story but of the book, where it lists all the publishing information. I like to know when the author was writing his or her story because it helps put things in perspective. This one said it was originally published in 1959. Dad would have been twenty years old, Mom fourteen. Then I remembered that Lorraine was a year older than Mom, meaning she'd been fifteen when it was published—exactly my age.

My mind wandered all over the place, thinking of Mom and Dad as teenagers in the 1950s. Although it was impossible to picture them growing up in an era I had no idea about, it was even harder to think of them meeting in 1964, a full decade before I was born. I had to remind myself that there was actually a moment in history when they liked each other, a time they were attracted to one another physically and maybe even in love.

Mom moved to Toronto from Oshawa to find work and was waitressing at a pub not far from where Dad was going to school. Apparently Dad was quite "dashing" in those days and pretty much swept Mom off her feet when they met. They hadn't been seeing each other for more than six months when Dad popped the question. As soon as he graduated the following year and got a job at an accounting firm, he wanted to start a family. Mom did too, but over the next few years she had some/a few/a lot of miscarriages (I was never really sure which). Fate, or at least biology, seemed to be set against Mom bringing life into this world.

Which is why, I suppose, Mom looked at me as a kind of miracle baby when I was born. "All I wanted to know," she would tell me C-O-N-S-T-A-N-T-L-Y over the years, "was if you had ten little fingers and ten little toes. Nothing else mattered."

Turning out the light, I rolled over and pictured Dad, who was away in Ottawa on business, learning of my birth. Mom's best friend had phoned his hotel to leave him a message: *It's a boy. Nine pounds, eight ounces. All his fingers and toes are in place.*

For some reason, I don't have many memories before I was ten years old. By then, Mom and Dad were fighting almost every day. I'll never know what exactly happened between them over that first decade of my life, but thinking of it triggered a massive sadness in me. I thought of the Frasers and wondered what their secret was. Why had they made it and my parents hadn't?

There are greener meadows on the other side, Lorraine had said. I turned over on my other side and adjusted the pillow under my head. *It's all about peaks and valleys.* She had to be right because I couldn't understand how this valley could get any deeper; things had to get better from here, I reasoned, which made me feel better as my breathing steadied and I drifted off to sleep.

22

We lost the next game, but I didn't really care. All I wanted to do was make up with Ali. It was almost ten o'clock when Dad and I got back to the apartment. My heart sank when Mrs. Blake answered the phone, thinking she'd bawl me out for calling so late. Luckily, she was all sunshine and rainbows and said she'd grab Ali for me.

"Hello?" Ali said, picking up another phone.

"Hey. Sorry for calling so late."

"How'd it go?"

"We lost."

Ali considered this for a moment. "Is it just me or do you not sound that upset?"

"Well, obviously I wish we'd won. But you're right. And that's because…Ali… when I hung up on you last night…I…it was stupid of me. I felt like such an A-hole last night and all day today." *Thump, thump, thump.* "I'm really, really sorry."

"You're a big jerk sometimes, you know?"

"I know. But—"

"But what?"

"But you're all I've got right now."

"Oh, don't be so melodramatic, Mr. Drama McDrama. You've got amazing friends and a father who idolizes you."

That last part threw me off. "He doesn't *idolize* me. The guy barely speaks to me half the time. We might say ten words to each other when we're in the same room together."

"Ugh. You're infuriating. You know that, right? I may have only met him a couple of times, but when your dad talks about you he lights up." I was about to shoot down her theory when Ali went on. "You really are daft!"

I let out a laugh. "Daft? Where'd you pick that one up?"

"Shut up! I know big words, too, okay?"

"*Daft!*" I repeated.

"Ugh. Fine. It was in a crossword I did today. But that doesn't change the fact that you're still daft!" Ali finally let it out and the both of us shared a light moment, which is exactly what we needed. Everything had been too over-the-top lately. "In all seriousness, can I say one more thing?"

"Of course." I had a stupid grin on my face.

"Justin, you know I'm here for you. I'm always here for you. But we can't be together all the time and I can't just cancel plans with friends because you ask me to."

"You're right."

"Thank you."

"Now, how about us getting together on Sunday and making up right and proper?"

"Right and proper?"

"Yeah, you know, like maybe get cozy or something."

She sighed. "You're ridiculous."

I'd just returned from the laundry room in the basement and was putting away my clothes when all the dead brown plant leaves on top of the dresser caught my attention. Dad was folding his own clothes when I asked him what you were supposed to do when a plant died.

"Throw it out."

"Yeah, well, it won't exactly fit into the garbage chute."

"Take it down to the garbage dump, then. There are several of them parked behind the building."

I was about to say, Why don't you take it out? But when I looked at Dad on the sofa and remembered what he'd been through recently, I told him I'd deal with it later.

"As you see fit."

Later, after getting through a bunch of heinous assignments and starting an English essay on *Great Expectations*, I asked Dad if he could bring my gear to the arena that evening.

"You're sending your equipment in place of you tonight, are you?"

"No, Rodney Dangerfield," I said. This made Dad chuckle. "Good to know you didn't lose your sense of humour while you were in the hospital. Anyway, Keith invited me over to watch a movie so we could get psyched up for the game."

"Dare I ask which movie this might be?"

"*Youngblood*."

"I can't say I'm familiar with it. Is it new?"

"Kind of. It came out on VHS a while ago."

"So you'll ride over with Keith and leave your father to lug your things to the arena?" Although Dad didn't rant and rave when he said this, he was really bad at hiding his emotions when he was hurt.

"How about I take my bag and sticks down to the car right now? That way all you have to do is drive over and I'll meet you at the arena."

"As you wish."

"And you know what time the game is?"

Dad looked up at me, his glasses halfway down his nose. "Ah-hem. Does a bear relieve itself in the woods, young man?"

"You could just say yes."

"And you could just stay home until the game."

"Anyway, just make sure you eat something before leaving, okay?"

"I'll do my best, Ambrosia. Now off you go. I'll see you shortly."

Keith had gone down to the Eaton Centre earlier and bought a new Nintendo game called *Airwolf*. It was okay and had some pretty cool graphics, but it was more Keith's thing than mine. A couple of hours before we had to take off, Keith started the movie. For dinner, Lorraine made us Caesar salad with homemade croutons that actually melted in your mouth, pork chops, scalloped potatoes and corn niblets. She even let us eat in front of the TV, a pretty rare event in the Fraser household. Mr. Fraser was at the office and Victoria was at a friend's place for a birthday party, so I guess she'd given up on trying to do the whole family meal thing tonight.

Watching Peter Zezel and Steve Thomas play Rob Lowe's hockey stunt double as they whipped up and down the ice and scored awesome goals did exactly what it was supposed to: Keith and I were fired up when Lorraine drove us to the game later on. When we got to the arena, the two of them headed inside while I waited for Dad near the entrance. It was a nice night for the first day of April, the sun just fading over the tree tops at the far end of the park. Normally, I like to start getting ready about half an hour before a game. While I don't do nearly as much talking or joking around as the other guys, I love the ritual of getting dressed at my own speed, maybe retape a part of my stick halfway through or take out a sharpening stone and go back and forth along each skate blade a few times.

Seven o'clock rolled around and Dad still hadn't arrived. I was starting to crap my pants. Fifteen minutes until puck drop, I rushed inside to the payphone only to realize I didn't have a quarter on me.

Mr. Wainwright was in the hallway outside the dressing room, talking to the assistant coaches, when I asked him for twenty-five cents.

"You're not dressed yet, Justin? The game starts in less than fifteen minutes."

"I've been waiting for my Dad. He's got my equipment."

He narrowed his eyes, reached into his pocket, and pulled out two dimes and a nickel. I knew what he was thinking as I raced to the phone: How did I get here without my equipment, and who the hell was going to centre the first line if I couldn't dress?

Please, please, please, I repeated as I called the apartment. Dad didn't pick up after the bazillionth ring, which seemed like a good sign. He must be on his way, I thought, walking outside again and locking my fingers around each other on top of my head. What was I thinking letting him come out here on his own? If I'd been at home we would have made it here in plenty of time and I wouldn't be going into this playoff game stressed out to the max.

Eyes glued to my watch, the minute hand went from five to six to ten to twelve. Just then the Volare slipped into the parking lot, slow and steady. Dad pulled right up to me.

"I thought you said you knew when the game started!" I said. Dad had his window rolled down, smoke funneling out of it, as I rushed to the trunk to grab my bag.

"I was caught up in a conversation with Alicia. She wouldn't let me go."

Somehow, I managed to throw all my gear on in three minutes, which left me with exactly no time to warm up or stretch. Mr. Wainwright put out the second line to start the game, and when Keith, Michael Bolton and I stepped on the ice for our first shift I could feel the tenseness in my legs and groin area. Our line got a couple of points by the end of the game, Keith and I both notching a goal each, but I never really found my stride. We ended up losing four-three and I was furious both at myself and at Dad.

"Not your team's finest hour, Churchill," Dad commented on the way to the car later on. "Look on the bright side, though." I waited for Dad's witty witticism about what lay on the other side. "At least you've still got a pot to piss in." While Dad may have said some weird things over the years, that one took the cake.

At the apartment, Dad drained a drink as quickly as he'd poured it, then told me he was heading to The Last Resort to finish his "tête-à-tête" with Alicia. I aired my bag out on the balcony and showered. When I got out, I couldn't figure out what to do. It was too early to go to bed and I didn't really feel like watching TV. What I wanted to do was hang out with Ali, maybe even just talk to her on the phone, but she was going to be out all night at Debbie's *thing*. I checked the time and thought of the one person I could talk to at this hour.

I phoned the operator and placed a collect call, knowing Dad would have a cow if this were on his dime. Although I could never wrap my head around the time difference, Dale told me when he moved to Tokyo that the two extremes of a day were usually safe to phone him, either early in the morning or late at night our time.

Dale accepted the charges and I caught him up to speed about all that had happened since we last connected. He listened thoughtfully, asking some basic questions like how I was doing, how Dad was recovering, etc. When I'd finished, he said, "It sounds as if you have your hands full."

"Kind of."

"Well, you know what they say: a leopard never changes its spots."

"That's what freaks me out, Dale. I don't know if he has the ability to change."

Dale thought about this, then told me he'd talk to his father and see if there was anything Uncle Adam might be able to do. Dale moved on and asked about Ali and hockey. I said things were going great with Ali and that we were playing in the City's, but that we were down two to one in the series.

"Justin," he said without skipping a beat, "if there's anyone who can lead his team to victory it's you. It's as much a truism as the Ginza has the finest collection of women on this planet, especially after dark, and doubly so when in a hostess bar."

I laughed even though I had no idea what a hostess bar (let alone the Ginza) was. That didn't matter. If Dale said those were cool things, I had to find my way to a hostess bar in the Ginza after dark.

"Listen, I've got to run in a couple of minutes, but I wanted to ask if you'd been in touch with your mother since we last spoke."

I hesitated. "No."

"Do you have any way of reaching her? A phone number? An address?"

"Ahh," I stumbled. While I was tempted to say no, I couldn't lie to Dale. "Yeah," I finally said. "I have her number and her address."

There was a sound in the background on Dale's end. He partially covered the receiver and spoke to someone in what had to be Japanese. "Sorry," he said when he returned. "My landlord's on my case about moving my car. I tell you, this country has been a godsend for me, but they need more land so people stop parking on top of each other. Anyway, that's neither here nor there. What I wanted to ask was if you had any desire to reach out to her."

"Shouldn't she have to reach out to me first?"

"Look, nobody knows more than me how fragile this situation is. You've got a father to care for and a mother who's AWOL. My point is, if you don't extend an olive branch it's very possible nothing will change. I know it's a lot to put on you, but I've always had a soft spot for your mother. Deep down she's a very caring person. She was like a second mother to me growing up. She did the best she could with what she had and I've always appreciated that. Now, I'm not saying you *have* to do anything. Tell you what," he continued after a moment's pause. "If there's anything you think I can do to help, let me know. Sound fair?"

"Yeah, I guess."

"All right, then. I should get out of here and hook up with this young vixen I met last night at a club. Let's hope she looks as good sober as she did through the lens of a Suntory bottle!"

We got off the phone and I poured myself a glass of milk. As I wandered around the apartment, I went over what Dale had said about Mom. For every reason to call, I thought of another not to. In the end, it was his comment about Mom being a second mother to him that hit me hard.

I pulled out a crinkly piece of paper from my wallet and dialed Mom's number. She picked up after a couple of rings and sounded as if she'd been woken up.

"Mom?"

"Justin? Baby, how are you?" she asked in a groggy voice.

Tremors vibrated softly down to my fingertips. "I'm okay. How are you?"

I could hear some rustling, like she was lifting herself in bed maybe, and turning on a light. She started to say something once, then twice. Both times she struggled to answer. "I'm getting by," she eventually answered. "Things could be better. Things could always be better," she added with a laugh, which relaxed me a little. "Things could also be worse, I suppose."

"Yeah."

"Baby, I was in bed when you called and can't put a single coherent thought together right now. Do you think there's any way I could... is there any way I could write you a letter maybe and explain everything?" When I didn't say anything, she went on. "There's so much to tell and I just think it would be easier to get across on paper."

Easier for who?

"Fine. Sure."

"Don't be angry, Justin. Please, baby."

Mom asked for my mailing address, which I gave her, but when it came to the postal code I drew a blank; there'd never been any reason for me to ask Dad what it was.

"That's all right. I'll get it at the post office. They can do that sort of thing there."

I'm not sure what I'd hoped to accomplish by phoning her out of the blue on a Saturday night, six months of no communication to get over. Maybe I needed to do it for a clear conscience. Or maybe I did it because I believed what Dale had said, that Mom was a good person deep down, a caring person who did the best with what she had.

Mom wasn't choked up or anything like that at the end of our call, saying she'd write me in the next few days and we'd take it from there.

"Fine," I said, bitterness lining that one word.

"I promise we'll be in touch real soon, K?"

"Sure."

"And Justin?"

"Yeah?"

"Thank you so much for calling. You're still the bravest b...young man I know."

I stayed on the line until that annoying *beep beep beep* forced me to put down the phone because I was hoping she'd tell me how this had all gone so wrong, and how and when and where we'd be able to fix it.

23

When I asked Ali if she could come to our game on Monday night, she said she'd do her best. Her grandmother was coming over for dinner and, remembering the lesson I'd learned the last time this same thing happened, I didn't accuse her of choosing anyone over me or hang up. I simply said it would be really nice if she could make it. She asked when it started, I told her seven-thirty, and that was that.

With or without my girlfriend in the stands, I was going to make sure we evened things up in the series. Dad headed upstairs when we got to the arena and I went to the dressing room, where Ryan was thumbing through his collection of tapes. I handed him one of my own and asked if he wouldn't mind putting it on.

"Who's on it, Baloney?" he asked, surprised because I'd never brought any of my music to our games or practices in the past.

"It's a mixed tape, a few songs to get us in the right headspace."

"Cool."

Metallica's "Master of Puppets" was followed by tunes from Slayer, Poison, Whitesnake and Firehouse. There was an instant buzz around the room.

Mission One: accomplished.

Before Mr. Wainwright came in to deliver his pre-game talk, I gave a short one of my own. "We haven't been getting enough shots," I began, feeling calm and at ease, not a tremor running through my body. "We need to get more pucks on this meathead goalie of theirs because so far he's proven we can beat him when we actually shoot it on net. We're dangling the stupid puck around him like a yo-yo and not letting it rip. And I'm just as guilty of this as anyone. I've got to get more shots on as well. We've all got to get more shots tonight." I wasn't standing up and trying to be some great speaker; half the time I wasn't even looking at anyone and just focused on lacing up my skates. "As the Great One said: *You miss 100% of the shots you don't take.* Let's bury this goalie in rubber and make him wish he never showed up tonight.

"I know you all want this series as much as I do. We've never won a City's together, and the fact is that these hicks from the sticks aren't nearly as good as us. And still they're beating us, what, two to one? That makes no sense. Let's even it up tonight, guys."

"Hicks from the sticks?" Michael Bolton repeated through a laugh. "I love it."

Mission Two: accomplished.

Mr. Wainwright started our line and we scored less than a minute into the game, Michael Bolton sliding it under the goalie's pads after a pass from Keith and me. We didn't look back for the next forty-four minutes and twelve seconds. At one point we were up six to nothing, but they scored in the third and the game ended seven-one.

Mission Three: accomplished.

Keith and I left the dressing room together, stinky and sweaty, bags hanging off our shoulders by one strap. Ali and Rachel were waiting for us in the lobby, huge smiles on their faces. Dad and Lorraine hung back, talking to each other as Dad pulled away on a cigarette.

Keith and Rachel had their own conversation while I asked Ali what had happened to Grandma Blake. Slipping my hockey bag down onto the floor, Ali gave me a peck on the cheek and said that was for having such a great game. "There never was a Grandma Blake coming over tonight," she said.

"Huh?"

"I wanted to surprise you."

I had a blank look on my face.

"What? Surprises are a good time!" Until then, I hadn't even noticed she had large Slush Puppies in each hand. "I wasn't sure which one you'd want, so I got both. This one is raspberry and this one's orange," she went on, extending them my way.

"Well, that's a no-brainer," I told her, reaching for the orange Slushie.

"*Really?*"

"What?" I said innocently. "Orange is a good time."

We took the next two games and won the City's on Friday night. While they weren't exactly cakewalks, we'd got our act together and dominated games five and six with a level of intensity we hadn't shown all season. Keith, Michael Bolton and I were on the ice for the final shift, and went cuckoo for Cocoa Puffs when the final buzzer went at the end. We were the MTHL AAA City Champions. Helmets and sticks and gloves went flying in the air as everyone poured onto the ice and mobbed Timmy Atkinson.

Afterwards, I gave my very first interview—a *press* interview. The *Toronto Star* had sent someone to cover the game and the reporter, Kevin DiManno, asked to have a word with me as we headed to the dressing room to celebrate. Guys were giving me a hard time as they passed by, screwing up my hair with their gloves and punching me. Although he asked me a bunch of questions, the only quotes that made it into the paper the following day (and by "into the paper" I mean the article was buried so deep it took me forever to find the blurbs) were: "I think we played a really balanced game. Timmy [the goaltender] stood on his head and our D got us the puck cleanly from our own zone."; "I think our line played three solid periods of end-to-end hockey. We capitalized where we could and the two wingers I play with…were awesome. The three of us were gelling tonight and had some great chemistry."

Unlike Stanley Cup champions, who got to spray champagne all over each other, we had soft drinks to dump on each other's heads, making our hair as sticky as glue. I guess because he had hoped/believed we'd end it tonight, Mr. Wainwright had cases of Coke, root beer and ginger ale, multiple bags of chips and a whole lot of other junk food just sitting in his car. That was all fine and good, but the nineteen of us were looking for something more than that.

When the coaches left us to celebrate on our own, Keith and Ryan went into organization mode. A plan was necessary, they said, asking around if anyone's parents were out of town. That was a negative. "All right," Keith said. "Plan B, then. Let's hit a park. The weather's warm enough, right?" Heads bobbed up and down.

"Park party!" Michael Bolton yelled

"We're going to need beer. And boatloads of it."

I don't think Keith had ever been this focused.

Timmy piped up and said his brother, a grade thirteen student who went to Ali's school, would buy us what we needed. "I'll get him to drive me to the park after we pay a visit to the beer store," he said.

"Everyone chip in ten bucks," Ryan ordered. He turned to Timmy and added, "Grab as much beer as you can with this. Right down to the last penny."

"And phone every single girl you know. Tell them where we're going," Ryan added. "We need at least a two-to-one ratio of girls to guys. Three-to-one would be better."

"What's it matter to you how many girls show up, Delacroy?" Michael Bolton said. "You couldn't get lucky if you had a four-leaf clover stuck up your ass and a hooker tied to the bed."

"Maybe if she was blindfolded he could," Dean said, the corners of his mouth barely turned up.

"Or unconscious," Keith added.

"Or mute," someone said from a corner of the room.

"Whatever. You turdballs won't be laughing so hard when the party's over and I'm getting my meatcane stroked and you fags are all choking your own chickens."

Timmy Atkinson came through for us and showed up at the park an hour later with six cases of beer. To Ryan's disappointment, only a handful of girls showed up. Not including Ali, Rachel, Debbie and Vicki, there were just two girls there. It might have been what Ryan called a sausage party, but we still partied like it was 1999, guys chugging beer as if it were water. Everyone was cheersing and clinking bottles. It didn't get boring either. We'd just won the City's. How could you over-celebrate that?

It was around midnight when the *fhit* hit the *san*. Ryan had brought his ghetto blaster, and what started on a decent volume, or decent enough not to wake up anyone whose house was nearby, only got louder as the night wore on. Soon, a few of the boys were getting rowdy, egged on by Keith, who was pretty schmased by that point. Then they started getting really loud. Then they started puking, first in the bushes and later right where they were standing. Then the cops showed up and you'd have thought we were a track and field team because you'd never seen a mass of people get the hell out of Dodge so quickly. Everyone scattered blindly, like points around a compass, as a police car inched its way into the park with a searchlight mounted on top of it.

Most of the guys had come alone, so they took off without a second thought. Keith and I, however, couldn't exactly leave the four girls behind; we had to go at their pace, which wasn't quite the sprinting speed of the others. Ali would've clobbered me if I'd actually said it, but Debbie was so drunk she could barely stand and was, in my opinion, the reason we got busted by the cops. There were around twenty-five people at the party, but it was only the six of us who got nabbed.

The male cop gave Keith and me a speech about underage drinking and disorderly conduct in public. The female cop was even harsher with the girls, treating them like derelicts and juvenile delinquents. By the time the stupid pigmobile left, each of us walked away with a fine for forty-two dollars and fifty cents, which, given the circumstances, wasn't so bad, I guess. Getting locked up in the drunk tank and having our parents receive a phone call at one a.m., telling them that their oh-so innocent children had been wreaking havoc in a public space with six cases of beer might have been a *tad* worse.

The next morning, I took two extra-strength Tylenol as soon as I woke up and heated up some premade lasagna in the oven. Dad was up but still horizontal on the couch, his eyes peeking out from the blanket like one of those Jawas from *Star Wars*. When I asked him if he wanted anything to eat, he said he was still digesting his meal from last night.

"What did you have?"

"Oh, a little of this and a little of that."

Dad wasn't home when I got back last night, so he had no idea how wasted I was. I'd passed out with my clothes still on, which explained why I woke up sweating my face off and my pillow soaked.

"Do you have any plans today?" I asked from the kitchen. Plate in hand, I shuffled over to the bed and took a seat on the floor.

"I'm going to visit my brethren later on."

"Uncle Adam?"

"He would be the one."

"How come?"

"What do you mean 'how come'?"

"Dad," I said, forgetting all about Uncle Adam as I turned on the TV. "What happened to the cable?" Only Global and CBC were coming through. Two freaking channels!

"It was taking up too much of our monthly expenditures. Those crooks at the cable company should be drawn and quartered for what they charge. At least now you will have more time to devote to your studies."

"Dad, please," I said desperately. "I'll die without cable."

"Consider this a lesson in frugality."

"Dad, I'll do anything if you call the cable company and get it reconnected. I swear."

"This isn't a case of you having to *do* anything, Justin. Besides, didn't you say we still have two channels?"

"They're Canadian channels!"

"Where's your sense of national pride?"

Argh.

"Justin, watching TV is a habit, not an addiction. Now stop complaining and be grateful we even have a television."

Without anything to distract me around the apartment, I went to Keith's place and played road hockey. What started out as two-on-two soon morphed into five-on-five, the nets getting pulled farther apart from each other on the street as each new person from around the neighbourhood joined in. Even after the Tylenol and the food and the fresh air and the exercise, though, my head wouldn't stop pounding.

"I've got to skedaddle," I told Keith an hour into the game.

The score was something like twenty-four to twenty, but nobody could be sure. Everyone kept arguing when a goal was scored about how it didn't count because of some ridiculous thing like the scorer was offside (there's no blue line in road hockey) or a penalty should have been called (we never called any penalties).

"Would you take off your skirt and stay a while, spaznuts?" I ignored Keith and headed to his garage, where I threw my stick into an empty garbage pail.

"I'll give you a shout tomorrow," I told Keith, walking past everybody as they yelled "Pussy!" "Fag!" and "Now the teams are uneven, dicksmack!"

Dad was out when I returned. I sat down on the floor and turned on the TV. Maybe I'd blocked out what had happened this morning, but it didn't lessen the pain of surfing through two stupid channels. Channel one, channel two. Channel two, channel one. My choices were a rerun of *Wheel of Fortune* and a black-and-white movie that made me sleepy.

I turned the stupid thing off and finished the lasagna I'd gotten halfway through at lunch. It would've been better heated up in the oven, but I was hungry and lazy and impatient, so ate it cold while standing up in the kitchen. There weren't any dirty plates or cutlery in the sink, which meant Dad hadn't eaten today. His massive weight loss these last couple of months was starting to worry me because I could see what it was doing to his body and his overall health. He was spending more time on the couch and barely had enough energy to drive me to games. And if I'm going to call a spade a spade, he looked God awful and was beginning to smell. His breath had gotten really bad lately and his BO was nothing short of rank, even when he put on deodorant.

Around eight o'clock, Dad wiggled the key out from the lock with an unsteady hand, barely getting inside and closing the door. I got up off the bed and helped him to the couch. He claimed to have done too much walking today.

"Would you be a darling and pour your father a drink?" he asked, slumped against one of the sofa's end cushions. A moral compromise, I only filled the glass halfway. Dad took a sip and closed his eyes. "One more thing, Justin. Would you put on my Pachelbel album? It should be at the very back of the collection."

Dropping the needle at the edge of record, the song I'd heard too many times to count began playing. Dad took another sip, relishing it as he pressed his lips together and kept his eyes shut tight. "Music is indeed the melody whose text is the world," he muttered, violins coming to life in the background. "You know, Schopenhauer once said that the effect of music is so very much more powerful and penetrating than is that of the other arts, for these others speak only of the shadow, but music of the essence. I love that line: for these others speak only of the *shadow*, but music of the *essence!*" He opened his eyes and looked into mine. "I'm convinced that if angels do actually exist, they might very well have come down to Earth and inspired the great Baroque artist to write this canon."

To be honest, I wasn't really listening to what Dad was saying. I was more concerned with his breathing, which seemed pretty uneven. That, of course, made me think of the stroke, or the mini-stroke, or whatever the hell the doctors dressed it up as. As if sensing this, Dad smiled and said he was okay. "When I hear this song played, I reach a state of being others call rapture." A second later he asked me to lower the volume. "Just a smidgen, will you?" Dad stretched out the length of the sofa. He reached for his blanket, which was lying in a heap on the floor. I picked it up for him and gave it a couple of good shakes to get the dust off. After carefully placing it over his body, I went to say good-night, but he was already passed out.

Ali and I made plans to get together the next day. "My parents are going to some wedding at their golf club, so we'll have the place to ourselves."

"Wicked!"

"And I was wondering..." Ali went on without finishing her thought.

"About what?"

"I was just thinking...maybe you could stop by a pharmacy on the way over? Only if you want to, I mean."

"Are you sick?"

"No, I'm fine."

"Because you sound all right to me."

"I am! It's not that, Justin. It's just, you know, we have the place to ourselves tomorrow and thought we might, you know..."

"Ali, what's going on? You're sounding like a crazy woman."

"Justin! What do they sell at pharmacies?"

Was this a pop quiz?

"I don't know. Band-Aids? Cough syrup?"

"Yeah, and what else?"

"Ali, you know me and tests don't like to be in the same room together."

"Ugh. Think about it, dumb-dumb. Pharmacy? My house? Us all alone for the day? Do I have to spell it out for you?" When I didn't answer she added, "I just thought we could, you know, get cozy."

"Oh..OH!!!" So I should pick up some—"

"Uh-huh."

"And bring them to your—"

"Yes!"

I should have been pumping my fist in the air. I mean, the hottest girl in the world was telling me I had a green light to round all the bases with her tomorrow, but all I could think about was how I'd ever find the courage to buy a box of condoms without dying of embarrassment.

When I got off the subway at Eglinton, I headed to the nearest pharmacy, a Boots two blocks north. From the moment I walked in, there was no doubt in my mind a stroke was imminent. Blood was filling my head from all the stress, making it hard to see clearly and even harder to think. Down one aisle, then up another, I went. Cruising down the third aisle, I saw them. *Sweet Jesus! It was like the cereal section at the supermarket!* There were small boxes, big boxes, shiny ones and dull, boring ones. Some of them had a picture of a couple at sunset, while others just had descriptions. One brand had Warm Sensations, Twister, Naked Sensations, and Fire & Ice. Another brand had a Pleasure Pack, Extended Pleasure, as well as different varieties: thin, very sensitive, ultra-sensitive, vibrating fling, lubricated, non-lubricated, and bare. One brand even asked on the cover of the box "Closest thing to wearing nothing?"

I stood there staring at them all, hypnotized and unable to reach a decision. The first time Ali and I had done it, I'd struggled just to get the stupid thing on. Figuring out what kind of condom to buy was like trying to solve a really hard math question while speaking French at the same time.

A woman started heading towards me from the other end. I panicked and fled the opposite way. She got what she needed and I returned to the same spot as before, picking up where I'd left off with my indecisiveness. When I was finally able to lift my arm, I was hit by a new fear: did they card people for condoms like they did with cigarettes and alcohol? It would be bad enough standing in line with a box of condoms only to walk away empty-handed because I was underage. It made sense. I mean, the government couldn't very well let ten-year-olds buy domers, could they?

A man started my way and, once again, I took off from the scene of the crime. The line to the registers snaked halfway across the small store and I knew there was no chance I could wait that long while holding a box of condoms on full display for everyone to see and silently judge me.

Up Yonge Street I went, my head swiveling all over the place as I looked for an out-of-the-way, non-descript pharmacy that I'd never have to visit again. As I quickly learned, pharmacies are not convenience stores, as in there's not one on every corner. I had to go five blocks before finding a Shoppers Drug Mart. It was hardly out-of-the-way and anything but non-descript. In fact, it was bigger than Boots and had even more choices in their condom section.

Inside, standing in front of the stupid boxes, an old guy started limping my way, a cane in one hand.

Don't move. Stand your ground. And breathe, idiot. Breathing is important, especially when you're freaking out and on the verge of a teenage TIA.

My cheeks burned as he passed behind me as quickly as a freaking snail.

Don't think. Just do it, I told myself as Nike's newest ad flashed across my mind's eye. I grabbed the box directly in front of me and hightailed it to the cash. With only three people ahead of me, the line moved quickly. There were two cashiers, a woman around Mom's age with coke-bottle glasses and curly grey hair, and a good-looking babe who was maybe a year or two older than me. I wanted the four-eyed lady, but ended up getting the hottie. Keeping my head angled down the whole time, I placed a ten-dollar bill on the counter. Beads of sweat started forming at the top of my forehead. A single drop slithered its way down the side of my face.

"Is that all?" she asked me.

"Yep."

"Did you find everything you were looking for today?" she went on in a bored voice, like reading from a script.

"Yes."

"Would you be interested in filling out a short customer satisfaction survey?"

Sweat was running down both sides of my face now. Some of it was dripping into my eyes and making them sting. "Nope. I'm fine."

"And would you like a bag for your purchase?"

Tremors started running along my arms.

"I'm all right."

The till opened and she took her time getting my change. "Mary," she said to the other cashier a second later, "do you have an extra roll of loonies? I'm all out."

"That's okay," I said frantically, stuffing the box into the front pocket of my navy blue K-Way windbreaker. "Keep the change."

I left the store and powerwalked to Ali's, half an hour late because of my pharmaceutical meltdown. When she opened her door, the dimples quickly disappeared.

"Oh, my God. You're soaked. Did you run here?"

"Something like that."

"Come on in," she said as I trailed her to the den, where the TV was on. "Bat Out of Hell" was playing on MuchMusic. We sat down on the couch and Ali commented on how red my face was.

"Say, do you have something I could use to wipe away the sweat?"

"Do you feel okay?"

"Never been better. You know me," I said with a forced smile. "The human furnace!"

"I'll be right back," she said. When she returned, she handed me a facecloth.

"Thanks. I'm sure my right arm will be nice and dry shortly."

"What?"

"I was kind of hoping for a towel."

Ali broke out laughing. "Did you shower after getting off the subway?"

"Yeah, I showered in that famous public shower at Yonge and Eglinton. Come on!" I traced the puny thing over my forehead, eyebrows, cheeks and neck. "You should probably burn this now," I said.

"You're hilarious. Here, give it to me. I'll put it in with the rest of the dirty laundry."

"I don't think you want to touch it without protective gloves."

Ali shook her head and called me a dummy. "By the way, do you want a bite to eat?" she asked, walking out of the den.

"Sure. What do you have?"

"My mom went to this swank deli yesterday," Ali said from the bathroom, "and stocked up on a bunch of goodies. Why don't I grab a little of everything and we can have a picnic here in front of the TV?"

"Sounds good."

For me, the funniest part of the whole thing was that I hadn't tried a single piece of food Ali brought out; I had trouble even pronouncing anything. There was sliced prosciutto, which Ali explained was a type of ham (but way better). We also had Niçoise salad and pitted cerignola olives stuffed with red peppers, three types of cheeses (gouda, brie, and some kind of way-stinky cambozola), crackers, a chicken pesto pasta dish that I devoured, and sundried tomatoes which made my taste buds explode. Ali had moved the footrest over, freeing up most of the den space for our lunch date. She'd also spread a blanket on the floor as we sat with our backs up against the couch.

Many music videos later, with pounds of Italian goodness swimming around our bellies, I asked Ali if I should put the food away. "Please! Get it away from me!"

"I thought you liked it," I said, picking up the plastic containers.

"I did, but look at me. I'm so fat!"

"Ali, I could still pick a lock with you you're so skinny."

"Whatever. I'm fat and bloated."

We watched *St. Elmo's Fire* after Ali put away the leftovers in the fridge and loaded the dishwasher. I'd seen it once and loved it, but this was Ali's first time. Her eyes were a little puffy at the end, so I slipped an arm around her shoulders, brought her in tight and asked if she liked it.

"I loved it," she said with a sniffle. "I'm such a crybaby when it comes to movies. You know I actually cried halfway through *Pretty in Pink*? I'm pathetic."

I told her she was anything but pathetic, then landed a kiss on top of her head, which smelled like a garden full of flowers in the middle of summer.

"I swear, I think I'd die without music and movies in my life."

"I know."

Ali nestled into me and sighed. "So…"

"So…"

"Did you…you know…have a chance to visit a certain store?"

My heartbeat increased and my blood pressure, I'm sure, went soaring through the roof. "I might have dropped by."

Ali moved a hand to my thigh and rubbed her head against my chest. "It's just, you're leaving for a week later tonight." Ali lifted her head and looked at me. "Do you want to go upstairs?"

Swallowing hard, I said, "Yeah."

In her room, we made out for a bit, arms and hands and legs and feet wildly exploring each other. When she asked if I had "it," I wanted to smack myself because I'd left my windbreaker in the den.

"Hold on a minute."

I literally sprinted both ways and was beside Ali on her bed again in record time, sweat lining my bangs.

"My little human furnace," Ali said as we locked lips and started kissing again. Then I pulled myself away, before she needed to ask me, and moved to the windows so I could close the drapes, knowing Ali hated getting cozy with any light on in the room.

"It's okay," she said from the bed, where she sat with one leg tucked into the side of the other.

"Yeah?"

She smiled. "I want to be able to see you for once."

"And you're okay with, you know, me seeing…"

She nodded.

Our second time around wasn't quite as disastrous, though it still felt like hard work. I was convinced Ali got no pleasure out of it whatsoever. Porn movies made it look so fun and hot and exciting. With me, there was so much stress to get around that by the moment it felt good it was over and I was taking off that stupid thing between my legs.

Last year in gym, we'd done a sex ed. chapter in the health portion of class, but it hadn't prepared me for any of this. We'd talked about AIDS, STDs, pregnancy prevention and about every other unsexy topic which did nothing to help me where it really counted. Could they really not have done one measly unit on how to make a girl happy in the sack? While I was glad to know how to protect myself from getting a venereal disease from a stripper who worked at Zanzibar or Cheaters, I was no better off making Ali happy. And in the end, that's all I wanted to do.

24

Reason No. 1 I love playing hockey: it's the greatest sport ever invented.

Reason No. 2 I love playing hockey: when you qualify for the Provincials, you get to miss a week of school.

On Sunday night, we boarded a bus for London, Ontario, host city of the 1989 All-Ontario AAA Championship. Seven teams from around the province would be there, six of them competing for the gold medal. With the tournament set up in a round-robin format, every game was a do-or-die one.

We were booked at the downtown Holiday Inn. Having lived in a big city my whole life, I was used to seeing people around no matter what time of day. But in London, the streets were deserted when our bus pulled up outside the hotel around eight-thirty and let us off. Mr. Wainwright had said we'd be two to a room. Naturally, Keith and I were together.

The coolest part about staying in a hotel is that there aren't any parents or adults in your room. In fact, Mr. Wainwright, the assistant coaches and the parents who'd tagged along for the week weren't even on our floor. There was a vending machine beside the elevators on every floor, so we could get chips, pop, gum, chocolate bars and a bunch of other crap without leaving the building. Also, as Keith quickly discovered, we could order movies in our room any time we wanted, including XXX ones.

Little surprise, then, that before going to sleep on Sunday night, Keith took the remote and asked me what we should watch. As he went through the menu, he read out each option, starting with *Throbbing Hood*—and here he began laughing like a little girl—*Hello Titty, Load Warriors, On Golden Blonde,* and ending with *When the Men Are Away the Sheep Will Play.*

"Dude," I said, lowering my book. "We've got to be up early tomorrow morning."

Keith shot me a look as if I'd just scored on our own net. "Since when did you get a sex change?" I put my novel on the nightstand. "Oh, I see, Mr. I've-already-poked-my-skinny-little-boner-in-my-girlfriend is too good for this shit now, huh?"

Keith took off his pants, got under the sheets and reached for a Kleenex.

"Tell me you are NOT—"

Keith blew his nose.

"What?" he said, wiping away some snot.

"Nothing. Fine. Just choose one, will you? I'm sure the sheep one has your name all over it."

"Whatever, buttmunch." Keith scrolled down to *On Golden Blonde,* but a second later a message came up on the screen saying YOU ARE NOT AUTHORIZED TO PURCHASE THIS MOVIE. This pissed off my best friend. I told him to relax and take it as a sign, but he was bent on watching what Dad calls "T&A."

Keith phoned down to the front desk: "Hey, we're trying to watch a movie in our room here and some message came up saying we're not *authorized*...402...Uh-huh...Yeah...Is he allowed to do that?... But we're eighteen...No, I left my license in Toronto...No...Not that either...Right. Okay, thanks."

Keith hung up and turned my way. "Mr. Wainwright blocked all the porns and R-rated movies from our rooms."

"I'm going to sleep."

"Wet dreams, J.R."

One of the assistant coaches knocked on our door in the morning to make sure we were out of bed. I told him we'd be downstairs soon. Keith was still dead to the world and snoring like a freight train, so we were going to need a little time. For breakfast, the Holiday Inn served Fruit Loops, Frosted Flakes, scrambled eggs, hardboiled eggs, sausage burgers, tea, coffee, milk, and juice. I'm pretty sure hotels don't account for hockey teams when they serve complimentary meals because we basically cleaned them out of everything. Nineteen teenagers and eight adults was all it took to shut down the place. If guests were coming down when we were through, they were in for an unpleasant surprise.

Suckas.

Practice started at nine-thirty and lasted an hour. Mr. Wainwright went over our schedule as we were getting ready, stressing how this was going to be the most grueling week of hockey in our lives.

Grueling? Who cares? We got out of school for a week to play the greatest sport ever!

Our first of six games was later that day. The top two teams would play for the gold medal five days later, on Saturday afternoon, while the third and fourth place teams would fight it out for the bronze medal that same morning.

At three p.m., we stepped onto the ice at the same arena the London Knights played out of. The stands were half full as we took on a team from Thunder Bay and ran away to a five-two victory. We celebrated by going over to the McDonald's close to our hotel and pigging out.

Keith and I hit the sack at a decent hour and woke up with our batteries fully charged. We won our lone game on Tuesday, slaying a team from Hamilton seven-one, and beat a team from Waterloo the following day five-one. Everything was clicking for us. The forwards were getting lots of scoring production, the D were stingy on the blue line, and Timmy Atkinson was standing on his head. We were at sixty percent on our power play and had let in just one goal on the penalty kill in ten tries. All that didn't matter to Mr. Wainwright, though. In the dressing room after our game on Wednesday, he reminded us of our hiccup in the winter. "Gas, gentlemen," he said. "Do you know what you do with gas?" No one said anything. "You step on it. You lean on it. You put your foot down on the gas so hard there's no mistake what you're trying to do. Full throttle. Nothing less. Because we're going to be playing on Saturday, not in the *morning*, but in the *afternoon*."

Sure enough, we got the jolt we needed on Thursday morning to keep the adrenaline flowing at Mach speed. Up against a team from Elgin, we played sloppy down low around our own net for the first thirty minutes, coughed it up in the neutral zone a ton and had trouble breaking out. We got called for three penalties, one of which was a five-minute major, which gave them plenty of chances to score. And score they did. Trailing four-two going into the last period, however, we somehow found the back of the net for three unanswered goals and stole it five-four.

By the four p.m., when we played our second game of the day, we'd gotten our act together again. Although London was hosting the Provincial championships, no team from the city had actually qualified for the tournament. Still, they got to play the six other teams competing here with an all-star team made up of the city's best players, kind of like a "Thanks for coming out, but please don't really come out" from the league. Needless to say, we wiped them off the face of the planet with a seven-one win.

The biggest test of the tournament for us came on Friday. We took on a team from Ottawa and they were pretty freaking good, I must say. They had a guy a year younger than all of us who did some pretty amazing things with the puck. We were locked at one-one for the better part of two periods, but in the third, with less than five minutes left, we scored, Michael Bolton sliding a pass over to me as the goalie went down and left a yawning cage to shoot at.

I'd kept Dad in the loop all week. I'd also been talking to Ali nightly, though the conversations were kind of stressful because Keith was on the bed beside me. He'd be watching TV and making stupid faces at me when I said something even remotely "gay," which is why I went straight to the hotel after dinner on Friday. Keith and a bunch of the guys were planning to go in search of an arcade and like always, Keith handled my decision with a maturity beyond his years: "Whatever, needledick. Have fun pulling your goalie. Just make sure you clean up."

I phoned Dad first because I knew it would be a short call.

"You're in the finals!" he exclaimed when I passed on the big news. "Congratulations! Who are the soon-to-be-vanquished?"

"Some team from Ottawa."

"Ha! I knew it. I *knew* this was your year."

"Yeah, well, we haven't won it yet."

"Nonsense. Money in the bank as far as I'm concerned. Now, what time does it start?"

"Three."

"I'll drive out for the game. What's the name of the arena?"

"The London Ice House."

"Consider me there."

"All right. See you tomorrow."

"And Justin?"

"Yeah?"

"*Res secundae.*"

Next, I called Ali. Aside from when she was in Florida last December, we hadn't spent more than a few days apart since we began going out. I was obviously stoked to be playing in the biggest game of my life, but I missed her a lot. Like, *a lot* a lot.

"Hiya," she said, picking up after the first ring. "How'd it go today?"

I told her about Ottawa and that tomorrow's gold medal game would basically just be a rematch of today.

"You must be so excited."

"I guess so, yeah."

"That wasn't such a convincing answer."

"It's just…I'd give my left arm to be with you right now. My other one too if you could make it to London tomorrow."

"You know I've got to do that fundraiser my dad organized at the hospital tomorrow. Washing cars for six hours in a row. Ugh. Shoot me now. Besides," she added, "you wouldn't be nearly as cute without any arms."

"You'd get over it in time."

"You wouldn't be nearly as good at hockey either."

"I'd get over that in time."

She laughed. "So when did you become so sappy?"

"Since forever."

"Hey! That's my line!"

"I mean it. I'm dying here without you." Being away from Ali the whole week and caught up in all the emotion surrounding the Provincials, I don't know, maybe it'd made me a little sentimental.

"You're sweet. Say, are you coming home tomorrow or Sunday?"

"Tomorrow. The finals are at three so we'll probably be back in the city sometime around six or seven."

"Do you want to come over to my place? My parents will be around, but we can still hang out. Maybe watch a movie or something?"

A very full grin took shape on my face. "That'd be cool."

"Okay. Listen, you, I should get going. I have a test on Monday and with my Dad's thing all day tomorrow and you coming by at night, I should put in at least an hour of studying right now."

"What's it in?"

"The test? Geography."

"Your favourite subject."

"Yeah, and I'm doing *sooo* well in it."

"Hey, Ali?" What I really wanted to do was end the call by saying *I adore you, Ali Blake.* But what actually came out of my mouth was, "I can't wait to see you."

"You, too. And good luck tomorrow!"

Sleep wasn't in the cards for me that night. Keith and I watched TV until midnight, neither one of us really tired. While Keith seemed pretty relaxed, I was way more anxious. It's possible I snuck in an hour or two of zzz's, but my eyes were wide open and alert when the alarm went off the next morning. Downstairs in the hotel's breakfast room, we all ate our body weight in food. I could tell I wasn't the only guy on edge; there was barely any conversation going on at the players' tables.

To relieve a little of the pre-game jitters, we decided to get out of the hotel. It was a gorgeous day and warm enough to be wearing just a T-shirt and jeans. We asked the girls at the front desk if there was somewhere nearby we could go and hang, and they directed us to a park a few blocks away.

Getting out of the hotel and doing something besides play hockey was the best thing we could have done. At the park, most of the guys played soccer. Four of us threw a Frisbee around, everyone doing their best not to freak out that we were playing for the Provincials in a few hours' time. On the way back to the Holiday Inn around noon, all of us seemed more relaxed. Guys were cracking jokes and giving each other noogies as we headed down Dundas Street, an army of fifteen-year-olds taking up half a city block.

We arrived at the London Ice House in time to catch some of Waterloo giving a spanking to Elgin in the bronze medal game. By the start of the awards ceremony, Mr. Wainwright walked into the dressing room and asked to speak with us. Ryan hit STOP in the middle of AC/DC's "*Back in Black*."

"There's only one thing I want to say, gentlemen," he began, looking pretty confident. "I want you all to have fun out there today. Don't treat this like the end of the world. What it comes down to is this: it's still a game. Have a blast out there this afternoon because this is a once-in-a-lifetime opportunity. Don't think about this as a gold medal game or a finals or a championship. It's a game. It's supposed to be fun. Keep in mind why you started playing hockey all those years ago. Remember playing shinny with your buddies? Can you remember the feeling of your first goal? Your first save? Your first bodycheck? Whatever that memory is, hold it close to you for the next forty-five minutes. Each and every one of you has worked incredibly hard to get here and I couldn't…" Mr. Wainwright chocked up a little bit. "You're the nineteen most talented hockey players in this province, gentlemen. I couldn't be prouder of you." He stopped himself again. "And it's been an honour this year to be your coach." There was one final pause. "Now go out there and kick some Ottawa ass!"

The stands were packed. All the guys' parents had made the drive to London, if not Saturday morning, then Friday night. After warming up, both teams stood on their respective blue line and some old dude on the PA system introduced us to the crowd. I craned my head sideways and looked for Dad. It took me a while to find him, but there in the back row, sitting, I assume, among the other team's parents, was Dad. He was kind of hunched over and taking long pulls from his flask.

In the opening period, Ottawa scored two early goals. We settled down after that and evened things up, eventually taking a three-two lead into the second. They answered with one of their own and soon pulled ahead again. They got another one early in the third, but we crawled our way back into it and scored two power play goals with four minutes left in regulation time. For those last 240 seconds, whenever either team skated across the blue line, you could hear a collective gasp around the arena. It felt like one lucky bounce, or mistake, was going to end this, and that's exactly what happened when Keith took a roughing penalty while trying to dig the puck out of the corner. He was too fired up for his own good, adrenaline flowing through him like electricity as he crushed a guy against the boards who needed to be removed with a spatula.

The face-off came back down to our end. I lost the draw and the Ottawa team passed it around the horn pretty well until, with just over a minute left, their fourteen-year-old captain took a pass from a defenceman and drilled a one-timer passed Timmy from the hash marks, making it six-five for the bad guys.

We dominated the last minute of the game. After gaining the blue line and pulling our goalie, we had a six-on-five advantage but couldn't get the puck in the net. In the dying moments, one of their guys shot the puck down the length of the ice and scored an empty-netter.

Final score: seven-five.

I'd been in my fair share of tournaments and league finals over the decade I'd been playing organized hockey. And while I'd been lucky to be on the winning side a lot of the time, I also knew the pain of losing a big game. Losing to Ottawa for the Provincial championships, however, was in a category all its own. You'd never seen so many teenage guys bawling their faces off. When they came out to present the medals, we were all standing there on the blue line like a bunch of mutes, our chins resting on the butt ends of our sticks. Keith was in especially bad shape because he blamed himself for the loss. I'd never actually seen my best friend cry. Today was different. Hockey was his life and we were his brothers in arms. His face expressionless, Keith's eyes were moist and raw with disappointment.

Dad offered to drive me back, as did the other parents with their own kids. I told him thanks but no thanks (though I did ask him to take my bag because I was going to head straight to Ali's later). None of the guys, in fact, went home with their parents. It wasn't an option. We'd played as a team all year, we'd won as a team, and now we'd suffer through a final bus ride together as a team.

When I got to Ali's place, Mrs. Blake let me in and asked how the week went.

"It was okay, but we lost in the finals."

"That's tragic," she said, frowning. "However, look on the bright side. Alison will be ecstatic to see you. She missed you terribly this past week."

"Oh…"

"Anyway, she's you know where, being sucked into a vortex of what else but music videos." Mrs. Blake angled her eyes upwards and sighed. "Would you like something to drink by the way? Some water or a soft drink? Perhaps some juice? We have apple, orange and grape."

"No, thank you. I'm okay."

As I began making my way to the den, Mrs. Blake called to me from the stairs. "By the way, I've been meaning to tell you for some time now, but thank you. For all that you've done with Alison, I mean."

"Umm…"

"Ever since you two started seeing each other, she's been eating like her old self again. Dare I say she even has a voracious appetite these days."

Was this Mrs. Blake's way of saying she knew that I knew?

Speechless (what does a guy say when his girlfriend's mother thanks him for helping out with her daughter's eating disorder?), Mrs. Blake added, "Anyhow, I won't keep you any longer. Enjoy yourselves."

"So? How did it…" Ali jumped to her feet when I got to the den. She didn't need to finish the question. The look on my face said it all. A Blue Rodeo song was playing on TV as she wrapped her arms around my waist. She pressed her head sideways against my chest, so the beating of my heart was probably coming through in Dolby Stereo. I lowered my chin so it rested on the top of her head and locked my hands around each other at the bottom of her back.

"I'm sorry," she said in a small voice.

"It's okay."

"I know how much this meant to you."

"Yeah."

"Sincerely, babe."

"Thanks." There was nothing more to say. We should have won and we didn't.

She pulled away and we looked at each other. "Can I tell you something?"

"Sure."

"Can I be totally honest?"

"Of course."

"You smell like…"

Ali was struggling to find the least hurtful way of putting it. She started using her hands to help her with the description and when that failed, I said, "A hockey bag that hasn't been aired out all season? A pair of used gym shoes?" Ali laughed. "A wet towel you left sitting in your closet for a few months? Tell me if I'm getting close here."

"Maybe a little of all those."

"Well, for your information, I would've showered earlier, but there was no way I was going another second without seeing you." I kissed her and tasted orange on my lips.

"Ugh," she groaned. "I wish my parents weren't at home right now."

"Oh? And why's that?"

"Would you get your mind out of the gutter, you!" Ali planted a kiss on my lips, then a second one, and finally a third. "Come on. I need your help with a crossword I was working on before you got here." She led me by the hand to the sofa, where we took a seat beside each other and she read the clues out to me.

Ali didn't notice me staring at her the whole time we were trying to figure out Eastern European capital names and puns that screwed with your brain. Each time I got one of the answers, which wasn't all that often, I'd score myself a kiss, pretty much the best reward system, I thought. When she'd finished filling in the last letters, she turned to me and said, "You killed that!"

"I did not. You got most of the answers. I got, like, three of them."

"Modest *and* cute, huh? Come here, you." She pulled me closer. "By the way," she said after a wicked kiss that made my jeans feel a little uncomfortable in a certain area, "I did something when you left last weekend that I hope you'll be proud of."

My eyes widened.

"I threw out our scale." It took me a second to figure out what she was talking about. "I know my mom will buy another one, but it's been a whole week and I haven't weighed myself once."

25

There was a letter addressed to me sitting on Dad's desk after school on Monday. I recognized the handwriting right away. I scooped it up, tore it open and took out the pages with shaky hands. The paper Mom had used was pink in colour, and she'd drawn flowers at the top.

My Dearest Justin,

I have been sitting here for what seems like an eternity trying to think of how to begin this letter to you. How over-welming it has been. May I start by saying how much I love & respect you? How proud of you I am?

You deserve an explanation for what has happened since September. I know you visited me when I was away & I am so truly sorry I did not come out & see you. The truth is that I did not have the strength to face you. Perhaps that sounds ridiculous to someone as strong as you, but I was consumed with so much shame & grief that I did not trust myself to gaze into those beautiful eyes of yours without turning into a complete basket case.

Ever since I was a teenager, depression has remained one close step behind me, strangling my soul. Years ago when things were good between me & your father, I could manage. Sometimes with medication & sometimes with prayer. But after going away last fall, my world began crumbling.

I fought hard not to let depression get the better of me. Those early weeks were so challenging because I wanted to make everything good again yet didn't know where to start. Morning after morning I would tell myself to get better for you. You were my light this entire time Justin. It may not seem like it, but I only made it through those two months because of you.

Against all of my prayers a new wave of depression set in when I was released, and I moved in with Maureen Arnott. Bless her heart, she had an extra room & said I could stay with her till I got back on my feet.

Even weeks after being released I had no desire to start my days & would often lie buried under my duvet until well past the noon hour. I ate very little & lost almost as much weight as Oprah did last year. (Maybe that is a bit of an exaggeration because if I lost 67 pounds I might very well float away.)

Anyways I had no will to face the world & had nothing to do all day except watch soap operas & game shows. Ocassionally I would take a walk by myself. Other than Maureen I lost all contact with my old friends.

I am sorry for rambling on like this baby. You probably want to throw this letter out & have nothing more to do with your old mom again. I only want you to understand why I disappeared into myself these last six months.

Now the good news! Bless Maureen's heart yet again because she helped me find a waitressing position at a restaurant nearby. I used to waitress before me & your father got married. Did I ever tell you that? Anyways it is not the most ideal job (I forgot how hard it is to be on your feet all day. My calfs & ankles kill me every night when I crawl into bed!) but it is OK for now.

Also can I mention that your mom has not had a single drink since September? I quit smoking on new years eve as well! Are you proud of me?

I hope so. I am trying to save some money & get my own place by the end of the summer. In the meantime would it be OK with you if we wrote to each other like this? Maybe just until things settle down a little more?

I know you must be furious with me & if you do not want to write back I will understand. My mailing address is below.

Depression is an ugly monster baby & I am having a tough go of it without hurting those around me. Just know that I love you with my heart & soul. I promise to do everything I can to make things right as rain again.

I know this probably won't make much sense but I came across something in my horoscope the other day in the newspaper that I liked.

LETTING GO DOESN'T MEAN YOU EVER STOP

299

CARING; IT JUST MEANS
I CAN'T SHOW YOU IN
PERSON HOW MUCH I DO
CARE.

Anyways I should let you go now. Thank you for having the courage to reach out & phone me last week Justin. Please bear with your old mom while she finds her way again. K? I know that we are going to figure this out. All we need is a little time and faith.

Love always,

Mom

I read the letter a second time. Then a third time, then a fourth, going over it until I'd memorized entire sections of the thing. It was hard to say how it made me feel. My first reaction was one of curiosity and hope. But there was a selfishness to her words that irritated me. She hadn't asked about my life or how Dad was doing or how we were getting by.

Wanting to keep the letter out of Dad's way, I folded the three pages and slipped them into the envelope once again. Restless, I tried to clear my head by watching TV. Both channels had the news on.

One was reporting on a polar bear attack somewhere in Manitoba, while the other was covering the sinking of a Ruskie sub that had gone down in a sea I'd never heard of and killed forty-one commies. I turned the stupid thing off and reached for my books.

When Dad walked through the door, I was on pins and needles. He'd obviously left the letter there for me to find and would have recognized Mom's handwriting just as I had.

"Hey. Good day?" I asked from the bed.

"Fine. Just fine," he said absent-mindedly.

He crossed the room and went shuffling through papers and drawers before taking off his blazer and throwing it on the couch. The back of his shirt had a sweat patch running down the length of it. He poked his head under the sofa, rifled through the kitchen cabinets, and when he still hadn't found what he was looking for, he came over to the bed and asked if I'd seen a letter lying around.

Uh-oh...

"Ah, yeah."

When I didn't say anything more, his eyebrows went up. "And?"

"And I opened it."

"Justin, we've been over this before," he said, growing frustrated. "The last time you went into my—"

"It was for me, though. It had my name on it."

This was strange. Dad didn't seem loaded or sober. He was, however, more intense than usual, his armpits soaked through and his hair damp.

"Anything sent from your mother goes through me first. You had no right to open it without my permission." When I didn't offer up the envelope, he added, "I want it, Justin. *Right now.*"

Dad was freaking me out. The way he was acting, the way he was speaking, his tone of voice, his crazy mood swing—something was seriously off.

"Do you want to know what she said? I'll read it to you."

"No. I want the evidence."

"What evidence?"

"*Der beweis!*"

"Dad—"

"Justin, so help me God, if you do not pass that letter over to me, you will find yourself without a roof over your head tonight. I'm going to count to five."

"Dad!"

"One..."

"Dad, listen to me. Mom wrote to *me.*"

"*Zwei...*"

Unable to think straight with a ticking time bomb staring me down, I said, "I'll read it to you. Every word. I swear."

"Three," he said, with a throaty evil that brought out my tremors. He moved a step closer. "Four..."

This is not happening.

"Five." Dad waited another second and then said, "Get out."

"Dad, what happened today? What did you...how much have you had to drink?"

"How dare you," he rumbled, raising a bone-thin arm and sweeping it down towards me. I caught it easily at the wrist. He tried to pull away, but he was as weak as a kid and couldn't free himself. He went to slap me with his other hand and I stopped that arm in mid-blow, too. With both of his wrists firmly in my grip, to the point it seemed one of them might snap, he turned frantic and told me to let him go, which I did right away.

Hunched over, Dad walked away and rubbed his wrists tenderly. He poured himself a drink, downed it in one swift gulp, then poured two more. When he was standing in front of me again, he took out his smokes from the pocket of his dress shirt. "The die is cast," he said, smoke funneling out of his nostrils.

Although my heart was pounding and the tremors were there in my arms and chest, I wasn't scared or intimidated. More than anything, I felt sorry for him. Whatever had happened today, whatever he'd done to himself, was beyond my control.

"Dad," I said quietly, so quietly I could barely hear myself, "I'm going to sleep at Keith's tonight."

He turned around and went back to the kitchen. I grabbed my school bag and stuffed Mom's letter inside. The last thing I heard while passing into the hallway was the *gulp, gulp, gulp* of liquid pouring into a glass.

In her letter, Mom said I wouldn't understand what it meant to let someone go and *not* stop caring. Now I did.

Something had broken long ago with Dad and me; tonight only crystallized it. He'd gone off the deep end earlier, yes, but that wasn't what had brought us to where we were now. I was done playing caregiver. When I got to the Frasers' place, Lorraine answered the door. He eyes grew large and she instinctively took a step forward, probably to hug me, but thought better of it before actually doing anything.

"Hey. Is Keith around by any chance?" I asked, arms wrapped myself, and my teeth chattering from the cold.

Instead of trying to be a second mother, which I knew she wanted to be, all she said was, "Let me get Keith. Why don't you go downstairs and have a shower. There are fresh towels in the bathroom. I'll tell Keith to meet you down there." Lorraine placed a hand on the top of my arm as she led me into the house.

"Thanks."

Heavy steps pounding down the staircase from the second floor could be heard all the way in the basement. I was staring at a blown-up photograph Lorraine had taken in Egypt. The picture featured an old man crouched on his hind legs in the foreground, smoking some kind of pipe deep inside a dark alley. High walls the colour of sand opened up at the other end of the picture, sunlight drenching the road ahead.

"What's up, dude?" Keith took a seat opposite me on the sofa. Herc trailed behind him, tail wagging.

"Can I crash here?"

"Sure."

"I mean, for a bit? Like, for a while maybe? I think my Dad's lost it."

"Lost it as in…?" I didn't say anything. Keith nodded. "You want me to talk to my mom?"

"If that's cool. Just make sure she's okay with me, you know, taking over the guest room for a while."

"Dude, you know as well as I do that if we were on a boat and it was going down, she'd hand you a life jacket before she gave me one."

I laughed. "Whatever."

"Anyway, I've got shit to take care of upstairs. Apparently Mr. Robertson isn't buying what I'm selling."

"What do you mean?"

"You know that paper due Wednesday on Great Sexpectations?"

"Yeah."

"I haven't even started reading the book. I tried telling him we were playing hockey all last week and that Saturday's game *traumatized* me. I asked him for a measly two-day extension—two days!—and you know what the asshat tells me?"

"What?"

"Then how come Justin handed in his paper this morning?"

Routines are funny things. They're pretty easy to get into, but as soon as you're in one it's almost impossible to imagine doing things differently, like the world might explode in a fiery explosion of explosiveness if you changed even the tiniest part of your day. As I learned after moving in with Keith's family, nothing is set in stone and a new routine was a heck of a lot easier to pick up than I'd thought.

Lorraine drove me over to Dad's on Monday evening. Unlike the time I'd gone to Tony's house last fall to get my things, Dad wasn't home, which was probably a good thing. I wrote a note telling him I'd be staying with Keith "for a bit" and that I'd call him soon. Fearing my emotions would get the better of me if I stuck around too long, I threw all my crap into two bags, books and clothes and toiletries all mixed together.

For me, my new routine took shape pretty fast. Most weekdays I'd go home with Keith and we'd watch TV for a couple of hours, have dinner and then do our homework. Ali and I would talk on the phone, and I'd read in bed until my eyelids got as heavy as dumbbells, which was usually around eleven or twelve. On weekends, Keith and I would hook up with buddies, or we'd rent VHS tapes and have movie marathons. Other times, Ali and I would get together. We'd either go to her place or look for somewhere to hang out in the city. Obviously spending time with Ali was epic, even if her parents were home, but it was also good to get away from Keith's. Although they'd never say a thing, especially Lorraine, I didn't want to be in their hair all the time.

Then there was Mom. It took me a couple of weeks just to work up the courage to write her. Even then, it took most of an entire Sunday afternoon to get down some thoughts. I decided to play it safe and write something kind of like a report you do in school. I gave her the gist of what life was like these days: how we lost the Provincials; I'd moved in with Keith's family; final exams were coming up; I had a girlfriend named Ali. Pretty boring crap if you ask me, but the kind of stuff I knew she'd want to know. The ending was the killer part. I wasn't sure how to sign off. Not wanting to be completely heartless (but also not sure exactly how I felt), I ended the letter by saying:

Justin
xo

Spring got off to an awesome start and only got more and more awesomer. At the beginning of May, with all the papers and TV being dominated by news about the first crack in the Iron Curtain (more than 200 kilometres of barbed-wire fence had been taken down along the border of Austria and Hungary), the weather was warm enough to put on a T-shirt and shorts.

Midway through the month, on a Saturday when it was twenty-six degrees out and only a few cotton balls dotted the sky, Ali, Keith, Rachel and I headed down to the Toronto Beaches. I hadn't been there in years and had forgotten how incredible it was, especially on a sunny day.

We got off the streetcar in the east end of the city and made our way towards the boardwalk with a whole bunch of other people. By the time our feet touched sand, the beach was already half full. There were families and kids and teenagers and babies and old people and dogs all over the place. After walking for a bit, we found a spot that gave us a little privacy, and the girls pulled two huge towels each out of their bags.

"Tell me this is not kick-ass, J.R.!" Keith said as he tore at his shirt, which wouldn't come off fast enough. The girls also took off their tops and jean shorts, revealing a pair of bikinis. Rachel's was purple; Ali's was yellow.

Holy mother of God.

Rachel was hot in her bikini, but Ali was *smoking*.

I kind of hung back from the three of them and, as Keith mauled his girlfriend, who fended him off with not a little difficulty, I wondered whether I could actually take off my shirt. I was scared Keith would poke fun at my pancake chest in front of Ali, and breathed a sigh of relief when he didn't seem to notice.

"Do you want some suntan lotion?" Rachel asked Keith.

"That shit's for pussies."

"Nice," she said. "Real classy."

"How about you, babe?" Ali asked me. She was spreading Hawaiian Tropic up and down her legs.

"Sure."

I heard the word "fag" muttered behind me.

After lubing up, Keith and I walked to the water's edge, where smooth brown sand gave way to a pebbly shoreline. The girls had said they needed more time to prepare lunch, but if I knew Ali, it was going to be nothing less than a feast fit for a king.

The sun was directly above our heads by this point, and although the weather was hot enough to make you sweat, Lake Ontario was *freeeeeeeeeeeeeeeeezing*. As the water lapped up against my feet, goose bumps popped up on my arms. Still, a couple of brave souls were swimming, which made me think of Jung-ho. Keith skipped stones along the surface of the green-grey/kind-of-murky-but-still-clean-enough-to-swim-in water as I considered how it would go down next Tuesday (Jung-ho and her family had been in Korea the last couple of weeks, so she didn't know what had gone down in that time). She'd go to Dad's apartment, only to discover I wasn't there. Dad probably wouldn't be there either. Jung-ho would just be left standing in the hallway, wondering where I was.

Damn.

"What's on your mind there, Fruit Loops?"

"Huh? Nothing." One guy was doing the front stroke a ways out, and the other was just floating on his back, not a care in the world as the sun sparkled all around his nearly invisible body.

"You got any idea what you're going to do this summer?" Keith asked.

"Get a job, I guess. You?"

Keith skipped a stone that was his best of the day and seemed to go on forever. "Probably the same," he said. "My mom said she'd send me to camp if I want, but camp's for fairies and fruitcakes."

"Yeah."

Another stone went sailing along the top of the water.

"Seven skips," I commented." Not bad."

"Whatever. So you have any leads yet?"

"Nope."

"Yeah, me neither. Maybe we should both get jobs teaching kids how to play hockey and then sign up for a summer league at night. How cool would that be?"

"Pretty unreal," I said with a grin, even if it was a pipedream.

We were quiet as the waves washed over our bare feet.

"So, ah," Keith asked a minute later, "are you planning to stay with us for the whole summer?"

This was the question I'd been dreading since moving in with the Frasers. Mom said she wouldn't have her own pad until August and I couldn't bring myself to go and live with Dad again, which kind of left me between a rock and a hard place. Plus, not only were Keith's parents putting a roof over my head and feeding me, but Lorraine was forking over pocket money to me every week.

"Hey guys! We're all done!" Ali yelled.

I couldn't take my eyes off the water.

She'd be standing there in the hallway, all by herself, with no one to hold her hand up to the pool.

"Come on," Keith said, giving me a bump on the shoulder. "Our chicks await us."

He turned around and started walking up the beach, but I didn't budge. It was almost as if my feet were stuck in the sand.

"J.R.! You coming or what?"

She'd ride the elevator alone, her pink swimsuit on, earplugs and nose plugs in place, then take those frightening steps into the water without anybody around to catch her.

"J.R.!"

Screw it.

I moved forward with sudden purpose. The pebbles underneath hurt, but the bone-chilling coldness, going from my ankles to my shins and soon to my thighs was worse. With a lungful of breath, I put my hands above my head and plunged into the lake. The air was sucked right out of me, and still I pushed on, my arms cutting through the icy water, my legs kicking with every ounce of strength I could muster. When I came up for air, what felt like hours later, I took another deep breath and then sank to the bottom like an anchor, bubbles streaming out of my mouth.

One Mississippi...two Mississippi...

Toes on sand as smooth as a desert; bubbles emerging from my nose; the water somehow warmer down here; hair lifted off my forehead by the lake's current.

Five Mississippi...six Mississippi...

When I couldn't hold my breath any longer, I launched myself up like a missile. Bobbing up and down on the surface, I could see the girls clearly, a look of shock on their faces. Keith was beside Ali and Rachel and waving an arm high in the air, his "Come on! Come on!" pleas muffled because of the distance. I did an easy breaststroke into shore. Ali was waiting for me when I got there.

"Feel better?" she asked, wrapping a towel around my shoulders like a cape. She pulled the edges of it to bring me closer so that our faces were almost touching. A drop of water fell from my eyelash and rolled down into my mouth.

"Much."

"Everything okay?"

Maybe it was the effect of the lake's Arctic temperatures on my brain, but when I stared into Ali's eyes just then, I was more sure of anything than I'd ever been, my tremors non-existent, my heart beating at a snail's pace. And that's when I was struck with the wildest, craziest, most fantastical thought, that this concept called "love" I'd heard about in hundreds of movies and TV shows, which I'd read about in novels and watched people say countless times must be...

Staring into your girlfriend's eyes...

and knowing her as well as yourself...

and feeling...

safe.

"Yeah," I said. "Everything's fine."

"Good."

Ali turned around, but I reached for her hand before she could take a step away. She spun my way, confused. "What, babe?"

I squeezed her hand three times as she pulled me in close, got on her tippy toes, and brought her mouth up to my ear. "I adore you," she whispered, even though nobody was near us. "You know that, right?"

I kissed her earlobe. "I really do."

Ali and I held hands as we strolled up the beach. Keith was lying on his side, a pair of Ray-Bans shielding his eyes from the sun. "What was that all about, J.R.? Trying to prove you're some kind of tough guy for your woman?"

"Like you'd have half the balls to go in the water," Rachel said, slightly annoyed with her boyfriend's cockiness. "You know, for someone who talks a big game, you sure don't put your money where your mouth is very often."

"Whoa!" Keith said, propping himself up on his elbows. "Do I detect a challenge?"

"Eat your sandwich, you goon," Rachel fired back, unimpressed, as she threw a sandwich wrapped in aluminum foil Keith's way.

On top of the PB&J, ham and cheese, and tuna sandwiches, Ali and Rachel had brought a salad, chips, pickles, soft drinks, bottled water and cookies. Even more amazing was that they'd brought a mini-stereo and a bunch of tapes. Peter Gabriel's *So* was playing as we unwrapped aluminum foil, popped open plastic container lids, and worked our way through a mountain of food.

Keith and I cleaned up after lunch while Rachel and Ali cruised down to the water. "They're pretty hot, huh?" Keith said in passing as we threw all the garbage into a single plastic bag.

"Say what?"

"The girls. They're pretty shit hot."

I looked towards the shore and saw Ali tracing a foot through the sand. Rachel was saying something while waving her arms all over the place.

"Yeah."

When they returned, Keith said I went to play a little soccer down the beach, where a bunch of guys around our age were in the middle of a pick-up game. The girls didn't really seem to care one way or the other because they just said "Uh-huh" from behind their magazines.

Like road hockey or shinny, the soccer game was disorganized and wild and there were basically no rules. That didn't matter, though. To be out in the sun on such a wicked day, running around with the sand under my feet, the hottest girl my age relaxing down the beach from us, my troubles evaporated like steam from a Zamboni's tail end as it floods the ice.

Until I got nailed in the honker by someone's shot and Keith took exception, that is.

At one point, the other team was pelting our goalie with shots and so I kind of got bored and looked around, which is when I noticed two older guys talking with Ali and Rachel. I couldn't hear a word of what they were saying, but Ali was laughing her ass off as she sat with both hands planted behind her on the beach towel. Rachel wasn't laughing quite as hard as she listened to Romeo No. 2 drone on about something probably gay and *so* not funny.

That's when one of the guys on my team launched the ball my way and expected me to take it off the chest, I guess. Thing is, I didn't see it until the last second, so when I turned to face the action again the ball nailed me right in the nose. I crumpled on the spot and put my hands over my face, blood spewing out of each nostril.

Keith, of course, took this is a personal affront and lost his marbles. As he mouthed off with his usual creative vocabulary, saying the guy had intentionally aimed for my face, a circle formed around us. Although the guy who'd kicked the ball at me had already said sorry, Keith still went at him. (Truthfully, he really didn't need to apologize. First, he was bigger and stronger and could have just told me to go stuff it. Second, it was technically my fault for not paying attention to the game and getting so caught up with those flirting Romeos). Keith and Buddy Boy ended up in a wrestling match, swinging at each other as a few of the other players tried to separate them. Keith spouted off a whole bunch of potty-mouthed insults the whole time. He only shut up and agreed to walk away when Rachel, who'd run over with Ali, arrived on the scene.

The trip home was pretty uncomfortable. Ali and I made small talk in a fake kind of way, not wanting to rock the boat because Rachel and Keith weren't talking. There was a part of me that wanted to ask about those dudes who stopped to talk with Ali and Rachel while we were playing soccer, but I figured now wasn't exactly the best time to bring it up. When we transferred from the streetcar to the subway, Rachel finally broke the silence and accused Keith of starting the fight at the beach. This set him off because all he did, he said, was stick up for his best friend. Rachel called him a goon. Those were the last words they said to each other before Keith and I got off at Rosedale Station.

Rachel phoned Keith after dinner on Sunday night and broke up with him.

"She said my anger is too out of control for her to handle," Keith said as we sat in the TV room, watching the Canadiens and Flames battle it out in Game Four of the Stanley Cup. "She thinks it's best if we walk away now so we can stay friends." Keith scoffed. "*Friends,*" he repeated in a mocking voice. "You know what she actually said to me?"

"What?"

"*For Justin and Ali's sake,*" Keith said in a girly voice. "Whatever. I hope I never see her again."

"That sucks, man."

"Doesn't matter. Summer's almost here. Then we'll meet more chicks than we know what to do with. We'll party, me and you J.R., and pick up tons of girls, maybe even some older chicks."

"Right."

Keith shook his head. "She didn't deserve me anyway, right?"

"No way. Not in a million years."

I felt bad because I'd never told Keith what Ali had said about Rachel having a problem with his temper. Maybe if I'd mentioned something before we went to the Beaches, Keith would have been less aggressive, at least when he was around Rachel.

I was still thinking about my best friend's breakup when Ali and I hooked up at McDonald's the next day. Ali got a cheeseburger made like a Mac and I ordered a Quarter Pounder with Cheese. We sat near the front, the same place we'd been when Ali told me I had an "eating problem" on our first quasi-date. We were munching away when I brought up Keith and Rachel, the fact that she'd dumped him and how much that sucked. Ali said it did suck, but that it was probably for the best. When I asked why, expecting her to say Keith was too angry or too immature, she instead told me that she and the girls would be gone for the entire summer anyway, so it didn't make much sense for Keith and Rachel to stay together if things weren't working out between them right now.

Until then, I hadn't asked Ali what her plans were for the summer, figuring now that she was in high school she'd get a job. (Camp was only for kids, right?) But when she told me it was "probably for the best" with Keith and Rachel, some part of my brain short-circuited. Ali asked me a question and I didn't respond. She asked again, but I was lost, thinking the same thing that happened to Keith lay in store for me.

"Justin?" she said, stealing one of my fries. "What is it?"

"What's what?"

"You're in another world. What's going on?"

"Nothing."

"Justin, everything was fine and good till a second ago and then all of a sudden you turned weird."

"I didn't turn weird."

"Yes, you did. What's going on?"

"How's your burger?"

"Don't try and change the subject. Why are you acting like this?"

"I'm not acting like anything."

"You are. Babe, please. What's racing through that brain of yours? I can tell you've got something on your mind."

"It doesn't matter," I said coldly. "The die is cast." I took my tray to the garbage, then walked to Eglinton Station, devastated Ali was going to break up with me for something as dumb as camp.

26

Regret is kind of a strange emotion. It's not like love, which is good, or hate, which is bad. It falls somewhere in between. I felt like a sack of horse manure about how it ended with Ali yesterday, but I also couldn't get over how she was going to do the same thing to me that Rachel had done to Keith.

To help resolve this linguistic dilemma, I opened up my dictionary and tracked down the word I was looking for:

re·gret
noun
3. a sense of loss, disappointment, dissatisfaction, etc.
4. a feeling of sorrow or remorse for a fault, act, loss, disappointment, etc.

Check, check and check. Ugh.
Ali didn't return my calls later that same night and probably only answered the phone the next day because she was sick and tired of listening to my lame messages. After a weak "Call me when you get this!" I dropped the whole ego/pride thing and left a slew of apologies on her answering machine, not really caring who in her house heard the

messages. All the better if Mrs. Blake was the one who got them because she might actually convince her daughter to forgive me.

When we finally did connect on the phone, Ali was pretty bitter from the get-go.

"Are you still pissed at me?" I asked, walking in circles around the bedroom and biting my fingernails.

"Justin, what's wrong with you? Is it your dad? 'Cause if it is that's awful. But guess what? Every family is a mess. I'm tired of you feeling sorry for yourself and taking it out on me."

"It's not that, Ali."

"Then what is it? Or what was it? You know I went home from McDonald's and actually cried?"

"I'm sorry. I swear. I didn't mean to make you—"

"Why were you such a jerkface, then?"

"Hey, you stole my line," I said through a deflated laugh.

"This isn't a joke, Justin. What's going on with you?"

I moved the cordless from one ear to the other. "Remember when we were talking about Keith and Rachel?"

"What about them?"

"You said it was obvious they'd break up because Rachel was going away for the summer."

"I did *not* say that!"

"That's exactly what you said."

"I said there was no point in them trying to make it work in different places if they couldn't make it work between them in the same city."

"Isn't that the same thing?"

"You're infuriating! No, it's not the same thing. And what does that matter anyway?"

"You'll be away with the girls all summer," I said. "You're obviously going to break up with me so you four can have a great time at *camp* together. I'm sure Debbie will be happy her best friend's single again."

I closed my eyes and sighed heavily at this last part, knowing right away it was a stupid thing to say, but the damage was already done.

"When did I ever say anything about breaking up with you because of camp, Justin? When? That's right. NEVER! I never said I wanted to end things because we'd be away from each other for two months."

Pause…extended pause…awkward pause…

"Ali, I didn't mean to screw this up."

"Well, you're doing a pretty good job of it, Justin."

"I really thought you were going to break up with me, though," I groaned. "It was stupid of me."

"*Ya* think?

"Will you let me make it up to you? In person? Can we get together tomorrow or Friday maybe?"

"I'm going to Rachel's cottage Friday for the long weekend. Why don't we just take the next few days to figure out where things stand."

"I know where things stand, Ali. And I said I'm sorry. Please, let's just get together for—"

"I'll call you on Monday when I'm back."

I opened the window beside the bed. My room felt like a prison cell, the air thick and suffocating. A siren in the distance was getting closer. "You really don't want to meet up—"

"Let's just talk when I'm home again."

"Right."

"Enjoy your weekend, Justin."

"Yeah. You, too."

Lorraine did a more convincing job than Keith of trying to get me to their cottage (with the same failed result, mind you). My best friend had asked if I wanted to do May Two-Four up north. When I said no, explaining how I had to start studying for finals or else I was going to fail grade nine, he didn't push. "Whatever. It's your life, twizzletits. If Jet Skiing around a lake watching hot, half-naked university babes drenched in sweat as they bake under the sun isn't your thing, then feel free to beat your meat here to your heart's content." His mom, on the other hand, had practically fallen on her knees to get me to go with them, saying I'd be lonely in the house by myself and that she was planning to cook so many wonderful meals for everyone and that the water was supposedly warmer for this time of year than ever before and wouldn't it be great to go swimming in May!

Only when the Frasers pulled out of their driveway, with a honk from Mr. Fraser and a hand out the window from Lorraine, did I actually believe they would leave without me. I buckled down to French vocabulary and math equations right away, playing video games for short spurts during study breaks. The weather was perfect all weekend, and while frustrated that I was cooped up inside for most of it, I was more depressed that Ali was still mad at me.

So, when Keith and the crew arrived home Monday night around dinnertime ("Dude! I saw the hottest chick I've ever seen in my life! Like, four hundred times hotter than that skank Rachel. And she waved at me!!!"), I waited for the phone to ring. At ten, I washed up and brushed my teeth, freaking out a little because we almost never talked past then. I tried making sense of this:

1. She was still on the road and hadn't arrived in the city yet.
2. She was in the middle of a fight with her mother and not in the mood to talk.
3. She'd gotten an incredibly rare form of poison ivy and was being airlifted to a small-town hospital.

The call never came Monday night, so Tuesday turned into one of those days where the second hand on the clock could not...move... f-a-s-t...e...n...o...u...g...h! As I wondered when to call Ali (right after school or later in the evening?), I was struck with an even better idea: I'd go and meet her at school and surprise her with flowers.

The final bell rang at three o'clock, a full half-hour earlier than Ali's classes ended. At a speed Flash Gordon would have been jealous of, I was in and out of a florist's and at the entrance to Ali's school. When Ali eventually flowed out the doors as part of a human tidal wave, she was joined by Debbie, Rachel and Vicki.

Great, I get to do this in front of the girls.

Rachel and Vicki were nice and commented on how beautiful the flowers were. Debbie was her usual dead-fish self, while Ali didn't seem to notice that I had brought her a dozen long-stem roses. After some meaningless chit-chat about how amazing the weather was up north on the weekend, the girls left Ali and me on our own.

"Thanks for the flowers," she said as we left the schoolyard.

"Do you like them?"

"Yep."

"How was the weekend?" I asked, deciding not to mention how she hadn't called last night.

"It was fun."

"Good."

"Yeah."

We kept going for a full block without saying another word, at which point I tried to break the ice(berg). "So—"

"What are you doing, Justin?" Ali snapped. "You think buying me roses—and I hate roses by the way—then showing up at my school is going to make things better?"

The roses comment stung. Then I remembered Christmas and the same stupid flowers I'd given Mrs. Blake.

"Sorry. I didn't know," I said. Tremors had begun running up and down my arms.

"You have a lot of nerve doing what you did today. Actually..."

Uh-oh.

"...I don't think I like the idea of you picking me up unannounced anymore and trying to be all Sir Lancelot or whatever."

"If that's what you want."

"What I *want* is to know why you get so mean with me. It's not fair."

"You're right. I get it now."

"No, I don't think you do because you make me do stupid things... stupid, *stupid* things when you act that way."

"Huh?"

We were on her street and not far from her house. Ali seemed confused by my question, saying, "I'm beyond angry, Justin, and fed up with how you treat me sometimes. You need to grow up because..." Ali was losing her train of thought. We were standing at the top of the path that led to her front door. A woman with a hot pink headband and a couple of Chihuahuas on leashes passed by us as those stupid mutts yapped away.

"Breathe," I said. Ali was struggling to keep the waterworks in check, her chest heaving. She couldn't get air into her lungs fast enough. She'd look at me for a fraction of second, shake her head, then just as quickly look away, as if I were some kind of pariah and my presence made her sick. "Breathe, Ali," I repeated in a sympathetic voice, tiny little pieces of my heart breaking.

"You're such an asshole!" The harshness of her comment caught me by surprise, as did the solid right she aimed at my chest and connected with perfectly. When I moved forward and tried to wrap my arms around her, Ali jumped back, disgusted. "No. Don't. Not now. I... don't." She wiped away a tear with a knuckle, opened her eyes wide and took a deep breath, in through the nose and out through the mouth.

"And take these," she said, handing me the flowers. "I don't deserve them."

"Ali, I dropped the ball with you last week. I understand that now." She looked down at the pavement, her head swivelling back and forth so many times I thought it would spin off. "I'm sorry. Truly."

"It's not that."

"Then what is it?"

She pulled a pack of tissues out of her bag and blew her nose. With glistening eyes, she looked up and that's when it hit me.

I'm about to be dumped.

"I know what you're going to say, so just say it. Get it over with." My words, like my soul, were hollow and lifeless. My arms were no longer shaking.

"It meant nothing. Absolutely nothing."

"Right."

"I didn't want it."

I folded my arms around the flowers, wincing as one of the thorns poked into my skin. "You didn't want us to be a couple?"

"No. I didn't want *it* to happen. I was just so…so angry with you. At first, I told myself you deserved it for treating me as badly as you did. But I was wasted and, I don't know, one thing led to another, and he—"

"Stop it," I said. "Stop right now. Don't say another word."

"I have to get this out. I absolutely have to, Justin. I've been a total insomniac the last two nights."

I'd had more than a week to get used to the idea of Ali breaking up with me. That was hard, but nowhere near as gut-wrenching as this news.

"Justin, please."

Ali went to give me a hug and instead pushed the roses into my arms. I winced at the sharp, sudden pain from the thorns and took a step backwards, refusing to look at her. I may have done some dumb things with Ali, but this was beyond shitty. I kept seeing Ali drunk and laughing and…touching some loser whose parents had an awesome cottage near Rachel's. He was holding her, groping her, smelling the same hair I did every time we kissed. My stomach revolted. I spun towards Ali's house and a stream of vomit went rocketing through the air like a puke rainbow.

"Thanks," I said when Ali offered me a tissue, hating myself and grossed out that chunks of chunky chunks were stuck up my nose. "I should get going."

"Wait, Justin. Don't you want to know what—"

I shook my head. "No, Ali. I don't."

She started stroking her hair at the bottom, like her hands were combs and could make it all nice and straight.

"So…what happens now, then? Between us, I mean?"

I frowned and said I had no idea.

"Then you're saying you still want—"

"I'm saying I don't know. That's all I'm saying. But I should take off," I said with finality, turning on a heel and speed walking all the way to Eglinton Station.

When I got home and handed Lorraine the roses, she couldn't stop gushing. "I don't think anyone has bought me flowers since Nathan and I were dating. Thank you, Justin. That's so kind of you."

I watched Lorraine chop a few centimetres off the stems and arrange the roses in a glass vase.

"Is Keith here?"

"Yes," she said, admiring the flowers.

Man, how could one woman go crazy for these things and another one actually hate them?

"He's upstairs in his room. Keith is on a strict diet of studying until final exams are over. I've limited his video game playing to thirty minutes a day. An hour on weekends." The fact she'd said "Keith" and not "you and Keith" wasn't lost on me.

"Okay, well, I'm going downstairs to do some studying myself."

Before I hit the first step, Herc came out of nowhere, tongue hanging out and demanding some loving. I patted his head and thought how much cooler he was than those stupid Chihuahuas.

"Justin?"

"Yes?" I turned around while scratching Herc's head and ears. You'd have thought the dog had died and gone to heaven.

"They're beautiful," Lorraine said, indicating the flowers. "But they weren't for me, were they?"

I flicked my bangs and looked away. "No."

"Regardless, it was very thoughtful of you."

Ali didn't call that night. She did, however, phone Wednesday. When Lorraine hollered from upstairs that the call was for me, I guessed who it was and asked her to take a message. Thursday night the same thing happened. Lorraine paused when I asked her to take a message, which she did, and then came down to my room in the basement. My chair was one of those swivelling things, so I made the hundred-and-eighty-degree turn with a push off one foot when she knocked on my bedroom door.

"That was Ali again," Lorraine said. "Do you mind if I have a seat on your bed?"

"Go ahead."

"This Ali girl must be pretty special." She took a seat on the bed and crossed her legs.

"I guess so." I didn't mind talking to Lorraine about Mom and Dad; when it came to Ali, I got a little weirded out.

"You know, it's one of the many paradoxes in life, but ignoring a girl when she likes you actually makes her like you more. Crazy, huh?" Lorraine said, smiling. I gave a fake laugh and flipped my bangs.

"But even the most lovesick girl won't wait around till the end of the world for a boy." She waited a second before going on. "Do you want to know a secret?"

"Sure."

"More than flowers or boxes of chocolates or diamonds, do you know what a girl really wants?"

"Shoes?"

Lorraine squawked so hard she almost fell on the floor. "Who told you that?" she asked.

"My mom always says that you can buy a girl's affection for a day with jewellery, or you can steal her heart for a lifetime with a nice pair of shoes."

"Your mother's a smart woman, Justin," Lorraine said through a laugh. "And while I'd tend to agree with her most of the time, you know what's the real secret to winning a girl's heart?"

"What's that?"

"Kindness." Not exactly the answer I'd been looking for. "Shoes and jewellery are fabulous, of course, but treat a girl kindly and she's yours forever. Anyhow," Lorraine said abruptly, standing up and heading for the door, "I should let you hit the books."

"Thanks."

"Oh," Lorraine added as she was about to close my door, "and in case I forgot to mention, that was Ali who phoned."

"Right. Thanks."

I spent Saturday cruising around downtown. Part of me just needed to get out of the house and have a few hours on my own. I kept my eyes open for NOW HIRING signs. Getting close to the bottom of Yonge Street, I came across a notice for job openings at McDonald's. I walked inside and a guy behind the till directed me upstairs, where they were holding interviews for what seemed to be an interesting possibility.

"Basically," explained the platinum-blonde woman in a navy blue pantsuit and scary amounts of mascara, "we're looking for young, ambitious people to work at SkyDome this summer. We've hired most of the people we need, but there are still a few openings left."

I asked what the job was all about, and Oxsana Fedotenko told me how McDonald's had won the right to do all the vending at SkyDome when it opened next month. Unlike Exhibition Stadium, where they'd sold nothing but popcorn, hot dogs, peanuts, and Coke in the stands, McDonald's would be going around with everything from hamburgers, fries and Chicken McNuggets to soft drinks, peanuts and ice cream bars. "Essentially," she continued, "every sales associate is assigned a product at the beginning of a game or event. You're paid five dollars an hour *plus* ten percent commission for whatever you sell. There are further incentives if you have sales totalling three hundred, five hundred or seven hundred and fifty dollars at a single event."

While the hourly rate was less than minimum wage, I'd only have to work from seven to ten or eleven at night, and only when there was a Jays or Argos game (or special event) scheduled. That left my days free to do whatever I wanted. As I filled out an application form, Mrs. Fedotenko asked me a few questions, starting with, "Do you have any sales experience?"

"Yes. I've worked at a coffee shop."

"Excellent. And do you feel comfortable in public settings? Public speaking? Talking to strangers? That sort of thing?"

"Oh, yeah," I said, thinking of my essential tremor.

"And how are you at math? Can you make quick calculations?"

"Top of my math class."

"And what school is it you said you went to?" She obviously knew the name because she then asked, "That's a private school, isn't it?"

"Yes."

Mrs. Fedotenko broke a few of the bones in my hand as she sent me off, promising to have someone get in touch with me by early next week. I spent most of the walk home thinking about what Lorraine had said. It was a good thing girls secretly wanted kindness over shoes and diamonds because it was a heck of a lot cheaper. Still, every time I thought of "him" with Ali, touching her body, feeling her up, kissing the same mouth I'd locked lips with so many times, my stomach got queasy.

Back in my room, I mulled over Lorraine's advice a million times, the cordless in my hand all the while. Eventually, Lorraine won out over "him." I dialed her number only to learn she was out. I thanked Mrs. Blake and hung up.

A few hours later, the phone rang. Lorraine didn't shout down that it was for me; she actually came to my room, knocked and told me Ali was on the line. I said I'd take it.

"Hello?"

"Hiya," Ali said in a softer voice than usual.

"How's it going?"

"Okay. You?"

"Same." Lorraine hung up the phone on her end.

"My mom said you called."

Damn. She was putting this on me to get the ball rolling?

Justin! Kindness...

I started slow, telling her about the job interview and the ridiculous amounts of studying I'd done since last weekend. She followed my lead and told me about her shopping extravaganza earlier with Rachel. "We spent a fortune," she said. "My dad is going to murder me when he sees his credit card bill. You know what the crazy part is, though? After all these years with my mom, the ultimate shopaholic, he still doesn't get what retail therapy is."

I laughed, and while we both did a pretty good job of avoiding the real issue for a bit, it eventually came up. This is where things got tricky. As much as I wanted to tell Ali I missed her so much it hurt, I wanted to know how she felt about us. She wasn't very clear, though, and recounted facts more than feelings: "This has been a tough month for us" was followed by "And we'll be separated for eight weeks this summer."

"Okay. But what do you *want?*"

"With us?" she asked.

"Yeah."

"I want to see you again."

"As in—"

"As in I want to *see* you again."

"And do what?"

"I was thinking we could go to a movie tomorrow. Get a big bag of popcorn and just, you know, not do anything heavy.

"Did you have a flick in mind?"

"Let me check the listings first, okay?

"Sure."

We met at the Cumberland Theatre in Yorkville. Ali said that all the big cineplexes were either playing jockstrap movies or war films. "But the *Star* and the *Globe* both raved about this one," she explained as we got our tickets to *Cinema Paradiso.*

"What's it about?" Ali and I shared a gargantuan bag of popcorn with extra butter on it, a diet Coke for her and a ginger ale for me.

"I'm not sure. It's an Italian film and won some big award. That's all I know."

When Ali had told me on the phone she didn't want to do anything heavy, she couldn't have been picked a worse movie. If *Beaches* had turned her eyes into a stream of tears, this one turned them into Niagara Falls. When the credits started to roll, Ali had her head buried in my T-shirt, both hands wrapped around my arm and squeezing it so hard she left nail marks. Now, to be fair, I was a wreck by the end as well. The only foreign movies I'd seen were Hong Kong martial arts ones that were badly dubbed over. With *Cinema Paradiso*, however, everything from the story to the acting to the music had me fighting back my own waterworks by the end.

Afterwards, we went to a diner down the street for a snack. Ali got a Caesar salad and I had a grilled cheese sandwich. The conversation flowed pretty smoothly, neither one of us bringing up May Two-Four weekend or the summer holidays. We joked around mostly. Ali even punched me on the arm a couple of times, a sure sign that things were getting better between us.

On the way to the subway, we got an ice cream cone. "*Gawd*, I'm so fat now," Ali complained as she polished off her lemon sherbet. We were coming up to Yonge and Bloor.

"Yeah, and I've got a bridge in Brooklyn for sale."

"What the? What does that even mean?"

"Nothing. It's a…nothing."

"You're weird."

"Taken a look in the mirror lately, Weirdy McWeird," I said, barely getting the last word out I was laughing so hard.

"No, no…NO NO NO! Seriously," Ali said, a pained expression on her face. "I don't know what's worse, that you steal my material and destroy it or that you blatantly laugh at your own jokes. Your own *lame* jokes, I might add."

"Well, you know what they say."

"Do I even want to hear this?"

I was buckled over laughing. "Takes one to know one." People passing by us on the street would probably think I was choking and in need of the Heimlich Maneuver. When I finally got it together again, my face was as red as a tomato.

"How old are you? I mean, seriously, did you graduate from kindergarten last week?"

"I run a comedy workshop if you're interested in attending." Ali grinned. "Really. They're once a month and last for two hours. I'll even give you a discount."

"To your comedy workshop?"

"That's the one."

She shook her head. "You're certifiably nuts, you know."

I wanted to say I was certifiably nuts about her, but thought that would be taking it too far on our first "re-date," so settled for "Yeah, I actually have the certificate hanging on my bedroom wall."

"I bet you do. Well," she added a moment later, "this is where I get off."

"Right."

"How are you going to get home?"

"I'm going to walk back to Keith's." A second passed as I tried to think of something meaningful to say. "So, uh…"

"Yeah?" Ali's eyebrows rose.

I shrugged. "Think I could maybe call you this week?"

Ali nodded and started playing with one shoe as if a ballerina getting ready to do a pirouette. "That would be nice."

There was no sentimental hug or long kiss goodbye. I'm pretty sure we both wanted to do either (or both) of those things. But I, for one, was still too raw. In place of some overly emotional send-off, we just said "See ya." Ali went down the stairs, arms wrapped tight around her body while I waited at the top. As she got farther and farther away from me, I hoped she would stop, spin on her heels, and look up at me. No words were needed, only a look, one that said, *It's all good. We'll make it through this together.* But that's what happens in movies like *Cinema Paradiso*, not in real life.

27

Mrs. Fedotenko called and told me the job at SkyDome was mine. That was the good news. The bad news was I had exams June fifth, sixth and seventh, the same dates as my first three shifts.

On the Sunday night before Hell Week kicked off with sociology, I was flipping through channels when I came across something on CNN. A reporter was talking over top a guy dressed in black pants and a short-sleeved shirt who was standing on a really wide street and blocking a column of tanks. Every time the lead tank tried to get around him, the guy moved as well. He was basically giving the tanks two choices: they could stay parked where they were or run him over. The reporter explained how a place called Tiananmen Square had been cleared out by the army yesterday morning and that nobody yet knew how many protesters had been killed. The Chinese dude wasn't budging as the reporter rambled on in his British accent: "This is a *revolutionary* moment in Chinese history. After the *bloodbath* that took place at the hands of the military yesterday on *innocent* civilians, you are *now* witnessing one man stand up to China's politburo in defence of more than a *billion* fellow citizens. This is *extraordinary*. Absolutely *extraordinary*. I have *never* in my twenty-seven years of journalism seen *anything* quite like this."

I hit MUTE.

Part of me was wondering if the tanks would roll over the guy on live television, making me think of the chapter we'd done in sociology (and fresh in my mind) about the "desensitization of society and how the Vietnam War being broadcast into the living rooms and dining rooms of 1960s and '70s America had forever changed how the public perceived war and, more importantly, death," as Mr. O'Connor had put it. When we'd done that unit it had all been theory, things I had to imagine, because I hadn't even been born when it was happening. Now, as I watched this skinny pecs Chinese guy tempting death, I had to turn the television off. Something about the scene made me ill.

With exams over (twelve weeks and one day of freedom ahead of me, not that anyone was counting) and the Jays in Milwaukee playing the Brewers, I headed over to Dad's apartment building. Ever since that day at the Beaches, I'd been meaning to give Jung-ho another swim lesson. On the walk over, I debated whether I should pop in and see Dad. I couldn't get that line Mom had written in her letter out of my head: *Letting go doesn't mean you ever stop caring; it just means I can't show you in person how much I do.* Although I hated admitting Mom was right, that's pretty much how I felt about Dad. While I still cared about how he was doing, there was nothing left to say at this point.

As I passed by 804, I noticed a whole bunch of flyers and menus sitting at the foot of Dad's apartment. I assumed that meant he hadn't left his place for at least a couple of days or hadn't come home in as much time. Strange, I thought, as I knocked on 802. Jung-ho lit up like a Christmas tree when she opened the door. "Justin!" she howled, wrapping her arms around my waist. Where did you go? Nobody ever answers your door anymore."

"Not even my dad?"

"No."

I explained how I'd moved in with my mom a couple of weeks ago, thinking a ten-year-old would find it weird that I was living with a friend and not with either of my parents. "Anyway," I went on, peeling off Jung-ho's arms, which clung to me like a couple of Fruit Roll-Ups. "How'd you like to go swimming today?"

"Eek! Really?"

"Really."

"*Omma!*" Jung-ho yelled as she spun around and raced towards the bathroom. "*Justin opparang suyung haraw kalgae!*"

I put on my trunks upstairs. Jung-ho and I spent a while puttering around the shallow end, splashing each other and basically having a good ol' time of it. Although her doggy paddle/gasping-for-air routine had gradually changed into something loosely called "swimming" over the last month, I was still surprised when she asked if we could go to the deep end.

"Are you sure?"

"Yes."

Jung-ho swum over to the stairs and got out of the pool.

"What are you doing?"

"I want to jump in together."

When we got to the edge of the pool, our toes curling around the tiles of the deep end, Jung-ho reached for my hand. She scratched her nose with the other hand as I looked off to the side and a noticed a NO DIVING sign for the first time (I'd been diving into the pool all year whenever I came up to swim by myself).

"On the count of three?" I asked.

Jung-ho nodded.

"Okay. One…two—"

"Wait!"

"What?"

"Start again," she said, moving her feet millimetres closer to the edge.

"All right. One…two—"

"Wait!"

I loosened my grip on her hand, but Jung-ho didn't let go. "You sure you want to do this?"

"Yes. Just one more time, okay?"

"All right. Here we go. One…two—"

"No!" Jung-ho shrieked, using her free hand to latch on to my forearm. "I'm scared, Justin."

"I know. And guess what?"

"What?"

"It's okay. We don't have to do this today. We'll try it another time."

"You don't think I failed?"

"No way. Never, ever, ever, ever."

We went to the shallow end again, though our lesson was cut short when the fire alarm started ringing. I told Jung-ho it was probably a false alarm, but took her downstairs just in case. On my way towards the staircase, curiosity got the better of me and I knocked on 804. When no answer came, I fished around for the key and let myself in. As the door closed behind me and I turned around, I froze in my tracks. My heart was beating, but I'd stopped breathing. There was a tiny figure lying chest down on the floor, his head turned to the left. Fully dressed, drool was pasted to the side of Dad's face. He looked as small as someone from those concentration camp pictures I'd seen in history books. Whether it was three seconds or three minutes later, when it finally dawned on me that he needed help, it was like being walloped in the facemask.

"DAD!" I screeched, collapsing to my knees. I touched his cold, pale, stubbly face, but he didn't move. "DAD!" I looked around once before running to the bathroom, where I got a towel and cleaned his mouth of all the crap around it. Lunging towards the phone, I hit three digits.

"911. What's your emergency?"

"It's my Dad. My dad…he's, I don't know, he's—"

"Sir, calm down," a bored, lifeless voice said. "Does your father need medical assistance?"

"Yes! Yes!"

"He's passed out or comatosed or…or…or…dead. I don't know. Just send an ambulance. PLEASE!"

"How long has been like that, sir?"

"I don't know. I…I…I just found him."

The woman asked for the address and apartment number, and said an ambulance was on its way.

I hung up and lay down on the floor beside Dad, talking quietly to him. "An ambulance is on its way. Everything's going to be all right… like it was…perfect…and normal." I stroked the hair off his forehead. He still wasn't blinking or showing any sign of life. "It's okay," I said as if lulling him to sleep. "Everything's going to be just fine."

Including Dad, there were three patients in the hospital room. His bed was nearest to the door. The only thing providing any kind of privacy was a white curtain hanging from the ceiling. Machines were whirring and buzzing. The other patients, both of whom had tubes going into their arms and hands and noses, were watching a TV show I didn't recognize from a mounted television set on the wall. In the couple of hours doctors had been dealing with Dad, I'd gone down to the cafeteria and had a meal. Dr. Phillips, a tall, lanky guy like me with spikey grey hair, said there was nothing to do but wait and see until the initial lab results came back.

Around four o'clock, I went up to Dad's room and moved slowly towards his bed. I figured he was sleeping, but maybe he was just passed out on whatever drugs they'd given him. He lay against a stack of pillows as white as snow, the thick sheets pulled up to his chest. It's funny, but whenever I'd looked at Dad in the past I'd never really *looked* at him. Now, with his forehead fully exposed, I got a clear view of the damage I'd caused in August of 1981 when we were driving home from Georgian Bay. I was seven and had broken out with chicken pox the last day of our summer vacation at a cottage Dad had rented for the three of us. Being cooped up in a car for hours, Mom later told me, let my chicken pox make their way to Dad. Only, he'd never had it as a kid and wasn't immune to the virus, so he got shingles in the weeks after we arrived home. I was too grossed out by the little red bumps all over my body to worry much about what was happening with Dad, but even when he got better, the pockmarks on his forehead never went away.

The door opened suddenly and gave me a jump. A black woman came in and checked over all of Dad's contraptions while making some notes. In a heavy Caribbean accent she said the doctor would be with me shortly and then made her way to another patient.

"Hi, Justin," Dr. Phillips said not a minute later upon entering the room. "How are we holding up?"

"Fine, thank you."

"Good."

Dad was awake. "Hello, Mr. Maloney. How are we feeling?"

"Never been better." As Dad coughed, you could hear the phlegm coming up from his throat.

"Excellent," Dr. Phillips said as he looked at me again. "Your father here wouldn't stop with the nurses earlier, Justin. If I were a betting man, which I'm not, but if I were, the smart money would be on you to be quite a successful hockey player in the future." I brushed my bangs aside. "Now, is there anything I can get you, Mr. Maloney?" Dr. Phillips continued.

"Something for the pain would be marvellous."

"I'll have a nurse take care of that right away."

The two of them talked a bit more and then Dr. Phillips asked to have a word with me outside.

"Justin," he said when we were alone in the hallway, the smell of creams and ointments inescapable, "we've only begun to run all the tests we need to. I'm going to have a pathologist look over his blood work. We should have some conclusive results in the next few days. But," he continued, his confident grin making me feel a bit better, "he's going to be receiving the finest care while he's with us." I stuck my hands in the pockets of my jeans. "From what I understand, it's just the two of you."

"Huh?"

"Your father told me you're an only child and that your mother is living overseas."

"Right."

"Is there anyone you want to call, family members or friends perhaps, who might be able to cheer your dad up?"

"Yes."

Dr. Phillips waited for me to go on. He could probably see I was a little out of it because the next thing he said was, "Well, on that note, I'll go and fetch a nurse for your father."

"Thank you."

Before returning to Dad's room, I headed to the payphone and called the only person I could think of.

Ali picked up on the third ring.

Ali poked her head in, a trail of blonde hair falling down the side of her face. My guess was she hadn't known there'd be two other people

337

in the room and that everyone else just came and went as they pleased. I rushed over and took her aside in the hall.

"Hiya."

"Hey."

"How's your Dad doing?"

"I think they've got him whacked out on a bunch of drugs. Listen, there's something I've got to tell you."

"Justin, I know. There's a lot I want to say about us as well."

"That's not it." I lowered my voice as a nurse breezed past us. "It's about my dad."

When I didn't go on, she put a clinched fist up to her mouth. "What is it?"

"Look, it's just…he's rough. He's in bad shape—*really* bad shape— and I needed to tell you that before you walk in there and see him."

This time, Ali wasn't as quick to say anything. "Okay." She breathed in deeply and nodded her head. "We'll get through this."

We?

Ali bowed her head. "A lot's happened in the last month, Justin. Like, *a lot* a lot." She looked at me again. "But *we'll* get through this."

I grinded my teeth, knowing my dentist and orthodontist would murder me. Then a random thought came to me and I smiled: *Now is the time to make circles with mints, do not haste any longer.* "All right. Let's go in."

"Hi, Mr. Maloney!" Ali said with a forced joy, striding towards his bed. I walked around so we flanked him. I knew the minute she spoke she was already choked up. With a glance at the clock on the wall, I gave her five minutes, tops, before I got her out.

"Ali, my dear, you are indeed the North Star in my night sky." Dad spoke slowly, each word a strain for him, it seemed. "You look as lovely and as resplendent as a cherry blossom in spring. Have you ever seen a cherry blossom…" Dad coughed up a lung. "…in spring?"

"No, I haven't." Tiny dimples might have surfaced on her cheeks, but cracks were running up and down Ali like hot water splitting through ice. Dad moved a weak hand to the side of the bed and asked Ali if she would hold it.

"Of course."

"I just want to feel the warmth of youth on my skin again." Dad closed his eyes. Then his lips parted and he said, "'Other men said they have seen angels,/But I have seen thee/And thou art enough'." He opened his eyes. "George Moore wrote that poem and…" Another lung was coughed up. "…I think I know for whom he penned it."

Ali struggled to swallow. I was about to say something, but she kept it together. "I, umm, was going to pop out and get a drink. Can I get either of you something?" she said, looking first at Dad and then at me.

"Yeah, I'll take whatever they have."

"My dearest, you're kind to offer, but your presence here today is all I could have asked for."

"Okay. So, I'll go and find a vending machine and…yeah."

"I'll come grab you in a minute."

"All right," she said and was gone.

I sat down beside Dad. He was resting again, but unlike those few seconds when Ali's hand was on top of his, there was no look of peace on his face. Soon, my eyes were closed as well, my head directed towards the floor. When I looked up, Dad was staring at me, his head turned sideways on the pillow.

How long had he been looking at me?

"Do you love her, Justin?" he asked. It was practically a whisper.

I waited out the question for as long as I could. "I'm not sure."

"There is no grey area in love." Dad wheezed and coughed. "May I have my cup of water, please?" He drank slowly and with difficulty, his arms shaking badly. "Do you and Ali hold hands?"

"Say what?"

"When you're together? Do you hold hands?"

I flipped my bangs. "Sometimes."

The corners of his mouth turned up. "I'm so glad to hear that. Don't ever stop. The moment you do, it's gone. The tactile sense is so deeply affecting."

"Okay. Umm," I said a second later, "I'm going to go and get Ali, okay? I'll be back in a jiffy."

At the nurse's station, I asked where the closest vending machine was. A woman who looked like she hadn't slept in days said there was one down the hall to my left, but Ali wasn't there. Scared she'd been too upset to stay, I became frantic in my search around the massive floor of the hospital. I eventually found her at the opposite end, where she was sitting alone on a four-chair bench. Her head, bobbing up and down, was buried in her hands.

"Ali!"

She looked at me with bloodshot eyes, got up off the seat and threw her arms around me. "I'm sorry, Justin. I'm *sooooo* sorry. I had no idea it was this bad. I didn't. I swear."

"*Shh...*" My neck was quickly warm with her tears. I stroked the back of her head as slowly as Mom used to with me sometimes. "Thanks for coming."

"Oh, you," she said, pawing at her eyes like windshield wipers. "You knew I'd come."

She's an angel, Justin. Someone fashioned in the heavens.

"Can I tell you something?"

"What's that?" she sniffled.

"It's a secret, though, so you can't tell anyone."

"Okay."

The lump in my throat squeezed its way down as I took a small, quiet breath. Then I moved my lips beside her ear and said, "Ali?"

"Yeah?"

"I adore you."

Summer

28

Dad died on June 26.

The pathologist came back with his blood work and said he had stage four cirrhosis and primary liver cell cancer as well as primary carcinoma of the lungs. "It's terminal," she told me the last time we spoke. "The cancer has advanced too far in his lungs and liver."

"Okay." I glided a hand slowly across my bangs. "So, what, umm…"

"My best guess," she said, folding her arms, "is that he has six months. It could be more, it could be less. I'm terribly sorry, Justin."

As I learned when Dad died, doctors are human, like everyone else. When you hear someone's got so many weeks or months left to live, it's a guess. Some are told they have a year and end up making it another decade; with others, like Dad, it's the opposite.

The Jays were out of town in late June, freeing me up to spend a lot of my days and nights with Dad. He rested more often than not, though we did take daily walks around the block or, on occasion, around the neighbourhood. We'd also go to The Last Resort now and again to say hi to Alicia and some of the other regulars Dad knew. I filled the remaining hours reading to him from his favourite book.

On Dad's first day back in the apartment, I was sitting with my feet on the bed as he pointed to the kitchen.

"What do you need?" I asked, not sure if he had anything in his fridge.

"A drink."

I looked at the glass of water on the table beside him. "Not water?" He shook his head.

"Dad..."

"*Please.*" It wasn't a request.

His hands shook so badly when I gave him his mixture of water, ice cubes and whiskey that he could barely keep it from spilling. "Hold on," I said, returning to the kitchen and finding a straw.

"Thanks, kiddo," he said in a weak voice.

Only then, with Dad lying in bed and taking sips from his drink, did I read from chapter one.

> Well, Prince, so Genoa and Lucca are now just family estates of the Buonapartes. But I warn you, if you don't tell me that this means war, if you still try to defend the infamies and horrors perpetrated by that Antichrist—I really believe he is Antichrist—I will have nothing more to do with you...

When Dad got sleepy, I'd slide down on the floor and put the TV on low. With the two channels he had left, I could usually find something half decent to keep me interested until he woke up and asked me to read again. Other times we'd just talk, debating things like whether Mario really was "the next One" or whether the "Maple Laughs" would ever win another Stanley Cup. One time Dad even asked which team I wanted to play for *when* I got drafted.

"I think every kid from Toronto wants to wear the blue and white." Then I thought of how much Dad loved Gordie Howe growing up and added, "But I think playing in Detroit would be pretty cool, too."

Dad smiled.

His final weekend was the only time we had company. Dad wanted Ali to join us. I hadn't told him how our relationship had changed over the last few weeks; Ali showing up at the hospital wouldn't have done anything to make him think differently. I asked him what he wanted to do and without hesitation he said, "I would love to visit the RCYC."

"Ahh…okay."

Years ago, Dad was a member of the Royal Canadian Yacht Club, and though he never had a boat to call his own, he would sail with friends on weekends. Now that I thought about it, sailing might have been the only hobby he had outside of reading. But when the bottom fell out and he lost his job at the accounting firm, he had to let the membership go, reluctantly, I'm sure.

I said I'd make a few phone calls. Deep down, I wasn't overly optimistic. The RCYC was one of those hoity-toity clubs where people had to dress up just to get on the damn boat over to the island, forget about crashing the club as an ex-member. Predictably, they weren't in the business of letting the public just saunter over for the day. When I pleaded with them, explaining the circumstances over the phone, they apologized and said there was nothing they could do. Policy was policy.

I got in touch with Ali later and asked if she wanted to hang with Dad and me on Saturday. She said sure, but from her tone I couldn't tell whether she was excited to get together or if she was doing this out of sympathy for Dad. Whatever the case, I told her about Dad's request. Ali thought about it and suggested going to Centre Island. Technically speaking, the RCYC was connected to Centre Island by a bridge, which seemed like a pretty good compromise. I ran the idea by Dad and he had just one question: "Did you ask Ali if she would be joining us?"

"Yeah. She said, and I quote, 'I can't wait to see your dad!'"

Lie? Fib? Who cares!

The weather, as Dad liked to say, "conspired in our favour" that Saturday in late June. The sky was a sea of blue, the temperature a perfect twenty-five degrees. Mr. Kim helped track down a wheelchair and a Wheel-Trans bus picked Dad and me up from the apartment. Dad looked as small as a kid in the wheelchair, his feet barely reaching the pedals. Even with the warm weather, he had me get him dressed up in his finest duds, complete with a navy blue sailor's blazer (and RCYC insignia), white slacks and a pair of brown Topsiders.

When we got down to the Queen's Quay area, Ali was waiting for us. "Sorry," I said as we got Dad off the mini-elevator thing. "These guys were late grabbing us."

"It's fine. I got down here late myself." She looked at Dad and mentioned how handsome he looked.

"Ali, dear, I would have knocked your socks off in my day." Ali and I laughed. Dad didn't flinch. "But as it stands, I'll have to accept nothing more than looking respectable for now. Thank you for your gracious comment because…" Dad cleared his throat and coughed. "I do feel somewhat debonair."

"You look *very* debonair, Mr. Maloney."

Dad reached back and patted her hand. "You're too kind, Ali. Much too kind."

When we got on the ferry, most people headed to the upper deck of the split-level ship. I wheeled Dad towards the front of the main deck and he was quiet as he took in Lake Ontario with a satisfied grin on his thin face. Halfway over, he said, "You know, there is one regret I have in life."

"What's that?" I asked, hoping this wouldn't start the day off on the wrong foot.

"Never having owned a boat. I would have liked that."

"Like a sailboat?" Ali asked from the opposite side of Dad's wheelchair.

"Yes. Perhaps a twenty-eight or thirty-two foot Catalina. Nothing ostentatious. But she'd be a fin keel beauty who'd take me to the farthest reaches of the Great Lakes." He paused and watched the boats in the distance, their wind-filled sails dotting the horizon. "And I would have called her *Euphemia.*"

"Who's Euphemia?" Ali asked.

"Ah! Now that you will have to ask my esteemed son," Dad said with a clap of his skeleton-like hands.

Ali looked over at me. I shrugged my shoulders.

The grass on Centre Island was so potent of whatever makes grass green that the smell of it hung as heavy in the air as Mom's perfume used to. We found a spot to have lunch in a shaded area under a tree. Ali took everything out from the basket she'd brought along and dished it out onto plates as I moved Dad onto flat ground. When he reached for his flask from inside his blazer pocket, I sighed. Ali looked at me, knowing everything I did about Dr. Phillips' warnings. I was standing behind Dad and shook my head, hoping Ali wouldn't say anything, which, thankfully, she didn't.

Before lunch, we did a *New York Times* crossword puzzle together. Every time Dad got one of the answers, Ali would light up. "Ah! You're so right, Mr. Maloney!" making Dad, I'm sure, feel like a rock star. For the rest of the afternoon, we pecked away at the lunch Ali had prepared, which included a filet mignon she'd made herself, garlic mashed potatoes, as well as club sandwiches. We chatted about everything from Ali's summer plans to next year's hockey season to politics (Dad was convinced the Soviets and Chinese were finished and would both rot from within by the end of the millennium).

Later on, they asked me to read from Dad's favourite book. Afraid I'd bore her to tears, I only agreed (and reluctantly) after Ali insisted (and insisted and insisted). Elbows planted firmly on the ground, she had her chin supported by the palms of her hands. Dad took a pull from his flask and closed his eyes.

How strange, how extraordinary and joyful it was to her to think that her son—the little son whose tiny limbs had faintly stirred within her twenty years ago, the son over whom she had so often quarreled with the count who would spoil him, the son who had learned to say 'pear' before he could say 'nanny'—should now be away in a foreign land, in strange surroundings, a gallant warrior, alone, without help or guidance busy doing his proper work.

All the universal experience of the ages, showing that imperceptibly children do grow from the cradle to manhood, did not exist for the countess. Her son's progress at each of its stages had seemed as extraordinary as though there had not been millions upon millions of human beings who had gone through exactly the same process. Just as twenty years before she could not believe that the little creature that was lying somewhere under her heart would one day wail and suck her breast and begin to talk, so now it was incredible that that little creature could be this strong, brave man, the paragon of sons and of men, that judging by this letter he was now.

Two days later, Dad would be gone. On the Sunday night before I left his apartment, I tucked him into bed and made sure he had a glass of water by his side and a heavily diluted half-glass of the golden liquid with three ice cubes and a straw. We were barely a quarter of the way through the book and truly believed that Dad would make it all the way to the end of the story. Dr. Phillips had told me I needed to give Dad a reason to keep going, "some catalyst to move on and brave the next day," as he put it. I figured it'd take at least six months to finish this tome, and that was my security blanket.

I kissed him on his scarred forehead before leaving. Actually, I can't be sure of that because I wasn't really paying attention. What I didn't see was that Dad wasn't looking for a reason to "make it" one or two or even six more months; he was looking for nothing more than a peaceful exit. When I arrived at his place on Monday morning, I thought he was still asleep. I sat down with my thermos of tea and sipped away while watching TV. He still wasn't up by eleven o'clock, so I pulled out my copy of *A Prayer for Owen Meany* from my knapsack. By noon, he still hadn't stirred. I took a seat on the edge of the bed and rubbed his arm over top of the sheet. He didn't move. "Dad," I said, brushing the frail grey hair off his forehead, which was stone cold. "Time to get up." I shook his body delicately. "Dad?" I placed a hand on his neck and when I needed further proof, I put an ear to his chest.

Nothing.

I stood up, my arms in an L shape, one hand covering my mouth and the other supporting an elbow. Dad looked like Hans Solo at the end of *The Empire Strikes Back*, frozen in time. When I eventually got my crap together and went to the phone, there was no dial tone. Dad must have let his phone bill go the same way as cable, I thought. Uncertain what to do next, I made my way to 802. When Jung-ho answered the door, she shrieked.

"Eek! Justin!" she said, piercing my eardrums as she wrapped her arms around my waist.

"*Nugusaeyo?*" came a voice from inside the apartment.

Mrs. Kim appeared from the kitchen with a dishtowel in her hands. "Justin's here!" Jung-ho went on, refusing to let go of me.

"Oh," she said and bowed slightly.

"Do you think I could use your phone?" I asked Mrs. Kim, who seemed confused by my request.

"*Omma! Junhwahaeya dwaendaeyo,*" Jung-ho muttered from beside my hip.

"Oh, yes. Please."

"But I have to show you," Jung-ho said as I moved forward and tried to peel her off me. "I can swim! I can really swim!"

"Give me one second, okay?"

"I can swim in the deep end, Justin! All by myself! You have to watch me."

"I will, Jung-ho. I promise. Just give me a minute."

I pulled out a number from my wallet and dialed it on the rotary phone, one long rotation of the stupid plastic circle at a time. A male voice answered.

"Hello?"

"Hi, Jeff?"

"Justin?"

"Yeah. It's, ah…something's happened…"

Dale picked me up from Keith's place at nine-thirty. He'd flown home from Tokyo a few days earlier. In his short time back he'd not only taken care of the funeral arrangements, but had also bought me a black suit and black necktie.

Although the service was scheduled to start at eleven, Dale wanted us to get to the church early. He said hi to Lorraine before we walked out to the car. Even from a couple of feet behind him, I could smell his cologne, one of those musky brands that make a guy seem old and wise and rugged.

"New hairdo?" he asked as he unlocked the doors.

"Kind of." I'd never been to a funeral, but I'd seen enough of them on TV to know you were supposed to look smart, so had combed the bangs off my forehead for the first time in forever, the Alps now on full display for everyone to see. "So whose wheels are these anyway?" I asked inside the black BMW, which had that brand-new car smell to it.

"My father's latest toy." He moved the stick shift into first. The engine purred as we flew down the street. "He'll be joining us for the service with my step-monster and the rest of the gang. By the way," he went on, flashing me a quick look. "The suit fits you like a glove."

I was fidgeting and biting my nails, the nervousness all but seeping out of my pores. Scenery whizzed by me, but I was too stressed out to think about much except the speech I had to make at the funeral. And the people who would be there. And the fact that Dad would never be at another one of my games or practices again.

Dale could see through me, I'm sure. He pulled over a couple of blocks away from Keith's place, turned off the ignition and put a hand on my shoulder. "Weren't those good times last summer out in the country when you drove my Datsun around like Gilles Villeneuve?" he asked.

"*Pff.* I nearly busted up your transmission."

"Far from it. You were actually pretty damn good."

"Whatever."

Dale took his hand off my shoulder. "Can you still remember everything I taught you about driving standard?"

"I guess."

"You sure?"

"I think so."

"That's good enough for me."

Dale got out and came around to my side. "Let's go," he said as he opened my door. "We haven't got all day."

I stood on the sidewalk like a goof, as if awaiting instructions. "Well," he went on, lowering the automatic window. "This thing's not going to drive itself."

My eyes widened. "You want *me* to drive!"

"Is the Pope Catholic?"

"My dad used to say that sometimes," I said with a grin.

"Where do you think I learned it? Now let's go."

"Dale, I don't have my license. I'm not even—"

"Are you going to tell me something I don't know, Justin? Because if not, it would be stupendous if you'd hop in the other side so we can get this show on the road."

"But I've only driven standard twice!" I'd driven the Volare a few times, but it was automatic and way easier than a manual car like this.

"Cousin, you're beginning to sound a bit like a broken record. We really do have to get going. Come on. Chop, chop."

When I got behind the wheel, I felt a huge rush of adrenaline.

"Ready?" Dale asked.

"I think so."

"Emergency brake on?"

"Yep."

"Car in neutral?"

I jiggled the gear shift and made sure it was where Dale taught me it was supposed to be. "Good to go."

"Clutch in and foot on the brake," Dale said. I turned the key to the right. The car came to life, the dashboard a cool bright orange colour. I exhaled slowly as my heart went into overdrive with anticipation. "All right, emergency brake off, ease up on the clutch as you put her into first and replace the brake with some gas."

The car started rolling forward. Those memories I had of the exhilaration from last summer came flooding back when....the car burped a couple of times and died.

Crap!

"No worries, no worries," Dale said calmly. "Let's try it again."

The second time around the car almost did the same thing, but I showed a little more finesse with the clutch, which saved me the embarrassment of another automobile belch. "Treat the clutch like a first date," Dale explained. "Be on your best behaviour, be patient, and most importantly, don't lose your cool, no matter how bad things might seem."

I put it into first gear and we glided smoothly to a stop sign. After looking both ways, I leaned on the gas again, getting up to second gear as we neared Bloor. "Where are we going?" I asked, nervous as hell now that there were other cars on the road.

"Hang a left at the lights."

My biggest fear with driving standard was coming to a stop, so when the light turned yellow at the intersection I gunned it and swung a hard left.

"All right. Let's get her into third. We're going to head onto the Don Valley Parkway. The entrance is going to sneak up on your right at the end of the bridge."

I aimed the stick shift up to third, convinced we'd be pulled over by the cops any minute. But damn this felt good. I'd gotten Dale's old Datsun 240ZX up to third gear last July and the feeling was unmistakable. Now, in his dad's Beemer, I felt like a pilot going from a commercial airliner to a fighter jet.

"Good. Good," Dale said. "Get in the right-hand lane. We're going to pull a hairpin turn to get on the Don Valley Parkway, so gear down, okay?"

"Got it."

The turn onto the DVP was nerve-racking. I had to fight with all my strength to keep the steering wheel steady as we turned and turned and turned. Then, just like that, the road straightened out and we were on the highway.

I was driving a frigging BMW on the highway!

Dale replaced the CD in the Blaupunkt stereo. "Take it back up again," he said. I put the car into third, holding my speed around 80 km/h in what Dad used to call the "old ladies' lane." "Check your rearview mirror, then your side mirror."

"All clear."

"Signal that you want to get into the passing lane, put her into fourth, and let's have some fun."

I looked over at Dale.

"Never forget, Justin, toys are meant to be played with. Now let's do it."

My left flicker went on and I checked my blind spot for the tenth time.

Clutch in, down to fourth, ease up, then pressure on the gas.

I veered into the passing lane and the clutch caught beautifully, the car surging forward with jet-like speed. Dale turned the volume all the way up as the sound of an organ began humming out of the car's speakers.

"Bring it up to fifth, and deke in and around the cars like they're pylons on the ice. Unless they're blocking both lanes, find a way around them!"

The clutch went in and I slid his dad's "toy" into fifth. The drums and guitar from "Where the Streets Have No Name" were coming through so loudly the dashboard was shaking. Dale looked pretty laid-back, bopping along with the song as if watching the tide come in to shore from his beachside chair. He used the buttons on his door to lower all the windows. My hair went flying all over the place as I watched the odometer go from a hundred to a hundred and ten to a hundred and twenty. I blew by a sign that read 90 KM/H MAXIMUM.

From the corner of my eye, I saw Dale tapping away to the drums on the glove compartment, the air blowing around us like a tornado. I was weaving in and out of traffic so fast I couldn't get my hand on the indicator. "Holy crap!" I yelled. "HOLY CRAP! HOLY CRAP! HOLY CRAP!"

Originally, it was the wind blowing into the car that made my eyes get all glassy. Then my thoughts turned to Dad and the funeral Dale and I were on our way to, which is when real tears started forming, snapshots flashing across my mind: finding him on the floor of his apartment; sitting beside him the morning he passed away; looking at him in the stands from the rink, a solitary figure drinking from a flask; driving in the Volare, my elbow up on the edge of the window as I ignored him; eating Kraft Dinner together as he emptied the salt shaker over his noodles, looking at me and saying, "What? It's devoid of taste without a pinch of salt."; listening to him read to me as a kid, his feet up on my bed, a dictionary at my side; the two of us carrying a stick over our shoulders, skates hooked onto the shaft, while trudging through the snow on our way to play shinny.

As the song came to an end and The Edge's guitar slowly faded out, Dale put the windows up. "Time to gear down, pal. Take it nice and slow." In the span of one song we'd ended up past Lawrence Avenue, six subway stops from where we'd turned onto the highway.

I went down to fourth, then third, the engine a series of rolling thunder. I put it in second as we got off the DVP and headed into traffic along York Mills. Dale told me to pull over at the closest gas station so we could fill up.

When he got back from paying the guy in the booth, he shut his door and said, "You know what those crooks charged me?"

"What?"

"Fifty-point-one cents per litre! Highway robbery, I say!"

I snapped my seatbelt into place and smiled to myself; Dad would've been proud of his favourite nephew's stinginess.

"So?" Dale asked me as he brought the car to life. He looked across at me and asked if that had been fun.

"Are you kidding? I'm…I'm…totally freaking speechless."

"Feel a bit better?"

I nodded.

"Well," he said, easing the car into first as we made the return trip downtown, "always good to go into something like this with a sense of purpose."

People started arriving at the church around ten-thirty. Not surprisingly, the Frasers were the first ones through the huge wooden doors. Keith and I talked for a bit, about nothing, really, and then he stepped aside. Lorraine, who was wearing a black dress and wide-brimmed hat, took off her sunglasses and hugged me so hard I could hardly breathe.

"Justin, I can't tell you how sorry I am for you. Your father was such a remarkable person. And so funny, a sense of humour like nobody else." Lorraine collected herself. "Just remember that we're here for you. We're always here for you."

"I know. Thank you."

She hugged me one more time before Mr. Fraser expressed his sorrow for my loss with a handshake and a pat on the arm.

Soon there was a lineup of people waiting to have words with me that snaked all the way to the entrance of the church. Everyone from the team showed up, as did a few people I recognized from The Last Resort, including Alicia. Uncle Adam came with his wife and kids. There were even people there I'd never met: "I'm an old colleague of your father's," one would say; "Your father was the wisest man I ever knew. Best guy at the firm if you want to know my two cents," said another.

When Jeff Brady showed up, he introduced me to his wife Jasmine, who looked like she had a bowling ball stuck to her stomach. "I'm sorry for your loss, Justin," she said with one hand on her tummy. "I can't imagine how hard this is for you."

"Thank you."

"What did I tell you?" Jeff said, looking at his wife, whose cheeks were round and rosy. "This one's a fighter. Tough as nails, eh, big guy? Jasmine's actually due to have a C-section on Tuesday, but she told me there was no way she wasn't coming here today to pay her respects."

"Thanks."

"And when *he* is born on Tuesday—" Jeff said.

"—Or *she*," Jasmine cut in.

"Jazz and I are thinking of maybe keeping the J name thing going in our family. You know, like, continuity or whatever they call it. Anyhow, you have any suggestions for a boy's name starting with J that sounds all dignified, let us know, okay?"

I grinned. "I'll do that."

"We're going to find ourselves somewhere to sit now. Be strong today, all right, big guy?"

Unlike the rest of the guests who'd formed a line, Jung-ho and her mother were standing towards the back and keeping to themselves. Jung-ho was dressed in a black one-piece dress, with matching Mary Janes on her feet. Her mother had a simple black dress on with a gold crucifix around her neck.

"Thanks for coming," I said to Jung-ho, then looked at her mother and added, "Thank you for coming, Mrs. Kim."

Jung-ho wrapped her arms around my waist, her head snug against my stomach. Mrs. Kim stepped forward and handed me a white envelope with two hands.

"I never got to show you my swimming in the deep end," Jung-ho moaned, refusing to leave my side.

"You will. We're going to go swimming together every Tuesday this summer."

Jung-ho pushed herself back and craned her neck up at me. "Really?"

"Really." I said, sticking out my hand for her to photocopy.

The only time I nearly lost it before the service was when Ali arrived; she was wearing her amethyst necklace.

"Hiya," she said as her mom stood a few feet behind us.

"Hey."

"How are you doing?"

I bent my head slowly each way. "It's probably not going to be my finest day."

"Why?" she asked, looking concerned.

"You know how much I *love* public speaking."

"You'll be fine."

"I'm not so sure about that."

"I disagree." She grabbed my jacket and gave it a tug. "I think today is going to be your finest day." She took a moment to give me the once-over. "And you look very handsome by the way." As she lifted herself on her tippy toes, Ali threw her flower-scented arms around my neck. "Do you remember *Euphemia*? Your Dad's sailboat?" she whispered.

I nodded.

"She was Justin's empress. I went to the library and looked it up." Her lips brushed up against the tiny hairs on my ear as she stepped back. Sniffling, she dabbed at each eye with a finger. "Okay," she sighed. "Now, where do you want us sitting?"

"In the front pew on the left side with me and Dale."

"Okay...okay." She ran her hands down the length of her skirt, turned around and said, "Let's go, Mom."

Mrs. Blake took a step forward. "I'm terribly sorry, Justin. My husband sends his...he would have been here if he could have."

When they were seated, I glanced at my watch and saw it was eleven-oh-four. "Justin?" Dale said, coming up from behind me. "Time to take a seat." When I didn't blink, he placed a hand on my upper arm. "Come on, buddy."

After Dale and I sat down, the reverend or priest or deacon (I had no idea what his title was) said some things about Dad, which was kind of weird because he never knew my dad. He quoted the Bible a few times and got philosophical for a bit. Then twelve kids shuffled onto a raised platform. I leaned over towards Dale and asked him what was going on.

"This is for your father," he said as their prepubescent voices hit the opening note to a song I knew only too well. There were no musicians backing them up, just a bunch of young boys singing that same canon I'd listened to countless times in the past. It made me think of something Dad once said: *Leave weddings for Wagner; Pachelbel wrote this piece, inadvertently perhaps, as his Death Chorus.*

When the kids were done, they filed off the stage, hardly a dry eye left in the place. Now it was my turn to speak. No hockey game I'd played had prepared me for this. My legs were like warm licorice as I headed up to the microphone. Behind the podium, I took out a piece of paper from inside my jacket. I looked down and read over a few of the opening sentences, then scanned the faces out in front of me and lost my train of thought. There was Ryan Delacroix and his hilariously oversized suit, definitely borrowed from his dad or older brother; Uncle Adam and his trophy wife; Alicia, the "light" of Dad's life; Ali, the prettiest girl I knew.

I was about to begin when the doors at the back swung open and in walked Mom. She slipped into the last pew, where no one else was sitting, but not for a moment did she take her eyes off me. I looked down at the notes I'd made and took a deep breath. It wasn't your usual speech, with every sentence written out, but instead a bunch of bullet points I wanted to touch on.

I waited to see if the tremors were on their way, and only continued when the coast seemed to be clear: "When a guy loses his dad..." I started. Saying those words out loud, in public, hammered me because it was only in doing so that I'd actually acknowledged his death and that he would never be coming back again. "He, ahh..." I cleared my throat. "He loses..."

Steady...

"...he loses a part of himself. My dad knew how to be an inspiration in his own unique way; he's the only guy who found the *'spiritus'* within us all." This drew a series of quiet laughs. "A son looks up to his father from the moment he's born. Nothing he does or says can ever make him proud enough. He's a teacher, a friend a...a..." I stammered, "a royal pain in the butt." More hushed laughter. "But, in the end, he's a father and you admire him in ways maybe nobody else can."

"With my own Dad, he was the reason I began playing hockey. He was the reason I started reading books—and not because I had to, but for fun!" I added, watching the smiles creep up on people's faces. "In short, he's a lot of the reason I am who I am today."

"There was a time when I was five or six years old," I said, remembering a story I hadn't thought about in years. "We were out playing shinny. My dad was taking a breather off to the side—more like a smoke break if you ask me—and watching the rest of us kids play. When it was over and I was taking off my skates, he sat down beside me on a bench and told me I had a gift. In fact, he said I had a very *special* gift. I considered what he'd told me and, in my own five- or six-year-old way, asked him if I could give this gift to Mom. Dad was confused, I think. 'Why do you want to give this gift of yours to your mom?' he finally said. 'Because Mom loves getting presents'." Tears were starting to fall down people's cheeks, Mom and Lorraine having an especially tough go of it. "'True', my dad said. 'But your gift is something you can never give to anyone else, not even your mom. It's for you and you alone. You can use it to help others and teach others and inspire others, but you can't give it away'. I don't know why, but I've never told anybody that story before."

I paused and looked at Ali. "You know, I can't recall the last time I told my dad I, ah...I loved him. It must have been ages ago. But, umm..." Overcome with emotion, I looked towards the back and into Mom's eyes, which glistened like a freshly flooded ice rink. "I'd just like to end this by saying one last thing." Although the next part took a while to get out, I eventually said the four words I should have told Dad when he was still alive, then walked down from the podium amid a golden silence, peace embracing me like a blanket. It was a feeling I hadn't experienced since the three of us lived under one roof together—when the three of us were a family—and I went to bed every night feeling safe and loved.

At the end of the service, everybody came to the pew where Dale, Ali, Mrs. Blake and I were sitting. They hugged me, imparted some words of wisdom or passed on their condolences once again. When the last person exited the church, I turned towards the front and wished there was a casket to go up to and bid a last farewell to Dad like people did in the movies. On Dale's advice, we'd chosen not to have a casket, opting instead to cremate Dad's body and scatter his ashes over Lake Ontario.

Pushing open the doors to the church, I was flooded with sunlight. Mom was at the top of the stairs, talking to Dale. Ali stood alone on the sidewalk. We looked at each other and I gave my head a flick in our direction. I mouthed the words *Come here* and gave my head another subtle tilt towards us.

"Well, Justin, what say you?" Dale asked me.

"I think I need a bit of time to decompress."

"Do you want me to wait around with you?"

"No, it's okay," I told him. "You go ahead. I'll catch up with you at your dad's." Uncle Adam was having a "wake" at his place, which is where some of the people who'd been here today were now heading.

When Ali reached the final step, I introduced her to Mom and Dale.

"So this is the one and only Ali? Ha ha ha." Dale had a smirk on his face. "My uncle Rick was quite enamoured with you, young lady."

Ali blushed.

"It's nice to meet you, Ali," Mom said. "I hope we have a chance to spend some time together in, well, happier circumstances soon."

"Me, too, Mrs.—"

"Merlyn. You can call me Merlyn."

"Well, Aunt Merlyn," Dale said (I loved how he still called Mom "aunt" even though she was technically not related to him anymore), "may I offer you a lift somewhere?"

"I'm fine, Dale. A friend of mine lent me her car. Thank you, though."

"Will we see you later at my father's?"

"I think I'll just go home. Get some rest and let you boys remember Rick together."

The two hugged before Dale moved towards me and lifted an arm around my neck. "Until later?"

"Yeah."

"Let's talk tomorrow, on the phone, K, hun?" Mom said.

I nodded. "Sure."

They said goodbye to Ali and then made their way down the stairs together, Dale with his hands in his pockets and Mom holding the inside of his right arm.

"So," Ali said, "what are you going to do now?"

"I don't know. Maybe go somewhere and sit. Think about the day, about Dad. Try and, you know, make sense of this."

Ali was quiet. "Right. Well, I should get going, too. I've got so much packing to do it's nuts." Ali was leaving for camp tomorrow. We still hadn't talked about how this was going to work, or not work, and with Dad's death there hadn't really been a good time to bring it up this past week.

Squinting at the sun above me, I said, "Listen, I was wondering..."

"About what?"

"...if you'd want to hang for a bit. In a park maybe? I noticed there's one up the street with a bench."

Ali traced a slow circle on the pavement with the toe part of her shoe. "I suppose I could put my packing off for a while." Our eyes met. "Plus, I've heard benches can be a good time."

Hold on to what is precious in your life with the strength needed to resist a gale-force wind. And never, ever let go.

I thought of "him" momentarily and for the first time since it happened, I wasn't jealous. It was in the past, a scar that might always be there but would fade, I hoped, with time. She was still my Ali, someone I loved spending time with more than anyone and the same girl who'd taught me that kindness won out over all else. More than that, she was the only person I wanted to hold on to when a gale-force wind came in and rocked my world.

Inching forward, I extended an arm in Ali's direction, dimples surfacing as our fingers locked themselves around each other and we took our first steps, together, hand in hand.

ACKNOWLEDGEMENTS

No book is an island. Without the love, support, help, and encouragement of so many friends and family members, there is little chance this novel would have seen the light of day. Or, as Louise Penny so eloquently once wrote, "I know that the real blessing here isn't that I have a book published, but that I have so many people to thank."

I'd like to begin by thanking Stephen Bentley, Tony Chan, Andrew Cole, Kyle Duffin, Adam Hay, Joel Hay, Claire Kilgour Hervey, Ji-young Hong, Vanessa Horsburgh, Lynne Hunter, Kyung-oak Jung, Eun-jung Kang, Hyun-kyung Kim, Ricardo Klassen, Tyler Levine, Jordana Lieberman, Todd May, Melanie McCreath, Patrick McEntyre, the McHughs, David Mitchell, Melissa Morgan, Randy Morgan, Andrea Poirier, Michael Posner, Susan Posner, Kevin Prozes, Rya Prozes, Sarina Ramnarine, Vicki Rivard, Melanie Rutledge, Angela Scott, David Scott, Karen Sweet, Jason Tannenbaum, Jen Trayner, and Jun-hee Yang.

I was very blessed to have Jaclyn Law edit several parts of this novel.

Fred and Jing, your steadfast faith in me and my cacography went further than you might care to admit.

Donna, many moons ago you made it possible for me to learn from great teachers, one of whom instilled in me a sense of confidence that I could do something productive with my writing one day. For that, and so much more, I owe you an incalculable debt of gratitude.

Thanks also to: Cousin John (your unflinching support when in the thick of it will never be forgotten); CJ (aside from planting the seed in Boracay, you made this book a reality in your own way); and Maria (you will always be my muse of choice when writing, for without you I would still be deconstructing tears that were once shed in a little place off Green Sidewalk Street).

A very special thanks to my mother for her (often) sage words and (equally as often) amazing ability to make me laugh as I finished this story and found myself in a Murakami-like well.

Finally, thank you to Barrie White for giving me the strength to write this novel. And for sitting behind me on a day when the rest of the room was empty.